Finance and Accounting for Nonfinancial Managers

Finance and Accounting for Nonfinancial Managers

All the Basics You Need to Know

Sixth Edition

William G. Droms

Jay O. Wright

BASIC
BOOKS

A Member of the Perseus Books Group
New York

Published by Basic Books,
A Member of the Perseus Books Group

Books published by Basic Books are available at special discounts for bulk purchases in the United States by corporations, institutions, and other organizations. For more information, please contact the Special Markets Department at the Perseus Books Group, 2300 Chestnut Street, Suite 200, Philadelphia, PA 19103, or call (800) 810-4145, ext. 5000, or e-mail special.markets@perseusbooks.com.

Library of Congress Cataloging-in-Publication Data
Droms, William G., 1944–
    Finance and accounting for nonfinancial managers : all the basics you need to know /
William G. Droms, Jay O. Wright. — 6th ed.
        p. cm.
    Includes bibliographical references and index.
    ISBN 978-0-465-01849-9 (alk. paper)
    1. Managerial accounting. 2. Accounting. 3. Business enterprises—Finance. I. Wright, Jay O. II. Title.

HF5657.4.D76 2010
657.024'658—dc22

                                                                            2010005528

10 9 8 7 6 5 4 3 2

To JoAnn, Courtney, and Justin Droms
To Janelle, Corinne, and Teddy Wright

CONTENTS

PREFACE

This book originally was written over thirty years ago in response to the demand by successful business people for additional education in the areas of finance and accounting. Over the last three decades, the demand for financial education by students, lawyers, public policy makers, and individual investors has increased markedly, and this book has evolved to help fill that demand. As this sixth edition goes to press, the recent events in the global economy, including the worst stock market drop since the 1930s, the highest unemployment in nearly thirty years, and widespread disillusionment with Wall Street due in part to the unearthing of history's largest Ponzi scheme perpetrated by Bernard Madoff, have made it more important than ever that nonfinancial executives, lawyers, public policy makers, individual investors, and citizens take the time to understand how corporations account for their financial operations and make (or at least should make) the financial decisions that affect us all.

While financial fraud and mismanagement garner headlines, it is important to remember that most corporations play by the rules. Those rules, including financial accounting rules, securities laws, and common law antifraud provisions, provide a framework for honest companies to account for and report their financial results to their investors and the public at large. This book is intended to provide readers with the fundamental skills needed to understand the rules of the game as played by the majority of those honest participants. The text is specifically designed to appeal to managers, students, and professionals who are relatively untrained in finance and feel the need to become better versed in order to enhance their business and managerial skills. Our experience in conducting executive-level seminars for this audience and interacting with business professionals without formal finance training suggests that the book will appeal to individuals in all types of organizations who currently work in various nonfinancial functional areas such as marketing, production, law, and human resources management. This book also will be useful for small business entrepreneurs who want to develop fundamental skills in financial control and financial planning. Finally, a variety of independent professionals, such as engineers, attorneys, and medical practitioners, may find the book useful for managing the financial side of their profession.

In addition to practicing nonfinancial managers and executives, college, law, and public policy students with no prior formal training in accounting and finance will find the book useful. The book could serve as the core text in a one-semester undergraduate course, or it may be assigned as supplementary or background reading for a more intensive finance course. The book may be particularly appropriate for finance courses with a heavy case-study emphasis where little straight text is normally provided. Finally, for graduate students planning to enroll in an MBA or JD program, particularly students with little or no formal education in finance, this book is an excellent source for learning the fundamentals of finance and accounting.

In keeping with the objectives of the book, the text does not purport to provide a comprehensive treatment of the fields of finance and accounting. The overriding objective of this book is to present the nuts and bolts of finance and accounting concepts in order to provide usable information with immediate practical significance. In this sense, every attempt has been made to provide a practical guide from which managers, investors, and executives may draw useful knowledge to be used in the normal course of business. In a similar vein, business students may find it helpful to use this book to develop a set of practical accounting and finance skills that may be applied to the analysis of business problems.

The first five editions of this book have been used successfully at a number of colleges and universities for continuing education courses in finance for nonfinancial managers, in business courses for nonbusiness majors, and in small business management and entrepreneurship courses. The book also has been used extensively for in-house corporate training programs in finance. The third and fourth editions of the book have been translated into Spanish and Portuguese, and these editions have achieved some success in Europe and Latin America. The book also has been purchased by thousands of individuals for independent study. The broad acceptance of the book, evidenced by sales in excess of 125,000 copies of the first five editions, has provided the motivation for this sixth edition.

With the preparation of this sixth edition, we would like to thank the many students and teachers who have provided feedback from their experiences with the first five editions of the book. To accounting consultant Leo Jubb, MBA, CPA, and treasurer of the Sherwood Forrest Club, many thanks for his detailed review of all the accounting chapters. To Steven Strauss, CPA/PFS, our thanks for his review of the tax chapter. Any remaining errors are in spite of Leo and Steve's best efforts to keep us on the straight and narrow and are our responsibility alone. Finally, we would like to thank Courtney Marie Droms, class of 1999 from the McDonough School of Business at Georgetown University, and PhD, 2009, from the Moore School of Business at the University of South Carolina, for her assistance with word processing and in putting together the spreadsheets that are available with this edition via our website at www.msb.edu.

WILLIAM G. DROMS
JAY O. WRIGHT

Washington, DC
December 2009

PART I

Introduction

1

Contemporary Financial Management

(R)EVOLUTION OF THE FINANCE FUNCTION

The field of financial management experienced significant change during the twentieth century, change that has accelerated in the first decade of the twenty-first century. From 1900 to 1920, financial managers were concerned mostly with the legal issues surrounding the issuance of stocks and bonds. This focus of attention reflected the primitive nature of the capital markets in the early 1900s, the wave of mergers and consolidations occurring at that time, and the lack of what now is considered routine full disclosure of accounting and financial information about companies offering securities to the public. The 1920s saw a wave of corporate expansion, new technologies such as the television, and new financial instruments such as the first mutual funds. With the Crash of 1929 and the Depression of the 1930s, the main focus of financial management shifted to the defensive aspects of business survival.

The early post–World War II period marked the beginning of the transition to the current emphasis on analyzing the financial implications of business decisions and maximizing the value of the firm. In the 1970s and early 1980s, experience with rapid inflation and high interest rates focused increased attention on the financial implications of long-term investment decisions. In 1974, the annual rate of increase in the Consumer Price Index hit double digits (12.2 percent) for the first time since the temporary inflationary surge following the end of World War II. Although double-digit inflation has not been seen again since 1979 and 1980 (13.3 and 12.4 percent, respectively), coping with the impact of inflation and managing the cost of capital continue to be important responsibilities of contemporary financial managers.

Beginning in August 1982, the world saw global stock markets enter a twenty-five-year bull market as disinflation, a revolution in telecommunications (including the breakup of AT&T, the privatization of many national telecommunications carriers, and the advent of the internet), and better macroeconomic management created ideal conditions for entrepreneurs, private equity managers, and public company executives to build value for shareholders. The early 1980s also saw the introduction of asset securitization on a large scale, a powerful process by which the cash flows of assets such as mortgages are repackaged and sold to investors through the capital markets. The full impact of this revolution is just now being appreciated.

As we end the first decade of the twenty-first century, several significant trends continue to affect corporate financial management. First is the continuing globalization of business in general and financial management in particular. No major U.S. or foreign corporations do business solely within the confines of their own country. Dealing with multiple currencies and capital markets in which investment capital moves across borders at an increasing pace, facing fewer and fewer barriers; a wide variety of accounting systems and tax laws; and a multitude of political risk environments is now a normal part of the responsibilities of a corporate financial manager. This globalization of business does not change the fundamental theories of corporate financial management, but it does have a substantial impact on corporate financial practice and domestic financial markets.

A second major trend impacting financial management in the early years of the twenty-first century is the fallout from the accounting and financial scandals of the past several years. Enron and Worldcom were the first two major corporate bankruptcies related to allegations of widespread fraud, cover-ups, and criminal behavior by senior executives of these corporations and their auditors. Since then, AIG, Bear Stearns, Lehman Brothers, Merrill Lynch, Washington Mutual, IndyMac, and Wachovia have either been sold in a fire sale or gone bankrupt because of excessive leverage and poor (and possibly fraudulent) financial management. Massive fraud on the scale of the Enron case has been shown to be the exception and not the rule, and new financial and accounting regulations imposed by the SEC (Securities and Exchange Commission) under the Sarbanes-Oxley Act have had a major impact on the conduct of corporate America. Nevertheless, new regulations did not prevent greed, stupidity, or poor financial management. And as the Bernard Madoff Ponzi scheme demonstrated, regulation with somnolent regulators is in many ways worse than no regulation at all. Restoring the public's trust in the integrity of public financial markets will take time and is predicated on crafting a new framework built on sound financial principles and transparency while accounting for human greed and fear.

The only thing certain about the future is that finance and industry will continue to change, offering new challenges and opportunities to financial managers. The importance of competent financial management to the success and even survival of the modern business organization cannot be overemphasized. It is no accident that presidents and board chairpersons of large, successful corporations increasingly rise to their positions by coming up the "finance side of the house." In smaller businesses, experience has shown that the early survival of a new business and prosperity in its developing stages are strongly dependent on effective financial planning and control. The most common reason cited for the high failure rate experienced by new ventures is lack of financial expertise. Similarly, financial administration is receiving increased attention by governmental units at all levels. Financial management in all types of nonprofit corporations and organizations is also benefiting from increased attention. Competent financial planning and management are critical components of success in any organization that brings people together to achieve a common goal.

A volatile stock market, turbulent economic times, and massive federal deficits have focused increased attention on the financial implications of nearly all business decisions. A knowledge of financial management principles and techniques has become even more important during our current era of economic uncertainty. Functional specialists in such diverse areas as marketing, production, and human resources management have become increasingly sensitive to the bottom-line implications of their management decisions.

GOALS OF FINANCIAL MANAGEMENT

This book adopts the conventional perspective that the primary goal of a corporate financial manager should be to maximize the value of the firm's outstanding common stock. The financial manager, along with other senior managers, has a fiduciary obligation to make decisions that are in the best interests of the owners of the firm—that is, the common stockholders. Management may best serve these interests by maximizing the value of the stock owned by these stockholders.

It is important to note that maximizing the value of the outstanding common stock is not simply a matter of increasing total profits. Management could simply issue additional shares of stock, for example, and invest the proceeds in long-term government bonds. The profits of the firm would increase, but there would now be more stockholders with whom these new profits would have to be shared. If the rate of return on the government bonds were lower than the firm's normal rate of return on investment, as is most likely, earnings per share would be diluted, and the common stock would decline in value. Hence, management must be concerned with the impact of its decisions on earnings per share rather than focus only on total profits.

The goal of value maximization cannot even be reduced to a matter of maximizing earnings per share. Management also must consider the timing of increased earnings. It is well-known that time is money, and management must consider the fact that a dollar of increased earnings received two years from now is less valuable than a dollar of increased earnings received six months from now. The timing of future earnings has a substantial impact on stock value, and management must consider the present value of future earnings in making decisions on behalf of the stockholders.

Management must also consider the risk that the firm assumes in its business affairs. Economic theory, common sense, and the recent history of firms such as Bear Stearns all argue that a dollar of risky profit is less valuable than a dollar of certain profit. When looking at the firm overall, management must contend with two general categories of risk: business risk and financial risk. Business risk is the risk imposed by the business and economic environment in which the firm operates. A high-technology firm, for example, faces a great deal more business risk than does an electric utility. Expected future demand for electricity is significantly less difficult to predict than expected future demand for most high-technology products.

Financial risk is the risk imposed by the manner in which the firm is financed. In general, the more debt a firm employs, the greater the risk of insolvency (temporary or permanent) and hence the riskier the operations of the firm. A firm that is heavily debt financed may not have the financial strength to ride out a prolonged sales decline, economic recession, or, in an age of mark to market, significant fluctuations in asset values. The degree of debt financing employed also has important implications for the dividend policy of the firm, which plays an important role in establishing the value of the stock.

In addition to considering business risk and financial risk in isolation, management must also consider the interaction of the two forms of risk. A well-run firm must strive to maintain an appropriate balance between business and financial risk. Thus, a firm facing a relatively low level of business risk can be much more aggressive in employing debt financing than a firm facing a relatively high degree of business risk. A firm such as McDonald's, which is relatively recession resistant, can safely employ a higher level of debt financing than a firm such as General Motors, which is severely impacted by the economic cycle.

As in all other areas of endeavor requiring judgment, successful financial management requires a fine balance of a number of factors. There are no cut-and-dried rules or regulations that will guarantee success or unfailingly point to the one correct decision. However, it is possible to at least describe the overall objective toward which corporate financial managers should strive: maximization of earnings per share of common stock subject to considerations of business and financial risk, timing of earnings, and impact on dividend policy. All the decision-making techniques described in this book are oriented toward the achievement of this objective.

ORGANIZATION AND STRUCTURE OF THE BOOK

This book is designed to present a set of fundamental concepts and techniques in accounting and finance and to do so in sufficient detail that the reader can extract usable information and develop practical skills. Every attempt has been made to make the book a hands-on text from which managers may draw practical knowledge to use in the normal course of business. Similarly, college students may be expected to use this book to develop a set of practical accounting and finance skills that may be applied to the analysis of a variety of business problems.

The book is divided into seven parts. This introductory chapter, along with a chapter concerning the tax environment of business, constitute Part I. Part II is composed of three chapters covering the fundamentals of financial accounting. The first two, Chapters 3 and 4, deal with the organization and interpretation of financial statements and the basic tenets of accounting regarding the use of financial statements as a financial information system. Chapter 5 provides separate treatment of a number of key accounting topics that have important implications for financial managers.

Part III deals with financial analysis. Chapter 6 provides the fundamental tools and techniques of financial statement analysis. A case study, drawn from experience with an actual company, illustrates the application of these techniques. In Chapter 7, techniques for forecasting the future financial condition of the firm are presented and illustrated with another case study. Fundamentals of breakeven analysis are presented in Chapter 8.

Part IV covers the important topic of working capital management. Chapter 9 deals with working capital policy, and Chapter 10 explores the major techniques of working capital management.

Part V deals with the analysis of long-term investment decisions. Chapter 11 explains the mathematics of compound interest. Chapters 12 and 13 discuss capital budgeting techniques, the cost of capital, and the application of capital budgeting techniques to a variety of practical problems.

Part VI focuses on long-term financing decisions. Chapter 14 deals with the process by which financial assets are valued in the marketplace. Chapter 15 discusses the theory and practice of valuing closely held businesses and presents a business valuation case study. Chapter 16 explores the major sources and forms of long-term financing.

Part VII covers selected special topics. Chapter 17 reviews some of the basic principles of sound corporate governance and risk management. Chapter 18 explores certain applications of finance in the international arena. Chapter 19 explains finance and accounting applications in the area of mergers and acquisitions.

CONCLUSION

Although this book is strongly oriented toward financial management of corporations, most of the principles espoused are equally applicable to nonprofit corporations and organizations and to governmental units. In particular, fundamental principles of accounting are similar across a broad spectrum of organizations. Similarly, analytical techniques for interpretation of financial data and basic budgeting concepts are of interest to a wide variety of organizational units. Control of the long-term financial course of the organization is also a vital area of concern for most organizations.

Most of the areas treated in this book are also of as much interest to small businesses as to large businesses. In fact, the three detailed case studies presented in Chapters 6, 7, and 15 are set against the background of small, growing businesses. Although financial management in the small firm often confronts a somewhat different set of problems and opportunities from those confronted by a large corporation, many financial decisions facing the small firm are actually quite similar to those faced by larger corporations. For example, while small firms do not normally have the opportunity to publicly sell issues of stocks or bonds to raise funds, the analysis required for a long-term investment decision such as the purchase of heavy equipment, or the evaluation of lease-buy alternatives, is essentially the same regardless of the size of the firm. Once the decision is made, the financing alternatives available to the firm may differ, but the decision process will be generally similar.

In any event, we hope that the following pages will provide you with helpful suggestions, techniques, and guidelines for successful financial management, which—when tempered with individual experience and the unique requirements of a particular industry—should enhance your ability to effectively manage or analyze the financial resources of an organization.

SUMMARY

Competent financial management is critical to the success and survival of a wide variety of organizations. In the business community, selecting the chief financial officer for advancement to chief executive officer has become increasingly common. For nonfinancial executives and managers, an understanding of the basics of financial management has become even more important during the current era of economic uncertainty. The goal of business financial management is to maximize the value of the firm. Successful financial management requires a balance of a number of factors, and no simple rules or solution algorithms will guarantee financial success under all circumstances. The overall goal toward which corporate financial managers should strive is the maximization of earnings per share, subject to considerations of business and financial risk, timing of earnings, and dividend policy. All the principles and techniques of this book are oriented toward that objective. Although the book is focused on business financial management for uniformity of illustration, most of the underlying principles are equally applicable to nonprofit organizations and governmental units. Such concepts as the fundamental principles of accounting, analytical techniques for interpretation of financial data, basic budgeting concepts, financial planning and control, and the analysis of long-term investment opportunities are applicable to many different types of organizations. Financial managers in business, government, and the nonprofit sector can profitably harness the principles and techniques offered in this book to manage the financial resources of their organizations effectively.

KEY POINTS	
MANAGERIAL FINANCE	Application of microeconomic theory. Goal is maximization of value of firm subject to risk constraints, timing considerations, and impact on dividend policy.
BUSINESS RISK	Risk imposed by the business environment and economic cycle.

ORGANIZATION OF BOOK

Introduction
- Scope and nature of managerial finance
- Tax environment

Financial accounting fundamentals
- Introduction to financial statements
- Accounting—a financial information system
- Special topics in accounting

Financial analysis and control
- Financial statement analysis
- Financial forecasting and cash budgeting
- Breakeven analysis for profit planning

Working capital decisions
- Working capital policy
- Working capital management

Long-term investment decisions
- Mathematics of compound interest
- Capital budgeting
- Cost of capital

Long-term financing decisions
- Valuation of financial assets
- Valuing closely held businesses
- Sources and forms of long-term financing

Special Topics in Finance
- Governance and rule management
- International finance
- Mergers and acquisitions

2

The Tax Environment

It is important to understand the tax environment within which the financial manager operates because few business decisions are unaffected by tax considerations. This chapter presents a brief overview of the major elements of the tax structure affecting financial planning and financial decision making. Providing a detailed description of the Internal Revenue Code or guidance relative to the preparation of tax returns is well beyond the scope of this book. The objective here is only to provide a brief sketch of the most important points of the tax system and an understanding of the necessary connection between financial planning and tax planning.

ORGANIZATIONAL FORM AND TAXES

There are four basic forms of business ownership in the United States: the sole proprietorship, the partnership, the corporation, and the limited liability company. Each form of ownership has various advantages and disadvantages. Perhaps the greatest advantage of the *sole proprietorship*, which is the most frequently encountered form of organization in terms of total numbers of businesses, is the ease with which it is formed. As the name implies, the sole proprietorship is owned and operated by a single individual. Formation of a sole proprietorship is extremely simple, and the profit earned by the proprietor is normally treated as ordinary income for tax purposes. The principal disadvantage of a sole proprietorship is that the owner is solely liable for all obligations of the business. Thus, if the business is sued, the owner is solely responsible for any liability resulting from the outcome of the suit. This liability extends to the owner's personal assets as well as business assets. Additional disadvantages of the sole proprietorship include certain tax disadvantages. For example, many fringe benefits such as medical insurance are not regarded by the Internal Revenue Service as a business expense to the sole proprietorship.

A *partnership* shares most of the advantages and disadvantages of the sole proprietorship. The main difference between a partnership and a sole proprietorship is that the partnership has two or more owners, each of whom owns a given percentage of the company. As one might expect, the addition of more owners often complicates matters. In the absence of a written agreement to the contrary, all partners share equally in the profits or losses of the company. Similarly, important decisions are also shared, sometimes complicating the decision-making process somewhat. An additional complicating factor is that, from a legal viewpoint, the partnership is terminated if one partner dies or withdraws from the partnership. The partnership must then be reconstituted as a new partnership following settlement of the terminated partner's account. (Such settlements are occasionally complex and difficult.) From an income tax point of view, partnership income is taxed the same as sole proprietorship income—that is, each partner's share in the profits of the partnership is treated as ordinary income for tax purposes.

The *corporate* form of organization is by far the most significant in terms of dollars of sales, assets, profits, and contribution to the gross national product. The most important legal aspect of the corporation is its limited liability. A corporation is a "legal person." It exists independently of its owners under the law. Personal assets of corporate stockholders (owners) generally cannot be seized to settle claims against the corporation, and capital can be raised in the corporation's name. Shares of stock are transferable among owners, and the corporation continues independently of stock sales or stockholder deaths. The limited liability and perpetual life characteristics of the corporation make this form of organization almost mandatory for large firms.

Limited liability companies (LLCs) are relatively new entities, the creation of new state laws passed over the past two decades. An LLC has the advantage of the flexibility and tax treatment of a partnership (for example, no double taxation), while conferring limited liability upon the LLC's owners (which are generally called "members"). LLCs are frequently used for start-up companies and real estate ventures, as they allow tax losses to flow to the members, subject to any passive loss limitations.

From an income tax point of view, the most important differences among the organizational forms described above relate to the way in which the income from a given business is taxed. The profits from sole proprietorships, partnerships, and limited liability companies are taxed as personal income to the proprietor, partners, or members. Corporate profits, however, are taxed at the corporate rate independently of the individual owners' income.

CORPORATE INCOME TAXES

The basic corporate income tax structure is actually quite simple, although the various tax laws governing how corporate taxable income is determined are quite complex. The laws also are subject to frequent revision by Congress. Major revisions of the tax code have been particularly numerous in recent years. The objective here is to introduce the fundamental characteristics of the tax system.

The current corporate income tax rate is 15 percent on the first $50,000 of income, 25 percent on the next $25,000, 34 percent on the next $25,000, 39 percent on the next $235,000, 34 percent on the next $9,665,000, 35 percent on the next $5,000,000, 38 percent on the next $3,333,333, and 35 percent on all income above $18,333,333. Exhibit 2.1 summarizes the current federal corporate income tax rate. The 5 percent extra tax in the $100,000 to $335,000 income bracket eliminates the benefit of lower tax rates on corporate income of less than $75,000. In an analogous manner, the extra 3 percent tax in the $15,000,000 to $18,333,333 bracket eliminates the benefit of the lower 34 percent tax rate on corporations with incomes below $10,000,000.

EXHIBIT 2.1   FEDERAL CORPORATE INCOME TAX RATE

TAXABLE INCOME		TAX RATE
$1 –	$50,000	15%
50,001 –	75,000	25
75,001 –	100,000	34
100,001 –	335,000	39
335,001 –	10,000,000	34
10,000,001 –	15,000,000	35
15,000,001 –	18,333,333	38
over $18,333,333		35

The structure of the federal corporate income tax rate provides a tax break for small corporations, since the first $100,000 of income is taxed at an average rate of only 22.25 percent. The increase in the tax rate once the first $335,000 of income is reached results in a progressive tax structure on the first $335,000 of income, after which the tax rate is a flat 34 percent for taxable incomes up to $10,000,000. At incomes above $10,000,000, the tax rate goes to a flat 35 percent rate. Exhibit 2.2 illustrates the marginal tax rate (tax on each additional dollar of income) and the average tax rate (total tax as a percentage of income) for corporate incomes up to $1,000,000.

EXHIBIT 2.2　MARGINAL AND AVERAGE CORPORATE TAX RATES

CORPORATE TAXABLE INCOME	MARGINAL TAX RATE	DOLLARS OF TAX DUE*	AVERAGE TAX RATE*
$1 –　$50,000	15%	$7,500	15.00%
50,001 –　75,000	25	13,750	18.33
75,001 –　100,000	34	22,250	22.25
100,001 –　335,000	39	113,900	34.00
335,001 – 1,000,000	34	340,000	34.00

*Assuming corporate taxable income equals the upper limit of the taxable income range.

The difference between the average and the marginal tax rates illustrated in Exhibit 2.2 may be best explained by an example. If a corporation has taxable income of $200,000, its tax liability is determined as follows:

First $50,000 at 15%　= $7,500
Next $25,000 at 25%　= $6,250
Next $25,000 at 34%　= $8,500
Next $100,000 at 39% = $39,000
Total tax liability　　= $61,250

In this example, the average tax rate is 30.63 percent ($61,250/$200,000), but the marginal tax rate is 39 percent, since the second $100,000 is taxed at the 39 percent rate.

Given this relatively simple corporate tax structure, one is often perplexed to find that the indicated tax rate actually paid by a given corporation (often referred to as the "effective tax rate") may be substantially less than the "statutory rate" indicated in the corporate tax rate schedules. There are many reasons for this discrepancy, the chief of which are listed in Exhibit 2.3.

EXHIBIT 2.3   DIFFERENCES IN ACTUAL VERSUS STATUTORY TAX RATES

1. Income less than $75,000 is taxed at less than 35 percent.
2. Earnings of some subsidiaries and affiliates—for example, foreign subsidiaries—may be taxed at rates of less than 35 percent.
3. Between 70 and 100 percent of income received from dividends paid on stock owned in other corporations is not taxable to the receiving corporation.
4. Net losses from prior years may be carried forward.
5. Some income may be from tax-exempt bonds.

Fortunately, any discrepancy between the tax rate actually paid (the effective rate) and the normal corporate rate (the statutory rate) is usually explained in the footnotes to the financial statements.

As can be seen from Exhibits 2.2 and 2.3, the corporate tax environment is much more complex when examined a bit further. While the objective is not for the reader to become an expert, some attention should be paid to a few of the more important details alluded to in the exhibits. A closer look at earnings from foreign affiliates, corporate capital gains and losses, operating losses carried forward (and backward), and intercorporate dividend taxation is appropriate.

Earnings from Foreign Affiliates

Some tax advantages are available to U.S. corporations doing business abroad through a foreign subsidiary. Income from a foreign subsidiary is normally not taxed in the United States until it is remitted to the parent corporation in the form of dividends. The obvious advantage to the parent is that earnings may be reinvested in the subsidiary and taxes deferred until a cash return is provided to the parent.

Under the Tax Reform Act of 1984, Congress removed most of the tax benefits formerly associated with domestic international sales corporations (DISCs) and established new tax benefits for foreign sales corporations (FSCs). In order for a corporation to qualify as a DISC, at least 95 percent of its gross receipts must be from exports, and certain other technical requirements have to be met as well. The 1984 act did not abolish DISCs but limited their tax benefits and imposed an interest charge to tax-deferred earnings. A DISC shareholder must now pay interest on the amount of the shareholder's DISC-related deferred tax liability.

Congress passed the FSC Repeal and Extraterritorial Income Exclusion Act of 2001 in order to comply with a ruling by the World Trade Organization that FSC provisions provide an illegal export subsidy to U.S. corporations. The old FSC tax rules have been replaced with new rules providing for partial exclusion of extraterritorial income from taxable gross income of U.S. corporations. The tax benefits of the new rules are generally comparable with the benefits available under the old FSC rules. Gross income for tax purposes may exclude extraterritorial income to the extent that such income qualifies under the act as qualifying foreign trade income. Qualifying foreign trade income is subject to a series of technical rules that limit the amount of foreign income that may be excluded from U.S. taxable income. The net result of the rules is to provide a lower tax rate on foreign income than on domestic income. However, on repatriation of foreign profits to the United States, a U.S.-based company may face a surtax that mitigates the benefit of foreign-sourced income.

Corporate Capital Gains and Losses

Corporate capital assets are defined as assets not normally bought and sold in the ordinary course of a corporation's business. Thus, security investments generally are capital assets, but items of real and depreciable property used in the business are not. Prior to the Tax Reform Act of 1986, corporate capital gains and losses were subject to a variety of special tax treatments. The most important one was that long-term capital gains (gains on assets held for more than one year) were taxed at a rate lower than the tax rate applied to ordinary income.

The 1986 act eliminated the preferential treatment given to corporate capital gains and applied the same tax rate to all sources of income. However, the Internal Revenue Code still requires that capital gains and losses be separately identified and reported.

Operating Loss Carry-Back and Carry-Forward

The provision of the tax laws commonly referred to as the *tax loss carry-back and carry-forward provision* was designed to avoid penalizing companies that have widely fluctuating profits and losses. This provision allows ordinary operating loss to be carried back three years and forward for up to fifteen years to offset taxable income in previous or future years. The law is written such that the loss must be carried back first to the earliest year (three years ago), then to the second earliest year, and then to the year immediately preceding the loss year. Any remaining loss may then be carried forward to offset profits in the succeeding fifteen years. Under some circumstances, it is possible for the corporation to "elect out" of the carry-back requirement and under other circumstances (set forth in Section 382 of the Internal Revenue Code) for loss carry-forwards and carry-backs to be sharply limited after a change of ownership control of the corporation.

To illustrate, suppose that Hoya Manufacturers earned annual profits of $100,000 before tax in each of the three consecutive years 2005, 2006, and 2007. If Hoya's effective tax rate were 20 percent in each of the three years, the corporation would have paid taxes of $20,000 in each year. If Hoya were to suffer a $450,000 loss in 2008, the loss first would be carried back to 2005, reducing the 2005 profit from $100,000 to zero and resulting in a refund of $20,000 in taxes. The remaining loss of $350,000 ($450,000 less $100,000 "used up" in 2005) would be carried back to 2006 next and then to 2007. Profits and taxes in each of these two years would also be reduced to zero, and an additional $40,000 in previous tax payments would be refunded. Finally, the remaining $150,000 loss ($450,000 less $100,000 [2005] less $100,000 [2006] less $100,000 [2007]) would be carried forward to offset tax liabilities in future years beginning with 2008.

Intercorporate Dividend Taxation

The tax rule on intercorporate dividend taxation is quite simple and easy to understand. If a corporation (investor) owns less than 20 percent of the stock in another corporation (investee), 70 percent of the dividends paid from the investee corporation to the investor corporation are generally tax free. If the investor owns at least 20 but no more than 80 percent of the stock of the investee, 80 percent of the dividends are tax free. If the investor owns more than 80 percent of the investee, all of the dividends are tax free, as the investee is considered a consolidated subsidiary.

The purpose of this provision of the tax law is to eliminate the possibility of triple taxation of a corporation's income. The investee corporation must pay corporate taxes on its income before paying out dividends—this is the first tax. The second tax would occur if the investor corporation had to pay a corporate income tax on the dividends received from the investee corporation. The third tax would occur when the investor corporation paid dividends to its stockholders, who would then have to pay their personal income tax on dividends received. The intercorporate dividend exclusion was designed to alleviate just this problem.

Corporate Taxes and Personal Taxes

From a financial management viewpoint, the major concern with the personal-tax structure is to compare personal taxes levied on sole proprietorships, partnerships, or LLCs with the income tax liability under a corporate form of organization. Accordingly, discussion of the personal-tax structure will be quite brief. No attempt will be made to discuss any of the details of the individual income tax structure, the various deductions allowed individuals, and so forth. Only a brief outline of the structure will be presented.

PERSONAL INCOME TAXES

An individual contemplating owning his or her own business must compare the expected tax rates on sole proprietorship, partnership, or limited liability company income to the corporate tax rate. Exhibit 2.4 presents the personal income tax rate schedules for 2008. Although most readers of this book are probably only too well aware of these rates, a brief comment is nonetheless appropriate.

The personal-tax rate starts lower than the corporate-tax rate in the lowest brackets (15 percent for corporate income of less than $50,000 and 10 percent in the lowest personal brackets for all filing statuses). At higher income levels, the highest personal rate of 35 percent never exceeds the highest corporate rate of 35 percent. In general, then, there is currently little tax incentive for forming a corporation as opposed to a limited liability company. However, future tax changes may shift the relative tax advantages of a limited liability company.

EXHIBIT 2.4 TAX RATE SCHEDULES FOR INDIVIDUALS AND MARRIED COUPLES

SCHEDULE X—SINGLE FILING STATUS

TAXABLE INCOME OVER:	BUT NOT OVER:	TAX RATE:	OF THE AMOUNT OVER:
$0	$8,025	... 10%	$0
8,025	32,550	$802.50 + 15%	6,000
32,550	78,850	4,481.25 + 25%	27,950
78,850	164,550	16,056.25 + 28%	67,700
164,550	357,700	40,052.25 + 33%	141,250
357,700	...	103,791.75 + 35%	357,700

SCHEDULE Y1—MARRIED FILING JOINTLY

TAXABLE INCOME OVER:	BUT NOT OVER:	TAX RATE:	OF THE AMOUNT OVER:
$0	$16,050	... 10%	$0
16,050	65,100	$1,605.00 + 15%	16,050
65,100	131,450	8,962.50 + 25%	65,100
131,450	200,300	25,550.00 + 28%	131,450
200,300	357,700	44,828.00 + 33%	200,300
357,700	...	96,770.00 + 35%	357,700

SCHEDULE Y2—MARRIED FILING SEPARATELY

TAXABLE INCOME OVER:	BUT NOT OVER:	TAX RATE:	OF THE AMOUNT OVER:
$0	$8,025	... 10%	$0
8,025	32,550	$802.50 + 15%	8,025
32,550	65,725	4,481.25 + 25%	32,550
65,725	100,150	12,775.00 + 28%	65,725
100,150	178,850	22,414.00 + 33%	100,150
178,850	...	48,385.00 + 35%	178,850

SCHEDULE Z—HEAD OF HOUSEHOLD

TAXABLE INCOME OVER:	BUT NOT OVER:	TAX RATE:	OF THE AMOUNT OVER:
$0	$11,450	... 10%	$0
11,450	43,650	$1,145 + 15%	11,450
43,650	112,650	5,975 + 25%	43,650
112,650	182,400	23,225 + 28%	112,650
182,400	357,700	42,755+ 33%	182,400
357,700	...	100,604+ 35%	357,700

Note: Tax schedules effective for tax year 2008

A realistic comparison of corporate- and personal-tax rates is somewhat more complicated than this suggests. If a sole owner were organized as a corporation, the corporation would pay that person a salary on which he or she would then pay a personal-tax rate. Corporate income remaining after the owner's salary would then be taxed at the corporate rate. And of course, if the corporation pays a salary to an owner, the owner can offset some of that salary with his or her allowed deductions from taxable income, such as home mortgage interest, real estate taxes, and other legal deductions. As a general rule, realistic tax comparisons require a detailed computation of potential tax liability under all options, taking all the current tax requirements into account. This is a job best left to professional accountants or tax advisers.

Profits reinvested in the corporation are available to finance future growth of the corporation or to pay future dividends. Corporate profits paid out as dividends are taxed twice: once at the corporate rate and once again when the dividend recipient pays his or her personal-tax rate on dividends received. Owners of a closely held corporation are almost always better off if they avoid dividend payments and draw profits out of the corporation solely in the form of salaries, reinvesting excess profits. Unfortunately, the IRS has guidelines as to what constitutes "reasonable" salaries and a "reasonable" level of reinvested earnings. If the IRS rules that the owners of a closely held corporation are paying themselves unreasonably high salaries or are reinvesting an unreasonably large amount of money in the corporation in order to avoid taxation of dividends, the IRS may require the owners to revise their tax returns and pay themselves a dividend. The interpretation of "reasonable" has been decided in relation to the value contributed by the owners and the legitimate future financing needs of the business.

SUBCHAPTER S CORPORATIONS

A final provision of interest in the tax law is the provision for Subchapter S corporations. Subchapter S of the Internal Revenue Code allows some incorporated businesses to elect to be taxed as sole proprietorships or partnerships. The main requirements to qualify for Subchapter S treatment are as follows:

1. The corporation may not have more than one hundred stock-holders, all of whom must be individuals, and the firm may have only one class of stock.
2. The corporation must be a domestic corporation and must not be affiliated with any group eligible to file consolidated tax returns.
3. The corporation may not derive over 20 percent of its gross receipts from royalties, rents, dividends, interest, annuities, and gains on sale of securities.

SUMMARY

The four forms of business ownership are the sole proprietorship, the partnership, the corporation, and the limited liability company. Profits earned by sole proprietors, partners, and members of limited liability companies are taxable as ordinary income to the proprietor, partner, or member.

Corporate profits are taxed at the corporate rate, regardless of the individual income of the owners.

The basic structure of the corporate income tax is quite simple, but the myriad laws governing the determination of corporate income are highly complex. The current corporate-tax rate progresses from 15 to 39 percent. Discrepancies between the statutory tax rate and the effective tax rate actually paid by a corporation are explained in the footnotes to the corporation's financial statements. The most common discrepancies stem from earnings from foreign affiliates, operating losses carried forward, and intercorporate dividend taxation.

Individuals starting their own businesses must compare the expected tax liability of a proprietorship, partnership, or limited liability company with the liability of a corporation. Sole owners or partners organized as a corporation draw a salary from the corporation and then pay their personal-tax rate on the salary. A Subchapter S corporation allows some corporations to elect to be taxed as a sole proprietorship or partnership. A limited liability company often combines the best of single-level taxation with limited liability.

KEY POINTS

SOLE PROPRIETORSHIP	Taxed at individual rate
PARTNERSHIP	Taxed at individual rate
CORPORATION	Taxed at corporate rate Advantage of limited liability
LIMITED LIABILITY COMPANY	Taxed at individual rate Advantage of limited liability
SUBCHAPTER S CORPORATION	Taxed at individual rate Advantage of limited liability
MARGINAL TAX RATE	Tax on each additional dollar of income
AVERAGE TAX RATE	Total tax due divided by income

PART II

Financial Accounting Fundamentals

3

Introduction to Financial Statements

OBJECTIVES OF FINANCIAL ACCOUNTING

The preparation and presentation of corporate financial statements is governed by the standards of financial accounting. Within the guidelines provided by generally accepted accounting principles (GAAP), the objective of financial accounting is to present fairly the financial position of a company to current and potential stockholders, creditors, security analysts, and other interested parties. Financial statements of larger companies normally are certified by independent certified public accountants (CPAs) as having been audited using generally accepted auditing standards and (in most cases) found to fairly present the financial condition of the company, in accordance with generally accepted accounting principles.

The term *generally accepted accounting principles* is somewhat debatable in the field of financial accounting. Although the phrase has enjoyed common usage for many decades, there is no single definition or all-inclusive listing of principles that are universally acceptable to theorists and practitioners. As a working definition, we may define GAAP as a set of objectives, conventions, and principles that have evolved over the years to govern the preparation and presentation of financial statements. These principles apply to the area of financial accounting as distinct from other areas of accounting, such as tax accounting, managerial accounting, and cost accounting.

This working definition of GAAP emphasizes the evolutionary nature of accounting rules and regulations. Generally accepted accounting principles are subject to varying interpretations and applications, and it is quite possible that two different companies in the same industry may account for the same transaction in different ways yet both be within the guidelines provided by GAAP. For example, within the area of depreciation accounting, one firm may account for depreciation of its capital equipment on a straight-line basis, while another in the same industry may account for depreciation according to one of several accelerated methods. Depreciation itself is a relatively complex topic that will be treated in some detail in Chapter 5. For now, it is sufficient to observe that depreciation in accounting is simply a means of allocating the cost of long-lived assets to the number of accounting periods in which the asset is expected to be used.

Several authoritative sources provide detailed guidance relative to what constitutes an acceptable accounting method. These principles are roughly comparable to a set of "rules" governing the preparation of financial statements. Chief among these rules are the various pronouncements of the American Institute of Certified Public Accountants (AICPA). From a historical perspective, the fifty-one Accounting Research Bulletins (ARBs) issued by the AICPA's Committee on Accounting Procedure and the thirty-one opinions of the AICPA's Accounting Principles Board (APB) represent a compilation of the institute's position on a wide range of accounting issues. Each APB opinion deals with a specialized topic and provides detailed guidance in that area. In a similar vein, the SEC provides a great deal of guidance in the form of SEC Accounting Series Releases.

The Financial Accounting Standards Board (FASB) superseded the APB in 1973 and is currently the most important source of authoritative pronouncements on accounting principles. The FASB is appointed by the Financial Accounting Foundation, an independent, nonprofit organization created in 1972 to oversee the establishment of accounting standards. The FASB has seven members, four of whom must be CPAs from the public accounting profession; the other three members may be accountants, financial analysts, or other qualified professionals. All seven members serve full-time in salaried positions on the board. The board issues Statements of the FASB that are responsive to the continuing need of accountants and financial analysts for full disclosure of the financial condition of corporations. The Financial Accounting Foundation also established the Governmental Accounting Standards Board (GASB) in 1984 to establish accounting standards for state and municipal governments.

A convenient summary, by no means all-inclusive, of the sources of accounting "rules" is as follows:

SEC Accounting Series Releases
AICPA Accounting Research Bulletins (ARBs)
AICPA Accounting Principles Board (APB)
Releases of the Emerging Issue Task Force (EITF)
Statements of the Financial Accounting Standards Board
   (FASB)

It is worth emphasizing that GAAP apply only to the field of financial accounting and not to other major accounting fields, such as tax, managerial, and cost accounting. These other fields of accounting have different objectives and thus should not be expected to conform to a set of principles designed to meet the needs of financial accounting. At the risk of oversimplification it may be said that the objective of tax accounting is to minimize a firm's tax liability within the constraints imposed by current income tax laws, while the objective of managerial accounting is to collect, report, and interpret information needed for managerial decision making. The major objective of cost accounting is to identify and assign relevant costs in a business organization.

These various objectives are obviously diverse, and one would expect to find widely divergent accounting techniques within the various fields. Thus it is quite understandable to find the same transaction accounted for in different ways according to different systems. A prime example of this diversity may again be seen in the area of depreciation accounting. It is quite common for corporations to report straight-line depreciation on their financial statements in order to present fairly the results of the year's operations to stockholders, while at the same time reporting accelerated depreciation to the Internal Revenue Service in order to minimize the firm's current tax liability. The accelerated depreciation does not, of course, allow the firm to escape taxes, but it does allow postponement of the tax liability to a future period and provide additional funds for current reinvestment.

At this point, it is becoming increasingly obvious that an apparently exact area such as accounting is subject to some degree of latitude in interpretation. It is important to understand the nature of the beast before undertaking a discussion of the various types of financial statements or exploring the mechanical techniques of accounting. We will therefore turn our attention now to the significance of the auditor's opinion and the fine art of footnote reading.

THE AUDITOR'S OPINION

The best way to begin a discussion of the auditor's opinion is to examine what is commonly called a *clean opinion*. Exhibit 3.1 shows a clean opinion (emphasis supplied by the authors).

EXHIBIT 3.1   CLEAN OPINION

To the shareowners and Board of Directors of the Ann Jubb Design Company:

We have examined the statement of financial condition of the Ann Jubb Design Company and consolidated affiliates as of December 31, 2008 and 2007, and the related statements of current and retained earnings and changes in financial position for the years then ended. Our examination was made *in accordance with generally accepted auditing standards, and accordingly included such tests of the accounting records and such other auditing procedures as we considered necessary* in the circumstances.

In our opinion, the aforementioned financial statements *present fairly* the financial position of Ann Jubb Design Company and consolidated affiliates at December 31, 2008 and 2007, and the results of their operations and the changes in their financial position for the years then ended, *in conformity with generally accepted accounting principles applied on a consistent basis.*

George R. Ruhl III
Certified Public Accountant

It is just as important to note what an auditor's opinion does not say as what it does say. It does not say that all transactions were audited; it does not certify the accuracy of the statements; it does not say that the company is soundly managed and that stockholders need not fear for their investment; it does not say that the auditors are confident that no misrepresentation or fraud is possible; it does not even say whether the company is profitable. None of these observations are meant as a criticism of the auditors—they simply reflect the nature of auditing and the state of the art in accounting. Given the complexities of the modern business world and the time and resource limitations on the auditing process, what the auditor's opinion does say is quite enough. Unless one is willing to accept a year or more time lag between the preparation of financial statements and the completion of an audit, the objectives of the auditing process must be judged as quite ambitious.

What the statement in Exhibit 3.1 does say is quite significant to the users of financial statements. The first paragraph, called the scope, indicates which statements were audited and informs the reader that generally accepted auditing standards were followed and that tests considered necessary by the auditors were undertaken. It should be fairly obvious that a complete audit of every single transaction in a large corporation cannot be done in a reasonable time or at a reasonable cost. Thus, one must be content with following generally accepted auditing standards and completing "necessary" tests. Similarly, in the second paragraph, called the *opinion*, one must be content with the opinion (not certification) that the statements "present fairly" the financial condition of the firm in "conformity with generally accepted accounting principles."

An opinion other than a clean opinion is known as a *qualified opinion* and usually indicates that there is some doubt as to whether the financial statements audited do in fact present fairly the financial condition of the firm. If a qualified opinion is rendered, it is important to users of the financial statement that they make an independent judgment of the meaning of the qualification in terms of the condition of the firm. It is also important to read the qualification carefully in order to be certain that the thrust of the problem is clear to the reader. The following excerpt from a qualified opinion, taken from an annual report of a corporation with total assets of approximately $9.5 million, is a good example of an important qualification:

As discussed more fully in Note 2 of the financial statements, at October 31, the Company's note and accrued interest receivable from . . . Manufacturing Corporation aggregated approximately $800,000. Recovery of the costs of these assets is dependent upon the net realizable value of the assets pledged as collateral, or the success of Manufacturing Corporation's future operations.

In other words, of the company's total stated assets of $9.5 million, approximately $800,000, or 8.5 percent, are composed of a note receivable that may be uncollectible! Doing a bit of detective work, one learns from Note 2 of the financial statements that the manufacturing corporation has already defaulted on some installments of the note, is currently operating at a loss, has a negative stockholders' equity amount, and is currently negotiating for a restructuring of the debt agreement. Thus, in analyzing the financial condition of the company, it would be reasonable to value the company's total assets at $8,700,000 rather than $9,500,000.

The moral of this short story is that care must be exercised in reading the footnotes to the financial statements. The footnotes are an integral part of the financial statements and provide an important and useful summary of the firm's accounting policies. Even if one is not qualified as an expert financial analyst, it makes good sense to read through the footnotes, even if only briefly, to develop a feel for the accounting policies of the firm. Many financial analysts read the footnotes to the financial statements before even looking at the actual statements. Armed with this information, one is prepared to undertake a serious examination of a complete set of financial statements.

EXHIBIT 3.2   HOYA MANUFACTURERS, INC.
STATEMENT OF FINANCIAL POSITION

	2008	2007
ASSETS		
Cash	$315,000	$297,000
Marketable securities	57,000	25,000
Accounts receivable	2,594,000	2,177,000
Inventories	2,257,000	1,986,000
Total current assets	$5,223,000	$4,485,000
Property, plant, and equipment	3,621,000	3,231,000
Other fixed assets	526,000	609,000
Total fixed assets	$4,147,000	$3,840,000
Total assets	$9,370,000	$8,325,000
LIABILITIES AND EQUITY		
Accounts payable	$696,000	$874,000
Notes payable	1,645,000	965,000
Accrued expenses payable	628,000	553,000
Accrued taxes payable	340,000	308,000
Total current liabilities	$3,309,000	$2,700,000

Long-term debt	$1,695,000	$1,429,000
Total liabilities	$5,004,000	$4,129,000
Stockholders' equity:		
Preferred stock ($100 par, 6%)	$425,000	$597,000
Common stock ($5 par value)	520,000	510,000
Paid-in capital in excess of par	420,000	405,000
Retained earnings	3,001,000	2,684,000
Total stockholders' equity	$4,366,000	$4,196,000
Total liabilities and equity	$9,370,000	$8,325,000

THE BALANCE SHEET

Exhibit 3.2 illustrates a typical balance sheet for a manufacturing company. The balance sheet may be thought of as a snapshot of the financial condition of a company at a given moment in time. In an economist's terms, the balance sheet is a stock statement, since it represents the stock of assets, liabilities, and equities as of a given instant—in this case we have comparative balance sheets as of December 31, 2008, and December 31, 2007, shown together.

The balance sheet has three major sections: assets, listed on the left-hand side (or top of the page on a "stacked" balance sheet); liabilities, listed on the right-hand side (or on the bottom half of the page); and equity, also listed on the right-hand side (or below the liabilities). That the two sides of the balance sheet "balance"—are equal to each other—is due to the essential logic of the balance sheet presentation. The assets side of the balance sheet lists the total resources of the firm in dollar terms. Here we find such items as cash, accounts receivable, inventories, plant and equipment, intellectual property, property under capital leases, and the other resources used to run a business. The right-hand side (or bottom half) of the balance sheet lists the various claims against these assets. Liabilities, such as accounts payable, notes payable, obligations under capital leases, and long-term debts, represent claims of various classes of creditors against these assets. The excess of assets over these creditors' claims represents the net worth of the firm's owners. This net worth account is expressed in the equity section of the balance sheet.

The balance sheet provides a detailed listing of accounts constituting what is called the *basic accounting equation*:

$$\text{Assets} = \text{Liabilities} + \text{Equity}$$
$$\text{Total business resources} = \text{Creditors' claims} + \text{Owners' claims}$$

The balance sheet is classified into a logical organizational structure. The asset section of the balance sheet is divided into two major sections: current assets and fixed assets. The current assets section includes cash and other assets that are normally converted into cash within a year or within one operating cycle, whichever is longer. Here one finds a listing of assets such as marketable securities, accounts receivable, and inventories.

Marketable securities represent short-term investments of cash in highly liquid, low-risk securities such as U.S. Treasury bills or prime commercial paper. The marketable securities investment has traditionally been carried on the balance sheet at cost (purchase price), with the market value of the securities listed in the notes to the financial statements. However, under FASB 157 and some international accounting rules, in certain cases companies are required to "mark to market" their securities investments. This change in accounting rules has introduced significant volatility in the financial statements of financial and other organizations. Further change to the accounting rules for marketable securities is likely in the future.

Accounts receivable represent amounts due the company for goods that have been shipped (or services rendered), but for which the company has not yet been paid. The accounts receivable figure is listed on the balance sheet less an allowance for bad debts. Allowance for bad debts represents the company's estimate, based on past experience, of the total dollar amount of current receivables that will eventually become uncollectible. This total dollar allowance is usually listed in a footnote to the balance sheet.

Normally, current assets are listed in order of liquidity, or nearness to cash. For Hoya Manufacturers, the least liquid of its current assets, inventories, are listed last in the current section. For a manufacturer, inventories have three components—raw materials, goods in process, and finished goods. Costing for purposes of inventory valuation requires the allocation of production and other expenses to inventories as they move from the raw-materials to the finished-goods stage. Inventory accounting is a rather complex subject that will be treated in some detail in Chapter 5. For now, it is sufficient to observe that inventory is generally valued at cost or at market value, whichever is lower. Details of the inventory valuation method used by a particular company are generally available in the footnotes to the company's financial statements.

The bottom section of the asset side of the balance sheet lists the company's investment in fixed or long-term assets such as property, plant, and equipment. These assets, compared with current assets, are highly illiquid and are used over long periods of time by the company. The generally accepted method of valuing fixed assets is to list these assets at historical cost, less accumulated depreciation as of the date of the balance sheet. *Accumulated depreciation* represents the cumulative total dollars of depreciation that have been "charged off" against the historical cost of the company's current fixed-asset base. Details relative to a given company's depreciation policy are available in the footnotes to the financial statements.

The right-hand side (or bottom) of the balance sheet, the liabilities and equity section, also follows a logical organizational format. The three major units of the liabilities and equity section of the balance sheet are current liabilities, long-term liabilities, and equity.

Current liabilities—debts that will fall due within one year, or one operating cycle—are listed first. *Current liabilities* include such items as accounts payable to the firm's suppliers, short-term notes payable, the currently due portion of any long-term debt, and various categories of accrued expenses. *Accrued expenses* in general represent expenses that have been incurred as of the balance sheet date but have not yet been paid in cash. Items such as salaries and wages due to employees, interest due on loans, accrued utilities expenses, and similar items would be included as accrued expenses.

One extremely important balance sheet relationship is that of current assets to current liabilities. Current assets are assets that are expected to be turned into cash within one year, and current liabilities are obligations that are expected to be paid in cash within one year. The relationship of current assets to current liabilities is of some importance in judging the short-term liquidity of the firm. Short-term liquidity refers to the ability of the firm to meet its current obligations as they fall due. The excess of current assets over current liabilities is called the *net working capital* of the firm.

A rule of thumb commonly employed by bankers and other lenders suggests that, for most firms, current assets should be approximately twice as large as current liabilities. It is easy to see why this relationship should be so. First of all, working capital represents the "circulating capital" of a firm. Marketable securities, accounts receivable, and inventories are continually being converted into cash in the normal course of business. This cash is, in turn, used to pay off maturing current liabilities, reinvested in new inventories, used to finance the growth of new accounts receivable, and, as excess cash balances build up, invested in new marketable securities. Additionally, new short-term liabilities are incurred as sales grow and additional investments in current assets are made. Accounts payable, in particular, are often referred to as "spontaneous financing," since they arise spontaneously with inventory purchases that are normally made on open accounts. Given the various lags in the conversion of inventories to receivables and then to cash, and given the necessity of paying current liabilities when due, normal prudence suggests that a margin of safety of current assets over current liabilities should be maintained.

A second margin of safety is dictated by the very nature of current assets. Marketable securities are subject to possible temporary or even permanent declines in market value. Accounts receivable are subject to bad-debt losses. Finally, inventories are subject to physical deterioration, unsalability, and declines in market value. In order to balance these possible declines in asset values against the fixed requirement to pay one's debts in full when due, some margin of safety of assets over liabilities is required. Experience indicates that a two-to-one margin is appropriate for most firms. In summary:

Net working capital = Circulating capital = Current assets – Current liabilities
Hoya Manufacturers' net working capital (2008) = $5,223,000 – $3,309,000 = $1,914,000

The second part of the liabilities and equity section of the balance sheet is the long-term liabilities section, which lists long-term debt owed to banks or other creditors and any obligations under capital leases. Detailed information relative to the specific characteristics of the long-term debt is disclosed in the footnotes to the financial statements.

Equity is the final segment of the liabilities and equity section and represents the common stockholders' interest in the corporation. This is known as the *stockholders' equity* section, or the *net worth* of the company. Here one finds the owners' interest in the company represented by various classes of shares of stock. Preferred stock, listed first, has preference over the shares of common stock as to payment of dividends or payment in the event of corporate liquidation. Most preferred-stock dividends are cumulative, meaning that if the dividends are not paid in a given year, they are considered in arrears and must be paid in full before dividends can be paid on the common stock. In Hoya Manufacturers' case, the $100 par, 6 percent preferred indicates that the stock was sold for $100 per share and pays a dividend of 6 percent, or $6 per year. This preferred dividend always must be paid before dividends can be paid to the common stockholders.

The next three segments of the equity section represent the common stockholders' interest in the corporation. Unlike preferred stock, the par value of the common stock has no particular economic significance but is merely the result of a bookkeeping necessity. When common stock is sold, it must be entered on the books of the corporation at an assigned or "legal" value, usually designated its *par value* or *stated value*. However, the dollar amount for which the stock can be sold is determined by investors' aggregate assessment of the value of the firm, not by the firm's bookkeeping requirements. Since in most states it is illegal for a corporation to sell stock below its par value, corporations commonly set a rather low par value on their common stock and, in some states, elect to have no par value. The amount for which the stock is sold over and above its par value generally is listed as "paid-in capital" or "amounts contributed in excess of par value." In the case of Hoya Manufacturers, the balance sheet figures tell us that 104,000 shares of stock are outstanding ($520,000 par value divided by $5 par value per share), and that these shares were sold by the corporation for a total of $940,000 ($520,000 par plus $420,000 paid-in capital).

The final common stockholders' equity account consists of *retained earnings*. This figure represents the firm's reinvested earnings over the years that have not been paid out in dividends. These earnings "belong" entirely to the common stockholders and represent the buildup of their equity interest over time. It is important to note the major difference here between preferred and common stock. The preferred stock has a priority claim to its $6 annual dividend and preference as to distribution of asset values in the event of a liquidation. In return for its preferred status, the preferred stock gives up any claim to earnings above the $6 per share to which it is entitled. These additional earnings accrue to the benefit of the common stockholder. In return for this benefit, the common stockholders accept the risk of variable dividends that are in no way guaranteed and the risk of changing stock values in response to the changing fortunes of the company. If residual earnings after payment of all expenses and preferred-stock dividends are insufficient to pay the common stock-holders, then the board of directors may vote not to pay common-stock dividends. Similarly, if a firm incurs a loss in a given year, the amount of this loss is deducted from the retained earnings account, and the common stockholders' equity decreases. Thus, common stockholders' equity is sometimes referred to as the firm's "equity cushion."

The legal form of the business is reflected in the presentation of owners' equity. The Hoya Manufacturers' financial statements illustrate the most common form of organization: the corporation. Three other forms may also be of interest: the sole proprietorship (single owner), the partnership, and the limited liability company. These ownership forms are generally reflected by a simpler method of presentation of the equity section. In a sole proprietorship, the entire equity section would be presented as the sole owner's equity in the business. Thus, if Hoya Manufacturers was owned by Ron DiLonardo, his equity at the end of 2008 would be reflected as follows:

Ron DiLonardo, Capital	$4,366,000

If Hoya Manufacturers was organized as a partnership, with Ron and Susan DiLonardo as equal partners, the owners' equity section would appear as follows:

Ron DiLonardo, Capital	$2,183,000
Susan DiLonardo, Capital	2,183,000
	$4,366,000

If Hoya Manufacturers was organized as a limited liability company, the members' equity section would appear as follows:

Ron DiLonardo, Member	$2,183,000
Susan DiLonardo, Member	$2,183,000
Total Members' Equity	$4,366,000

Of course, a business organization the size of Hoya would often be organized as a corporation, so these examples are presented as illustrations only. Small businesses, real estate ventures, and professional organizations such as law firms, CPA firms, and the like typically are organized as sole proprietorships, partnerships, or limited liability companies.

BOOK VALUE OF SECURITIES

A final item of interest in the balance sheet is the *net book value*, or *net asset value*, of a company's securities. The net book value of a bond, share of preferred stock, or share of common stock represents the value of the corporation's assets to which each class of security has a claim, based on the book value of these assets. Book value represents the value at which an asset is carried on the company's balance sheet ("the books"). Stated alternatively, assuming that all assets could be sold at book value and all current liabilities paid off, the net asset value, or book value, represents the dollar value of the remaining assets that would be available to pay off each class of security in order of its preference in liquidation-first bonds, then preferred stock, then common stock.

Perhaps the best way to understand book value is by means of an example. Assuming that Hoya's $1,695,000 of long-term debt consists of 1,695 bonds with a face value of $1,000 each, then the net asset value per bond is determined as follows:

Net asset value per bond

Total assets	$9,370,000
Less: Current liabilities	(3,309,000)
Net assets available to meet bondholders' claims	$6,061,000
Net asset value per bond = $6,061,000/1,695 =	$3,576

Since bonds have first preference in liquidation, they will have the highest degree of safety. As seen in the previous example, there are $3,576 of net assets available to meet the claims of each $1,000 bond, based on the book value of the company's assets.

Preferred stock is next in order of preference in liquidation. Its net asset value per share is computed as follows:

Net asset value per share of preferred stock (4,250 shares)

Total assets	$9,370,000
Less: Current liabilities	(3,309,000)
Long-term debt	(1,695,000)
Net assets available to meet preferred claims	$4,366,000
Net asset value per share of preferred stock = $4,366,000/4,250 =	$1,027

Finally, the net book value per share of common stock is computed by determining the amount of money, based on book values, that each share of common stock would receive in the event that the company were liquidated. In Hoya's case, a net book value per share of common stock equal to $37.89 is computed as follows:

Net book value per share of common stock (104,000 shares)

Total assets	$9,370,000
Less: Current liabilities	(3,309,000)
Long-term debt	(1,695,000)
Preferred stock	(425,000)
Net assets available to meet common claims	$3,941,000
Book value per share of common stock = $3,941,000/104,000 =	$37.89

Alternatively (and equivalently), the net book value per share of common stock could be calculated as follows:

Net book value per share of common stock (104,000 shares)
Alternative calculation

Common stock ($5 par)	$520,000
Paid-in surplus	$420,000
Retained earnings	$3,001,000
Total common stockholders' equity	$3,941,000
Book value per share of common stock = $3,941,000/104,000	$37.89

Both calculations must, of course, yield the same answer since common stockholders' equity is by definition equal to total assets less all liabilities and preferred stock.

One should not be misled by book value calculations, particularly values calculated for common stock. First of all, in most cases it is reasonable to make what accountants call the "going concern" assumption. One may assume that there is no imminent danger of liquidation, and therefore the liquidation value of the company is not the most relevant variable in determining the value of its securities. Second, one must bear in mind that book value computations implicitly assume that all assets may be sold at book value to satisfy the various claims. Depending on individual circumstances this may or may not be the case. If liquidation were to occur, assets might in fact be sold at more or less than book value. Finally, one must observe that market values of securities are determined by market forces that may be only marginally related to book values. For bonds and preferred stocks, market values are determined mainly by the credit rating of the company, prevailing interest rates, and, for larger issues, the probability of default implied by the prices on a company's credit default swaps.

For common stocks, corporate earnings and future economic outlook are the key to value. However, even given the limitations of book value calculations for common stock, many stock analysts and investors look at the ratio of stock market price to book value as a measure of the reasonableness of the stock's market price. Several recent empirical studies in finance have shown that stocks with low ratios of market price to book value (so-called value stocks) outperform stocks with high ratios of market price to book value.

THE INCOME STATEMENT

Exhibit 3.3 presents a common form of the income statement. The income statement format shown in the exhibit also shows changes in retained earnings at the bottom of the statement and therefore is entitled a "Statement of Current and Retained Earnings." If the balance sheet is visualized as a snapshot or stock statement, then the income statement can be thought of as a moving picture or flow type of statement. The income statement presents the flow of revenues, costs, and expenses through a business in a given year. The relationship of the income statement to the balance sheet can be depicted as follows:

Stock of financial resources on December 31, 2007 $\longrightarrow$ Flow of revenues and expenses during calendar year 2008 $\longrightarrow$ Stock of financial resources on December 31, 2008

Balance sheet December 31, 2007 $\longrightarrow$ Income statement calendar year 2008 $\longrightarrow$ Balance sheet December 31, 2008

This diagram conveniently expresses both the major difference and the key relationship between the balance sheet and the income statement. The balance sheet represents the financial position of the firm at a given instant, whereas the income statement portrays the results of operations for a period of time.

In terms of this example, the two balance sheets show the position of the firm at the end of 2008 and 2007, whereas the income statement provides information relative to how the firm got from where it was at the end of 2007 to where it is at the end of 2008.

EXHIBIT 3.3 HOYA MANUFACTURERS, INC.
STATEMENT OF CURRENT AND RETAINED EARNINGS

	2008	2007
Sales	$13,413,000	$11,575,000
Operating expenses:		
Cost of goods sold	7,467,000	7,194,000
Depreciation	376,000	334,000
Selling and administrative expenses	4,575,000	3,092,000
Total operating expenses	$12,418,000	$10,620,000
Operating income	995,000	955,000
Other income	186,000	184,000
Total income	$1,181,000	$1,139,000
Interest expense	180,000	184,000
Earnings before tax	1,001,000	955,000
Provision for income taxes	382,000	371,000
Net income	$619,000	$584,000
===		
Common shares outstanding	104,000	102,000
Net earnings per share of common stock	$5.71	$5.38
===		

STATEMENT OF ACCUMULATED AND RETAINED EARNINGS

	2008	2007
Retained earnings at January 1	$2,684,000	$2,390,000
Net income for year	619,000	584,000
Total	$3,303,000	$2,974,000
Less dividends paid on:		
Preferred stock	25,500	35,000
Common stock	276,500	255,000
Retained earnings at December 31	$3,001,000	$2,684,000

The upper half of the statement of current and retained earnings shows the firm's annual sales revenue, various categories of costs and expenses, net earnings before and after tax, and earnings per share of common stock. The sales figure represents the firm's total sales revenue for the year, net of any sales returns or discounts allowed. Cost of goods sold represents such items as materials costs, direct factory labor, and factory overhead costs. Depreciation represents the total dollar amount of plant and equipment depreciation for the year, while selling and administrative expenses represent all other categories of operating expenses. Deducting total operating expenses from sales results in operating profit, or the amount of gross profit earned from the normal operations of the company. Other income normally represents miscellaneous income from sources other than normal operation, such as interest on notes receivable held by the company, capital gains and losses, and similar items. Next comes the interest expense account. This item is normally listed separately, since it represents a financing expense—that is, an expense resulting from the firm's decision on how to finance the company (debt versus equity), rather than an expense resulting from the normal operations of the company.

Finally, deducting interest expense yields the "bottom line"—net income for the year. Since the owners of the company normally are most concerned with earnings per share of common stock, the bottom line is expressed on a per share basis. This conversion is made by deducting any preferred-stock dividends paid from net income and dividing the remainder by the average number of shares of common stock outstanding during the year. Preferred dividends are deducted because, unlike interest paid to bondholders, they are not a tax-deductible expense of doing business. Just like common stock, preferred stock is an ownership security, and any dividends paid are considered a distribution of profits to the legal owners of the company. In Hoya's case, earnings per share is computed as follows:

	2008	2007
Net income	$619,000	$584,000
Less: Preferred dividends	(25,500)	(35,000)
Earnings available to common stockholders	$593,000	$549,000
Common shares outstanding	104,000	102,000
Earnings per share of common stock	$5.70	$5.38

SUPPLEMENTAL "PRO FORMA" OR "OPERATING" EARNINGS

Over the past few years, many public companies have provided what are commonly called "pro forma" presentations of supplementary earnings computations in addition to earnings per share as calculated according to GAAP. The intent of these supplementary computations is to present the core operating earnings of the company independent of the impact of what the company may consider to be nonrecurring, unusual transactions. For example, a loss incurred from closing a plant may be excluded from core earnings computations on the grounds that this is a nonrecurring event and does not affect core earnings. Although Standard and Poor's Corporation has announced guidelines that S&P will use in calculating pro forma operating earnings for credit analysis done by S&P, most companies have developed their own standards, and it is necessary to carefully read the footnotes to a company's financial statements to determine what rules they have applied.

ACCUMULATED AND RETAINED EARNINGS

The bottom section of Exhibit 3.3, the statement of accumulated and retained earnings, illustrates a key relationship between the balance sheet and the income statement. Retained earnings for the year just ending must be equal to retained earnings at the end of the previous year (same as the beginning of the current year), plus net income (or minus net loss) for the current year, less any distribution of net income, usually dividends. Occasionally distributions of losses, such as final settlement of prior years' income taxes, may be deducted from the retained earnings account. Hoya Manufacturers illustrates the more typical case (note that retained earnings at December 31, 2007, are the same as retained earnings at January 1, 2008):

Retained earnings	+	Net income	–	Dividends	=	Retained earnings
December 31, 2007		2008		paid 2008		December 31, 2008
$2,684,000	+	$619,000	–	$302,000	=	$3,001,000

Having examined the income statement, we may now direct our attention to the second important category of flow statements, the statement of cash flows.

STATEMENT OF CASH FLOWS

Exhibit 3.4 presents Hoya Manufacturers' *statement of cash flows* for the year 2008. This statement shows all of the sources and uses of cash during the year and details the overall change in the total of cash and marketable securities (often referred to as "cash equivalents") during the year. The bottom section of the statement for 2008 shows that Hoya began the year with $322,000 in cash and marketable securities and ended the year with $372,000, for an increase of $50,000 in cash and marketable securities. The top sections of the statement show changes in cash from three major sources: cash flows from operating activities, cash flows from investing activities, and cash flows from financing activities.

The first section of the statement, cash from operating activities, always begins with net earnings as the initial source of cash from operations. To reconcile account earnings with cash flow requires that we first add back depreciation to net earnings, because depreciation is a noncash charge against earnings. If Hoya had other noncash charges (which it does not), these charges also would be added back at this point. Next, changes in current asset and liability accounts that impact cash must be accounted for. In Hoya's case, both accounts receivable and inventories increased, resulting in a decrease in cash. On the current liabilities side, accounts payable decreased, which requires a use of cash, and accrued expenses and accrued taxes increased, which causes cash to increase. As the exhibit shows, total cash from operating activities contributed a $236,000 cash increase.

**EXHIBIT 3.4   HOYA MANUFACTURERS, INC.
STATEMENT OF CASH FLOWS, 2008**

Cash flows from operating activities:		
Net earnings	$619,000	
Adjustments to reconcile net earnings to cash provided from operating activities:		
Depreciation	376,000	
Decrease (increase) in receivables	(417,000)	
Decrease (increase) in inventory	(271,000)	
Increase (decrease) in accounts payable	(178,000)	
Increase (decrease) in accrued expenses	75,000	
Increase (decrease) in accrued taxes	32,000	
Cash from operating activities		$236,000
Cash flows from investing activities:		
Additions to plant and equipment	(766,000)	
Disposal of other assets	83,000	
Cash used for investing activities		($683,000)
Cash flows from financing activities:		
Increase in notes payable	680,000	
Increase in long-term debt	266,000	
Sale of common stock	25,000	
Refunding of preferred stock	(172,000)	
Dividends on preferred stock	(25,500)	
Dividends on common stock	(276,500)	
Cash from (used for) financing activities		$497,000
Increase (decrease) in cash and marketable securities during the year		$50,000
Cash and marketable securities at beginning of year		$322,000
Cash and marketable securities at end of year		$372,000

Cash flows from investing activities were negative in 2008, resulting from a use of $766,000 for additions to plant and equipment, less $83,000 from disposal of assets. Cash flows from financing activities contributed $497,000 to cash. Cash was provided by an increase in notes payable of $680,000, plus an increase in long-term debt of $266,000, plus a $25,000 sale of common stock. Cash was used to buy back $172,000 of preferred stock and to pay a total of $302,000 in preferred- and common-stock dividends.

We can see that the cash flow statement provides both important information about the company's management of stockholders' resources and a useful picture of how cash flows through the business. In this chapter we have seen the three major categories of financial statements. The next chapter will show the structure of the financial information system that allows the collection, reporting, and intelligent interpretation of financial information.

SARBANES-OXLEY AND FINANCIAL STATEMENTS

The reforms introduced by the Sarbanes-Oxley Act have had a significant effect on the process of financial reporting in four primary areas. First, Sarbanes-Oxley introduced a requirement that public company CEOs and CFOs "certify" the company's quarterly and annual financial statements, stating that, to the executive's knowledge, the financial statements are accurate. Making a false certification can result in significant penalties to the executive. Second, Sarbanes-Oxley requires that public companies and their accountants review the company's "internal controls" and provide a public statement as to the effectiveness of those controls. Third, accounting firms have become much more proactive in requiring corporate executives to certify to the accounting firms themselves the quality of the information provided to the accounting firms, a direct fallout from the Arthur Andersen collapse. Finally, Sarbanes-Oxley requires public companies to minutely detail the firm's processes under Section 404 of the act. This requirement has added hundreds of thousands of dollars (for small companies) to millions of dollars (for larger companies) of cost to public companies.

SUMMARY

The objective of financial accounting is to present fairly the financial condition of a business organization. Generally accepted accounting principles (GAAP) provide guidelines for the preparation of financial statements. GAAP apply only to the field of financial accounting and not to other major fields of accounting such as tax, managerial, and cost accounting. CPAs audit financial statements and render opinions on whether the statements present fairly the financial condition of a firm. A "qualified opinion" normally indicates some lack of conformity with GAAP.

The balance sheet provides a snapshot of the financial condition of a firm as of a given date and lists the assets, liabilities, and equities of the firm. By definition, assets must equal the total liabilities plus equity. The income statement may be thought of as a moving picture representing the flow of revenues, costs, and expenses through the firm over the course of a given year or accounting period. The cash flow statement shows the sources and uses of cash and cash equivalents (such as marketable securities) during the year and the resulting change in the company's cash position. It also shows the changes in the individual cash accounts that resulted in the overall change in cash.

KEY POINTS

GAAP   Generally accepted accounting principles, a set of objectives, conventions, and principles that have evolved through the years to govern the preparation of financial statements. The objective of the statements is to present fairly the financial condition of the company.

BALANCE SHEET   A "snapshot" or "stock" statement showing the financial condition of the firm at a given instant. The basis of the accounting equation:

Assets = Liabilities + Equities

INCOME STATEMENT   A "moving picture" or "flow" statement showing the flow of revenues and expenses through the firm over a given period of time. The results are usually expressed on a per share basis for corporations. Generally includes a statement of accumulated retained earnings, providing the key link between the balance sheet and the income statement:

Retained earnings last year
+ Net income this year
− Dividends paid this year
= Retained earnings this year

STATEMENT OF CASH FLOWS A second "flow" statement showing the flow of cash through the firm during a given year. Provides an important "moving picture" of the total sources and uses of cash.

SARBANES-OXLEY A federal law that increases management accountability for the financial statements of public company issuers by requiring certification of financial statements and testing and reporting on the internal controls of the company.

4

Accounting—A Financial Information System

THE ACCOUNTING PROCESS

Accounting is often referred to as the "universal language of business," and for good reason. The accounting process is a financial information system designed to record, classify, report, and interpret financial data of interest to organizations of all varieties. In the previous chapter, an introduction to basic financial reports—the balance sheet, the income statement, and the statement of cash flows—was provided. In this chapter, we will examine the logical structure of these statements in more detail. Specifically, we will examine the fundamentals of the double-entry accounting system, which is used as the framework for our financial information system.

Before proceeding to the mechanics of the double-entry accounting system, we must examine one very important accounting concept. This concept, called the accrual concept or matching principle, forms the basis for the measurement of accounting income. Understanding this concept is a prerequisite for an understanding of the double-entry system and of nearly all financial records.

THE ACCRUAL CONCEPT

A short and meaningful statement of exactly what the accrual concept means is difficult. For a working definition, we may begin by noting that it has three aspects that relate to the measurement of revenue, the measurement of expenses, and the matching of revenues and expenses in the calculation of income.

The first aspect of the accrual concept states that revenue earned does not necessarily correspond to the receipt of cash. One often reads statements in introductory accounting texts to the effect that "revenue is recognized at the time it is realized," meaning that earned revenue is measured by the asset received in exchange. The asset received in exchange for goods delivered or services performed is most often cash or an account receivable. Thus, when an individual buys an item from a department store and charges it on a store credit card, the department store considers the sale consummated and revenue earned even though no cash has yet changed hands. Further, if the sale occurs in December and the customer does not pay for the purchase until February, the sale will be considered part of earned revenue for the calendar year ending in December, even though the cash is not received until two months later.

A simple example of a hypothetical service firm will make this point clearer. Assume that Rusty Gardner, the sole proprietor of RAG Limited, a management consulting firm specializing in small business management, has a balance sheet on March 31, 2008, as shown in Exhibit 4.1. During the month of April 2008, Rusty performs $2,500 worth of services for his various clients and bills them for services rendered. No other transactions take place during April. At the end of April, his balance sheet would appear as in Exhibit 4.2.

EXHIBIT 4.1 RAG LIMITED
BALANCE SHEET, 3/31/08

ASSETS		LIABILITIES	
Cash	$12,000	Accounts payable	$4,000
Accounts receivable	1,000	Total current liabilities	$4,000
Total current assets	$13,000	**Owner's equity**	
Building and equipment	20,000	RAG, Capital	29,000
Total assets	$33,000	Total liabilities and equity	$33,000

Note in Exhibit 4.2 that the $2,500 worth of services performed appears on Rusty's balance sheet as an increase in accounts receivable of $2,500 on the asset side and an increase in Rusty's equity of $2,500 on the liabilities and equity side. This is the point of revenue recognition. For purposes of recognizing accounting revenue, the accounting revenue is earned at the time the services are provided and the client is billed. Even though no cash has yet changed hands, the revenue is already reflected in Rusty's accounts. When the cash does change hands (that is, when the accounts receivable are paid), no additional revenue is "booked." The payment of the accounts receivable is a "swap" of one asset for another—namely, of the accounts receivable for cash. Assuming that the accounts are paid in full during the month of May, Rusty's balance sheet at the end of May would appear as shown in Exhibit 4.3. Note that in the May balance sheet, no change in owner's equity has occurred, and no change in total assets has occurred. The only change reflected on the balance sheet is the shift in current assets shown by the $2,500 increase in cash and the $2,500 decrease in accounts receivable.

EXHIBIT 4.2   RAG LIMITED
BALANCE SHEET, 4/30/08

ASSETS		LIABILITIES	
Cash	$12,000	Accounts payable	$4,000
Accounts receivable	3,500	Total current liabilities	$4,000
Total current assets	$15,500	**Owner's equity**	
Building and equipment	20,000	RAG, Capital	31,500
Total assets	$35,500	Total liabilities and equity	$35,500

The second aspect of the accrual concept is related to the first. This aspect states that *expenses are not necessarily related to the expenditure of cash.* Expenses are costs incurred by the firm in earning revenue and are measured by the cost of the asset consumed or services used. One of the most common and readily understood illustrations of this concept deals with the purchase of multiyear fire-insurance policies. For example, if a company purchases a three-year fire-insurance policy for $1,800 cash on January 1, 2007, the insurance expense associated with that policy properly belongs to 2007, 2008, and 2009, the years during which the policy will be in force. Thus, from an accounting standpoint the $1,800 expenditure of cash should be "charged off" over a three-year period beginning in 2007. Without going into accounting details at this point, what occurs is that an $1,800 asset called "prepaid insurance" is recorded on the balance sheet on January 1, 2007. At the end of 2007, one-third of the value of the asset ($600) is recorded on the income statement as an expense. The value of the prepaid expense on the balance sheet is reduced to $1,200—the difference between the original value of $1,800 and the amount "used up" during the current year. At the end of 2008, an additional $600 is charged off, with the final $600 charged off at the end of 2009. At this point, the value of the prepaid insurance asset on the balance sheet would be reduced to zero, and a new insurance policy would be purchased.

EXHIBIT 4.3   RAG LIMITED
BALANCE SHEET, 5/31/08

ASSETS		LIABILITIES	
Cash	$14,500	Accounts payable	$4,000
Accounts receivable	1,000	Total current liabilities	$4,000
Total current assets	$15,500	**Owner's equity**	
Building and equipment	20,000	RAG, Capital	31,500
Total assets	$35,500	Total liabilities and equity	$35,500

The final aspect of the accrual concept states that accounting income for a given accounting period is determined by matching the expenses incurred in that period with the revenues earned in that period. The difference between revenues and expenses constitutes income for the period. In short, income is what is obtained through matching revenues and expense and may be only coincidentally related to cash flows. Flows of cash will be addressed later on, in the chapters dealing with financial analysis and control. For the present, we will move ahead with our explanation of the double-entry accounting system.

DOUBLE-ENTRY ACCOUNTING

Double-entry accounting is a rather clever bookkeeping system that provides a set of techniques to keep track of accounting data while minimizing the probability of an arithmetic error. The mechanics of bookkeeping can become quite complex, and the probability of an error of some sort is quite high. Perhaps the greatest virtue of double-entry accounting is the requirement that accounting records always be "in balance," so that an arithmetic error is automatically exposed by a lack of balance.

Reduced to essentials, any accounting system requires a means to keep track of five fundamental categories of data:

Balance sheet accounts
1. Assets
2. Liabilities
3. Owners' equity

Income statement accounts
4. Revenue
5. Expenses

As a first step toward understanding the accounting system, recall the accounting equation from Chapter 3:

$$\text{Assets} = \text{Liabilities} + \text{Equity}$$

$$\text{Total business resources} = \text{Creditors' claims} + \text{Owners' claims}$$

It is this relationship that requires that the balance sheet always balance, since by definition the total resources of an organization must always be equal to the sum of the creditors' and the owners' claims against those resources.

The accounting equation, which forms the basis of the double-entry accounting system, contains the first three categories of data to be accounted for—assets, liabilities, and equity. The basic accounting equation can be expanded to include the last two categories of data, revenues and expenses. Recall from the RAG Limited example that the effect of revenue on a business is to increase owners' equity. Just as revenue increases owners' equity, the effect of an expense is to decrease owners' equity. Noting this effect of revenue and expense on the owners' equity account, we can see that the accounting equation can be expanded to account for changes in equity brought about by the earning of revenue or incurring of expenses as follows:

$$\text{Assets} = \text{Liabilities} + \text{Equity} + \text{Revenues} - \text{Expenses}$$

Alternatively, by using a bit of simple algebra one can restate the accounting equation in its common form:

$$\text{Assets} + \text{Expenses} = \text{Liabilities} + \text{Equity} + \text{Revenues}$$

This last form of the accounting equation is the basis of double-entry accounting. The double-entry accounting system is designed such that the accounting equation is always kept in balance: the left-hand side (assets plus expenses) must always be equal to the right-hand side (liabilities plus equity plus revenues). The basic component of this system is the *account*, which is an individual record of increases and decreases in the dollar amount of specific assets, liabilities, equity, revenues, and expenses. An individual account may be kept on something as simple as a ruled sheet of paper with a line down the center. As the accounting system becomes more complex, it may be kept on a computer. To illustrate, an individual account is usually represented by the so-called T-account, a simple representation of an accounting record with a line separating the left- and right-hand sides, such as the following:

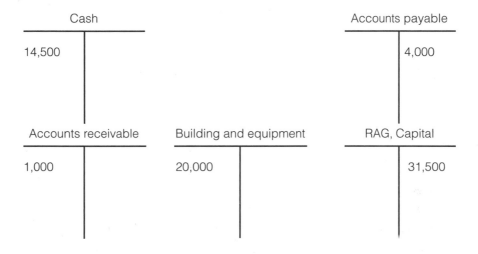

Making entries, or notations, in various accounts is called posting the account. Double-entry accounting provides a system for posting accounts so that the accounting equation remains in balance. Those accounts on the left-hand side of the accounting equation (assets and expenses) are posted on the left-hand side in order to increase the amount of the account. Decreases to the account are posted on the right-hand side. Conversely, those accounts on the right-hand side of the accounting equation (liabilities, equity, and revenues) are posted on the right-hand side to increase the amount of the account, and on the left-hand side to decrease the amount of the account. Overall, when accounts are posted, a sufficient number of entries must be made so that the dollar amount posted on the left-hand side of various accounts balances the same dollar amount posted on the right-hand side of one or more accounts. Following this simple rule ensures that the accounting equation will always be in balance. The term *double entry* merely reflects the fact that whenever accounting records are posted, at least two entries must be made—one or more on the left-hand side and one or more on the right-hand side. As a shorthand method for noting whether entries should be made on the left-hand or right-hand side of a given account, the system of debits and credits was developed.

The System of Debits and Credits

The system of debits and credits often creates quite a bit of unnecessary confusion among persons who are not familiar with accounting rules. Actually, the use of debits and credits is quite simple and is nothing more or less than a shorthand method developed to aid in writing down instructions for making accounting entries. The word *debit* refers to an entry on the left-hand side of an account, while the word *credit* refers to just the opposite—an entry on the right-hand side of an account. Whether a debit or credit has the effect of increasing or decreasing the amount of a particular account depends on the type of account. For example, if the account is an asset account such as cash, the account is a left-hand side account and would be increased by a debit entry and decreased by a credit entry. If the account is a right-hand side account, such as revenue, the opposite is true. In sum:

$$\text{Debit (Dr.)} = \text{Left-hand side entry}$$
$$\text{Credit (Cr.)} = \text{Right-hand side entry}$$

$$\left.\begin{array}{l}\text{Debit} \neq \text{Increase} \\ \text{Credit} \neq \text{Decrease}\end{array}\right\}\quad \begin{array}{l}\text{Increase or decrease} \\ \text{depends only on type of account}\end{array}$$

To determine the effect of a given entry on the balance of an individual account, one must refer to the accounting equation. The left-hand side accounts (assets and expenses) normally carry a debit balance, are debited to increase, and are credited to decrease. Conversely, right-hand side accounts (liabilities, equity, and revenues) normally carry a credit balance, are credited to increase, and are debited to decrease. The chart below summarizes the foregoing:

Debit side (Dr.)	Credit side (Cr.)
Assets + Expenses	Liabilities + Equity + Revenues
Debit (Dr.) to increase	Credit (Cr.) to increase
Credit (Cr.) to decrease	Debit (Dr.) to decrease
Normal balance = Debit	Normal balance = Credit

For the accounting equation to be in balance, the sum of the debit entries must always be equal to the sum of the credit entries. To determine whether the accounts balance at any given time, one need only add up the sum of the debits and the sum of the credits. If the two totals are not equal, then an error has been made somewhere and should be located immediately.

The process described above is called taking a trial balance. The system, of course, is not foolproof. For example, the correct number and amount of debits and credits might be made, but one or more entries may be posted to the wrong accounts. The accounting records will still balance, but they will not be correct. Errors of this type are much more difficult to find.

A few simple accounting entries will illustrate the double-entry accounting system. Since the objective is for readers to understand the system, not to become bookkeepers or accountants, a minimal amount of space will be devoted to these examples. Readers requiring further information on this subject may refer to any introductory-level accounting text.

Some Simple Examples

To illustrate, let us assume that Tommy Termite, who is currently employed by Bugsey's Pest Control Service, is leaving Bugsey's employ to start his own business. The new business, Tommy Termite Pest Control, will be operated as a sole proprietorship and will begin operations on June 1. Tommy's first "official act" will be to open a checking account in the name of Tommy Termite Pest Control by depositing $10,000 in that name in his bank. The accounting transaction would be recorded as follows:

Dr. Cash   10,000
    Cr. Tommy Termite, Capital   10,000

Tommy now has two accounts, one asset account (Cash) and one equity account (Tommy Termite, Capital). If Tommy keeps his accounts in a loose-leaf notebook with one page devoted to each account, his accounts would be represented by the following T-accounts:

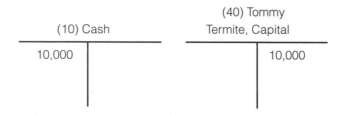

Note that the T-accounts are numbered. Accounts are often numbered in order to facilitate the recording of transactions in journals—if journals are used to record transactions prior to posting the actual accounts. A journal is nothing more than a chronological record of transactions that are to be posted later in the actual accounts. The accounts themselves are kept in books referred to as ledgers. For a small operation such as Tommy's, a journal probably would not be used, and transactions would be posted directly to one "general ledger." The process of recording transactions in journals is referred to as journalizing.

The number system used above is not a random process. Each account is assigned a number of at least two digits with the leading digit established according to the order of appearance of the account in the accounting equation. Asset accounts always begin at number 1 and proceed roughly in balance sheet order. Thus, cash would be number 10, accounts receivable 11, inventory number 12, and so forth. For an extremely large number of assets, cash might begin with 100, 1,000, or even 10,000. Similarly, expense accounts begin with 2, liabilities with 3, equities with 4, and revenues with 5. The advantages of using systematic numbering should be fairly obvious.

To continue the Tommy Termite example, let us journalize Tommy's first month's activities and then post these journal records to his general ledger. Each journal entry will have a number, which will be noted on the simulated ledger sheets so that the reader may examine each transaction. The previous $10,000 transaction will be treated as transaction number 1. Additional transactions during June, with appropriate journal notations, are as follows:

2. Tommy purchases a new delivery van for $10,000. He makes a down payment of $2,000 in cash and borrows the remaining $8,000 from the Friendly National Bank:

Dr. Delivery van	10,000	
Cr. Cash		2,000
Cr. Bank notes payable		8,000

3. Tommy purchases $2,500 worth of various pest control supplies on open account from Pete's Pest Products, a local wholesale distributor:

Dr. Supplies inventory	2,500	
Cr. Accounts payable		2,500

4. Tommy completes an extermination job for the Cliffdweller Apartment Complex, billing Cliffdweller for $4,500:

Dr. Accounts receivable	4,500	
Cr. Service revenue		4,500

5. Cliffdweller sends Tommy a check for $3,000, which he deposits in his checking account. The remaining $1,500 will be paid at the end of July:

Dr. Cash	3,000	
Cr. Accounts receivable		3,000

6. Tommy pays $1,500 on his account at Pete's Pest Products:

Dr. Accounts payable	1,500	
Cr. Cash		1,500

7. Tommy takes an end-of-month inventory of pest control supplies in order to determine how much was used up during the month. He notes that $1,500 worth of the original $2,500 inventory is left. Therefore, $1,000 worth of supplies must have been used up in the Cliffdweller job:

Dr. Supplies expense	1,000	
Cr. Supplies inventory		1,000

If transaction number 7 is Tommy's last transaction for the month, it can be seen that Tommy now has a total of nine accounts to maintain as follows:

Assets

(10) Cash
(11) Accounts receivable
(12) Supplies inventory

(13) Delivery van
Expenses
(20) Supplies expense
Liabilities
(30) Accounts payable
(31) Bank notes payable
Equity
(40) Tommy Termite, Capital
Revenue
(50) Service revenue

T-accounts for the nine accounts above would appear as shown in Exhibit 4.4. All seven transactions are numbered and posted to the appropriate T-accounts. We will return to the accounts shown in Exhibit 4.4 following a brief discussion of the major steps in what is generally known as the accounting cycle and an explanation of the closing process.

THE ACCOUNTING CYCLE

The *accounting cycle* is a logical series of steps that accountants follow to keep necessary accounting records and prepare financial statements. In this section, the Tommy Termite example will be continued in order to illustrate the steps in the cycle, and a one-month income statement and balance sheet will be presented for Tommy.

The first two steps in the accounting cycle are very closely related and are accomplished during the month as transactions occur. Step 1 involves sorting business transactions into an appropriate number of debits and credits to be entered on the accounting records. Thus, in Tommy Termite's first transaction, we conclude that depositing $10,000 in his checking account involves a debit to cash and a credit to Tommy's capital account. Step 2 in the accounting cycle involves recording this transaction (as debit and credit entries) in a journal for later posting to the general ledger. As previously noted, a small operation such as Tommy Termite's may not even bother with a journal. In this case, one would proceed directly to Step 3 in the accounting cycle and post the general ledger directly.

Posting journal entries to the general ledger, Step 3 in the cycle, is generally accomplished at the end of each month. If no journal is

**EXHIBIT 4.4   TOMMY TERMITE PEST CONTROL
SAMPLE T-ACCOUNTS**

(10) Cash	
(1) 10,000	2,000 (2)
(5) 3,000	1,500 (6)

(11) Accounts receivable	
(4) 4,500	3,000 (5)

(12) Supplies inventory	
(3) 2,500	1,000 (7)

(13) Delivery van	
(2) 10,000	

(20) Supplies expense	
(7) 1,000	

(30) Accounts payable	
(6) 1,500	2,500 (3)

(31) Bank notes payable	
	8,000 (2)

(40) Tommy Termite, Capital	
	10,000 (1)

(50) Service revenue	
	4,500 (4)

maintained, transactions would simply be posted to the ledger as they occurred. For Tommy Termite, we have already seen examples of journal entries in the previous section, and the general ledger was posted in Exhibit 4.4.

Step 4 in the accounting cycle involves making what are called adjusting entries to the general ledger. Perhaps the best way to describe an adjusting entry is by means of an example. Recall from the earlier explanation of the accrual concept the example of an $1,800 prepaid insurance policy good for the next three years. At the time of purchase of the asset, the appropriate entry would be:

Dr. Prepaid insurance (an asset)   1,800
Cr. Cash   1,800

As noted previously, when the end of the year arrives and financial statements are drawn up, it will be necessary to charge off $600, or one year's worth, of the cost of the policy. The appropriate accounting entry would be:

Dr. Insurance expense   600
Cr. Prepaid insurance   600

Thus, $600 worth of an asset, prepaid insurance, is "moved over" to the income statement as the year's insurance expense. Adjusting entries in general result from the need to match expenses with revenues in accordance with the accrual concept. In Tommy Termite's case, there are no required adjusting entries. Adjusting entries are normally prepared at the end of each quarter or at the end of the year, although many firms prepare monthly financial statements. In practice, accountants normally prepare a worksheet showing the current balances for all of a company's accounts and then prepare financial statements from this worksheet. In the simple case of Tommy Termite, financial statements will be prepared directly from the general ledger accounts.

Step 5 of the accounting cycle is commonly referred to as "closing the books" and is undertaken at the end of the year. At year's end, all temporary accounts are closed out. *Temporary accounts* are those accounts that begin the new year with a zero balance—generally, the income statement accounts. All revenue and expense accounts are "closed" into an account called an income summary or profit-and-loss summary. This account in turn is "closed" to the owners' equity account. Expenses are subtracted from revenues to determine net profit (or loss), and this amount is then added to (or subtracted from) owners' equity. Remaining accounts—generally, the balance sheet accounts—are then balanced, and the balance is brought forward to begin the new year. The balance sheet accounts are therefore commonly referred to as permanent accounts. The next section provides a detailed illustration of this process for Tommy Termite.

Step 6 in the accounting cycle follows immediately after the closing process. In this final step, financial statements for the period are prepared.

The Closing Process

In the simple Tommy Termite example, a worksheet is not necessary to prepare financial statements for the end of June. To prepare Tommy's statements, we will first close out his revenue and expense accounts, transfer these balances to the income summary account, and close the income summary account to Tommy's capital account. Next, all his permanent accounts will be balanced and double ruled, with the balances brought forward to the beginning of the next ac-

EXHIBIT 4.5   TOMMY TERMITE PEST CONTROL CLOSING PROCESS

(20) Supplies expense		Income summary		(50) Service revenue	
(7) 1,000	1,000 (C1)	(C1) 1,000	4,500 (C2)	(C2) 4,500	4,500 (4)
		(C3) 3,500			

	(40) Tommy Termite, Capital
	10,000 (1)
	3,500 (C3)

counting period. Finally, in the sixth and final step, financial statements will be developed for the period ending June 30.

Exhibit 4.5 illustrates the closing process. Tommy's supplies expense and service revenue accounts are listed, along with a new account, income summary. The closing process can be seen as a result of the following three accounting entries:

(C1) The first closing entry transfers the $1,000 supplies expense to income summary:

| Dr. Income summary | 1,000 | |
| Cr. Supplies expense | | 1,000 |

(C2) The second closing entry transfers the $4,500 service revenue to the income summary account:

| Dr. Service revenue | 4,500 | |
| Cr. Income summary | | 4,500 |

(C3) The final closing entry transfers the $3,500 profit ($4,500 less $1,000) to Tommy's capital account:

| Dr. Income summary | 3,500 | |
| Cr. Tommy Termite, Capital | | 3,500 |

The remaining steps of the closing process are straightforward. The debit or credit balance in each account must be determined and brought forward to begin the next accounting period. Exhibit 4.6 illustrates the mechanics of this process. For example, in Tommy's

**EXHIBIT 4.6   TOMMY TERMITE PEST CONTROL
CLOSING PROCESS**

(10) Cash		(11) Accounts receivable		(11) Supplies inventory	
(1) 10,000	2,000 (2)	(4) 4,500	3,000 (6)	(3) 2,500	1,000 (7)
(5) 3,000	1,500 (6)		1,500 (B2)		1,500 (B3)
	9,500 (B1)	(B2) 1,500		(B3) 1,500	
(B1) 9,500					

(13) Delivery van		(20) Supplies expense		(30) Accounts payable	
(2) 10,000	10,000 (B4)	(7) 1,000	1,000 (C1)	(6) 1,500	2,500 (3)
(B4) 10,000				(B5) 1,000	
					1,000 (B5)

(31) Bank notes payable		(11) Tommy Termite, Capital		(50) Service revenue	
(B6) 8,000	8,000 (2)		10,000 (1)	(C2) 4,500	4,500 (4)
	8,000 (B6)	(B7) 13,500	3,500 (C3)		
			13,500 (B7)		

Income summary	
(C1) 1,000	4,500 (C2)
(C3) 3,500	

cash account there is a total of $13,000 in debit entries (increases in cash) compared with $3,500 in credit entries (decreases in cash). The difference between the two, $9,500, represents the current (debit) balance of the account. The debit balance is brought forward by means of two balancing entries. First, the account is credited for $9,500 (balancing entry number B1) and is double ruled to show that both sides are now equal. Next, an offsetting debit for $9,500 is "brought forward" to show the beginning balance of $9,500. A similar procedure is followed for all other open accounts. Balancing entries B1 through B7 are shown in the exhibit.

EXHIBIT 4.7 TOMMY TERMITE PEST CONTROL
INCOME STATEMENT, JUNE

Service revenue	$4,500
Expenses:	
Supplies expense	<u>1,000</u>
Net income	<u>$3,500</u>

An income statement and balance sheet can now be constructed directly from the accounts. The resulting income statement, Exhibit 4.7, is essentially a written statement of the closing process. Expenses of $1,000 are deducted from revenue of $4,500 to show a profit of $3,500. Since Tommy is a sole proprietor, no tax expense is shown because the profit will be taxed directly on Tommy's personal income tax return along with his other sources of income, if any.

Exhibit 4.8 shows Tommy's balance sheet as of June 30. The balance sheet lists the balances of Tommy's asset, liability, and equity accounts as determined by the T-accounts illustrated in Exhibit 4.6. As can be seen from Exhibit 4.8, the accounts must, of course, balance, and we see that Tommy's equity in the business has increased to $13,500. The $3,500 increase is the result of the month's profit. Recall that this $3,500 found its way into Tommy's equity account through the closing process described earlier.

Having examined the basic tenets of accounting, we have one final task. In the next chapter we explore a few special topics in accounting, including changes in the equity account, depreciation accounting, and accounting for inventories.

EXHIBIT 4.8 TOMMY TERMITE PEST CONTROL
BALANCE SHEET, JUNE 30

ASSETS		LIABILITIES	
Cash	$9,500	Accounts payable	$1,000
Accounts receivable	1,500	Bank notes payable	<u>8,000</u>
Supplies inventory	<u>1,500</u>	Total current liabilities	$9,000
Total current assets	$12,500	**Owner's equity**	
Delivery van	<u>10,000</u>	Tommy Termite, Capital	<u>13,500</u>
Total assets	<u>$22,500</u>	Total liabilities and equity	<u>$22,500</u>

SUMMARY

Accounting is a financial information system designed to record, classify, report, and interpret financial data. The accrual concept states that accounting income is measured by matching the expenses incurred in a given accounting period with the revenues earned in that period. Double-entry accounting is a bookkeeping system that provides a set of techniques to keep track of accounting data while minimizing the probability of an arithmetic error. Debits are entries on the left-hand side of an account; credits are entries on the right-hand side of an account. Using the double-entry accounting system, the sum of the debits must always equal the sum of the credits. The accounting cycle is a six-step process: (1) analyze transactions from source documents; (2) journalize transactions; (3) post general ledger; (4) adjust general ledger; (5) close and balance ledger; and (6) prepare financial statements.

KEY POINTS

ACCOUNTING PROCESS

Record
Classify
Report
Interpret
} Financial data

ACCRUAL CONCEPT

Revenue earned does not necessarily correspond to the receipt of cash. Expenses are not necessarily related to the expenditure of cash.
Income = Revenue − Expenses

ACCOUNTING EQUATION

Assets + Expenses = Liabilities + Equities + Revenues

DEBIT-CREDIT SYSTEM

Debit = Left-hand entry
Credit = Right-hand entry

THE ACCOUNTING CYCLE

1. Analyze transactions from source documents
2. Journalize transactions
3. Post general ledger
4. Adjust general ledger
5. Close and balance general ledger
6. Prepare financial statements

5

Special Topics in Accounting

This chapter addresses five special topics that are important to developing a working knowledge of financial accounting: changes in the equity account, depreciation accounting, inventory accounting, accounting for leases, and intercorporate investments. We will focus on the importance of these topics to a conceptual understanding of accounting as a financial information system.

CHANGES IN THE EQUITY ACCOUNT

In the previous chapters, it was shown that the majority of *changes in the equity account* are the result of earning revenue or incurring expenses. Other changes in the equity account also are possible. The two most common changes are the result of owners' contributions of additional equity capital and owners' capital withdrawals or profit distributions.

The nature of equity account changes is the same regardless of the organizational form of a given firm, but the organizational form does affect the method of accounting for a change. For a sole proprietorship, a partnership, or a limited liability company, contributions of additional equity capital normally take the form of direct cash (or occasionally some other asset) contributions to the firm. The amount of the contribution is reflected as a direct increase in the owner's capital account for a sole proprietor, or as an increase in one or more partners' capital accounts for a partnership or members' accounts for an LLC. For example, if Tommy Termite should find that his business requires an additional $5,000 cash for some reason, the appropriate accounting entry for this contribution would be:

| Dr. Cash | 5,000 |
| Cr. Tommy Termite, Capital | 5,000 |

For a corporation, capital contributions take the form of stock sales, and the associated cash inflow is treated in a comparable manner. Thus, if Hoya Manufacturers were to sell 10,000 shares of common stock with a par value of $5 at a market price of $15 per share, the appropriate accounting entry would be:

Dr. Cash	150,000
Cr. Common stock ($5 par)	50,000
Cr. Amounts contributed in excess of par	100,000

Withdrawals of equity capital are treated in a comparable manner. Sole proprietorships and partnerships (and some LLCs) maintain accounts known as drawing accounts to account for owners' withdrawals of cash from the business. The drawing account is the accounting mechanism through which an owner withdraws his or her share of the company's profits. Unlike the owners of a corporation, sole proprietors and partners do not draw salaries as such. Owners are taxed according to their proportionate share of the firm's profit. Thus, in our Tommy Termite example, if Tommy withdraws $8,500 from his drawing account, the appropriate accounting entry would be:

| Dr. Tommy Termite, Drawing | 8,500 |
| Cr. Cash | 8,500 |

At the end of the year, the drawing account would be closed to the capital account. Total drawings for the year would be deducted from capital.

For a corporation, profit distributions to the owners (stockholders) take the form of dividends. From an accounting point of view, a dividend payment is a two-step process. First, the board of directors must meet and vote to pay a dividend—only the board has this power. In the case of Hoya Manufacturers, if the board met and voted to pay a cash dividend of $1 on each of the 104,000 outstanding shares, the appropriate accounting entry would be:

Dr. Retained earnings	104,000
Cr. Dividends payable	104,000

The second entry, which would be made on the date of payment, would be:

Dr. Dividends payable	104,000
Cr. Cash	104,000

There are many possible additional entries to the equity accounts, such as stock splits and stock dividends, but an exploration of the details of these entries is not critical to understanding the big picture. Readers interested in further details may consult any standard financial accounting textbook.

DEPRECIATION ACCOUNTING

The second area of interest is depreciation accounting. Depreciation is a major expense for most businesses, and the treatment of this expense can have important tax implications. From an accounting point of view, depreciation is handled through a special type of account called a contra account. The account is entitled "accumulated depreciation" and is maintained to offset its associated asset account. For example, if a $10,000 machine is purchased, the machine would be recorded as an asset, and the depreciation applicable to that machine would be recorded in an accumulated depreciation account for the machine. (The owner's drawing account discussed previously is also considered a contra account. It acts to offset the owner's capital account.)

Depreciation provides a method of allocating the cost of an asset over time in an attempt to match this cost to the period in which the asset is being "used up" to earn revenue. Thus, it is the accrual, or matching, concept of accounting that makes depreciation necessary. If an automobile is purchased for business use, for example, the automobile is normally expected to have a useful life of more than one year. Therefore, the automobile is recorded as a capital asset (it is "capitalized"), and its cost is allocated over its entire expected useful life. Any asset with an expected useful life of more than one year is normally considered a capital asset. Depreciation accounting is simply a technique used to allocate the cost of a capital asset over its expected useful life.

Depreciation accounting may be thought of as a simple four-step process. First, the value of the asset must be determined. This is normally the cost of acquiring the asset and preparing it for use—the "delivered and installed" price. Second, the expected useful life of the asset must be estimated. The third step is to make an estimate of the asset's salvage value—that is, the asset's estimated value at the end of its expected useful life. Fourth, a method is selected to allocate the dollar value of the asset expected to be used up (its depreciable balance, which is equal to the cost minus the salvage value) to its expected useful life. Four of the most common methods of depreciation cost allocation are:

- Straight line
- Units of production
- Sum of the years' digits
- Double declining balance

A single example can explain the four methods. Suppose that Pete and Judy Smith open a small bakery business outside of Baltimore, Maryland, and they need to buy a compact pickup truck to deliver cookies. Suppose further that the bakery buys a used truck costing $10,000, that the truck is expected to have a useful life of five years, during which time it will be driven 100,000 miles, and that the expected salvage value of the truck at the end of five years is $2,000. The depreciable balance of the truck is $8,000 (the $10,000 cost less the $2,000 salvage value), because the asset provides benefits evenly over its expected life of five years.

Straight-line depreciation is generally the easiest method to use. As its name implies, straight-line depreciation requires only that depreciation expense be written off in a "straight line," or at an even rate. Thus, the $8,000 depreciable balance would be expensed at the rate of one-fifth per year for five years, or $1,600 per year.

The units-of-production depreciation method also is relatively straightforward. Under this method, the depreciable balance is simply allocated according to the number of units the capital asset is expected to produce. In the truck case, a "unit" would be an individual mile of service and the $8,000 depreciable balance would be allocated over the expected total usage of 100,000 miles at the rate of $0.08 per mile ($8,000 divided by 100,000). Assuming that the truck would be operated approximately the same number of miles per year (20,000 miles per year for five years), the amount of depreciation written off each year would be the same as in the straight-line method (20,000 × $0.08 = $1,600).

The next two depreciation methods are common types of accelerated depreciation. Under the sum-of-the-years'-digits (SYD) method of depreciation, one first sums the digits of the number of years over which the asset is to be depreciated. In the present example the sum is 15 (1 + 2 + 3 + 4 + 5 = 15). The depreciable balance of the asset is then depreciated by establishing a series of depreciation fractions that have the sum of the years' digits—15 in this case—as their denominator. The numerator of each fraction is then the reverse order of the years—5, 4, 3, 2, and 1 in this case. Each year's depreciation expense is then determined by multiplying the appropriate depreciation fraction times the depreciable balance. The example for the truck, shown in Exhibit 5.1, should make the process clearer.

EXHIBIT 5.1   SUM-OF-THE-YEARS'-DIGITS DEPRECIATION

YEAR	DEPRECIATION FRACTION	DEPRECIABLE BALANCE	YEAR'S DEPRECIATION
1	5/15	$8,000	$2,667
2	4/15	8,000	2,133
3	3/15	8,000	1,600
4	2/15	8,000	1,067
5	1/15	8,000	533
15	15/15		$8,000

Under the fourth commonly used method of depreciation, the double-declining-balance (DDB) method, a firm may write off up to double the straight-line depreciation rate. Thus, in the truck example the straight-line depreciation rate over a five-year period allows the total amount of depreciation to be written off at the rate of 20 percent per year. Double this rate would allow the total amount of depreciation to be written off at the rate of 40 percent per year. The depreciation rate allowed under DDB is applied to the declining balance of the cost of the asset, rather than to the depreciable balance.

However, the firm may not write off more total depreciation than the amount of the depreciable balance.

Exhibit 5.2 illustrates the application of DDB depreciation to the truck example. In year 1, the 40 percent allowable depreciation factor is applied to the $10,000 cost of the asset to produce a $4,000 depreciation expense for year 1. At the end of year 1, the balance of the asset account (its "book value") is $6,000, the difference between the original cost ($10,000) and the total amount of depreciation written off so far ($4,000). In year 2, the 40 percent allowable depreciation factor is applied to the $6,000 balance, the declining balance of the asset, to yield $2,400 in depreciation for year 2 and an ending book value of $3,600. This process continues until year 4, when the firm "runs out" of depreciation. In year 4, 40 percent of the declining balance equals $864, but only $160 in depreciation can be taken because this amount will reduce the book value of the asset to $2,000, its original estimated salvage value. In year 5, no depreciation is allowed.

EXHIBIT 5.2   DOUBLE-DECLINING-BALANCE DEPRECIATION

YEAR	DEPRECIATION FACTOR	DECLINING BALANCE	YEAR'S DEPRECIATION	ENDING BOOK VALUE
1	40%	$10,000	$4,000	$6,000
2	40	6,000	2,400	3,600
3	40	3,600	1,440	2,160
4	40	2,160	160	2,000
5	40	2,000	-0-	2,000
			$8,000	

Choice of Depreciation Method

Given the variety of allowable depreciation methods available, one might logically ask how to select the appropriate one. In general, the answer to this question is that the depreciation method that most closely matches the rate at which the asset actually depreciates should be used. The most obvious example of this principle would be the depreciation pattern of most new American automobiles. It is a well-known fact that new autos depreciate very rapidly in the first two years of life and depreciate much more slowly thereafter. An accelerated method of depreciation is clearly appropriate for such an asset.

Depreciation for Tax Purposes

Tax deductions for the depreciation of assets used in a trade or business or for the production of income have been allowed by the Internal Revenue Code in one form or another since 1913. A major modification to the allowable options for tax depreciation was enacted in the Tax Reform Act of 1986 (TRA 86). TRA 86 ushered in a system called MACRS (pronounced "makers")—modified accelerated cost recovery system. Under MACRS depreciation, the number of years over which an asset is depreciated is not tied to the expected useful life of the asset, and the salvage value of an asset is disregarded. The entire cost of an asset is depreciated over its MACRS life. Businesses are generally required to use the accelerated depreciation schedules provided by MACRS.

MACRS prescribes depreciation lives of 3, 5, 7, 10, 15, 20, 27.5, and 39 years. For tax purposes, most asset categories must be depreciated under MACRS, depending upon when the asset was placed in service. Some special categories of assets not required to be depreciated under MACRS can be depreciated using straight-line, double-declining-balance, or sum-of-the-years'-digits rules. There are also special rules for depreciation of real estate.

A simple example will illustrate the MACRS system. Suppose Smith's Bakery buys a new compact truck for $15,000 in February 2008. Under the MACRS rules, light trucks are specifically assigned to the five-year recovery property class. Optional tables provided by the IRS can be used to compute the depreciation. In this case, the table using the so-called midquarter convention would be used (the asset is assumed to have been placed in service during the middle of the first quarter of the year). The depreciation allowed under MACRS is as follows:

Year	Depreciation percentage	Dollars of depreciation
1	35.00%	$5,250
2	26.00	3,900
3	15.60	2,340
4	11.01	1,652
5	11.01	1,652
6	1.38	206
	100.00%	$15,000

One additional option is allowed under the IRS code. Up to $250,000 of the cost of some classes of business assets (defined in the code as Section 179 property) may be expensed in the year placed in service rather than depreciated. For property placed in service after 2008, the $250,000 maximum expense allowed is reduced if the cost of the property exceeds $800,000.

Under generally accepted accounting principles, companies may use straight-line or one of the accelerated methods of depreciation for financial accounting purposes. Most companies prefer to use MACRS depreciation over straight-line depreciation since they allow faster write-offs for tax purposes. However, MACRS cannot be used for financial accounting purposes since this is not an acceptable depreciation method under generally accepted accounting principles. Hence, nearly all companies will use a depreciation method for financial accounting purposes different from the one they use for tax purposes.

It is quite common practice for firms to use straight-line depreciation for financial accounting purposes. The choice of straight-line depreciation on the firm's financial statements recognizes the gradual erosion in the value of an asset that is expected to be used over its entire useful life. Straight-line depreciation also minimizes the impact of depreciation on a firm's reported earnings per share. If a firm uses straight-line depreciation for financial accounting purposes and MACRS depreciation for tax purposes, MACRS depreciation will generally exceed the straight-line rate. As a result, taxable earnings will be less than earnings reported on the firm's financial statements. The difference in taxes (called a tax timing difference) results in the creation of a liability account entitled "deferred income taxes."

INVENTORY ACCOUNTING

The method a firm uses to account for its investment in inventory is often of major concern to users of financial statements because, for many companies, inventory makes up a major portion of the firm's assets. The method the firm employs to account for its inventory investment can have an important impact on its reported income. The accounting method selected will have an impact on the dollar value at which the inventory is carried on the balance sheet and on the dollar value of the cost of goods sold on the income statement. This impact is particularly important during periods of rising prices.

There are four commonly used inventory accounting methods that will be examined here:

- Specific identification
- Weighted average
- First-in, first-out (FIFO)
- Last-in, first-out (LIFO)

The *specific identification* method of inventory accounting is commonly used to account for "big ticket" items such as automobiles, jewelry, and heavy equipment. Under this method, each item is specifically identified, often by an individual serial number or RFID device, and is carried in inventory at its actual cost. This method of accounting is most often employed when a perpetual inventory is maintained—that is, when inventory records are perpetually updated. When a perpetual inventory is maintained, inventory records are updated whenever new items are received and old items are used up or sold.

The three other inventory accounting methods are commonly used when a periodic inventory accounting is employed. Under this system, inventory is counted periodically (monthly or quarterly, for example) and the quantity used up or sold is determined by subtracting the current quantity on hand from the prior inventory on hand plus purchases since then, if any. A periodic inventory system is often the only practical way to account for inventory when large quantities of inventory are held, when inventory turnover is high, or when a large number of very similar items are maintained in inventory.

The *weighted-average* inventory system is a fairly straightforward method that is often used to account for fungible goods, such as wheat or other products that are physically indistinguishable. Under this method, each unit in inventory is priced as a weighted average of the cost prices of the items at the time of purchase. For example, if thirty units were purchased in three lots of ten each at costs of $3.00 per unit, $3.50 per unit, and $4.00 per unit, the average price of the units would be $3.50 each. When the items are used up or sold, each will be costed at the $3.50 price. The next time inventory is taken, a new weighted-average price will be computed, counting any "leftover" items from the original thirty as $3.50 each.

The last two inventory accounting methods should be discussed in tandem. FIFO (*first-in, first-out*) and LIFO (*last-in, first-out*) inventory accounting have complementary advantages and disadvantages in a period of changing prices. FIFO inventory accounting corresponds most closely to the actual physical flows of inventory since inventory is costed on a first-in, first-out basis. It is assumed that the oldest inventory is used up first, so that ending inventory is priced at the newest, and presumably higher, prices. As a result, ending inventory is valued on the balance sheet at prices that are closest to current prices, but inventory that is used in production is charged against income at older (and lower) prices that are less than replacement costs.

The result of this process is the earning of what are often called "phantom profits." Simply stated, if a wholesale distributor buys an item for $50, sells it for $60, and then finds the replacement cost of the item has risen to $55, what is his profit? Under FIFO, the dealer will report a profit of $10 but have only $5 in the till after replacement. Critics of FIFO refer to the "missing" $5 as "phantom profit" (the "missing" $5 is, of course, invested in inventory). The critics further point out that if the distributor is in a 30 percent tax bracket, there is actually only $2 in the till after a $3 tax is paid on the reported profit of $10.

It is often stated that FIFO accounting results in the balance sheet being "accurate" in the sense that inventory is priced closest to replacement value, but that it causes the income statement to be "distorted" to the extent that "phantom profits" occur. LIFO accounting was devised as a means of dealing with this problem. Under LIFO accounting, inventory is costed on a last-in, first-out basis. It is assumed for cost and valuation purposes that the newest (and higher-priced) items are used first and that the oldest (and lower-priced) items remain in inventory. Although this is obviously an artificial assumption about physical inventory flows for most items, it is a more realistic method of measuring the cost flows on the income statement. Over a number of years of rising prices the value of inventory on the balance sheet can become substantially understated. Thus, it is often said that LIFO inventory accounting "distorts" the balance sheet but makes the income statement "more accurate" in the sense that LIFO more closely matches current costs with current revenues than does FIFO.

Exhibit 5.3 provides a simplified illustration of the difference between the two methods. The exhibit is instructive for two reasons.

EXHIBIT 5.3 FIFO–LIFO INVENTORY EXAMPLE

Assumptions:

Beginning inventory	10 at $ 5 = $ 50
Purchases	10 at $10 = $100
	10 at $15 = $150
Sales	20 units at $25 each = $500

Ending inventory = Beginning inventory + Purchases – Units sold

$$= 10 + 20 - 10 = 10 \text{ units}$$

Value of ending inventory (FIFO) = 10 at $15 = $150
Value of ending inventory (LIFO) = 10 at $ 5 = $ 50

	FIFO			LIFO	
	INCOME STATEMENT	CASH FLOW*		INCOME STATEMENT	CASH FLOW*
Sales		$500	$500	$500	$500
Cost of sales:					
Beginning inventory	$ 50			$ 50	
Add: Purchases	250		(250)	250	(250)
Less: Ending inventory	150	150		50	250
Gross profit		$350		$250	
Other expenses		50	(50)	50	(50)
Earnings before tax		$300	$200	$200	$200
Tax (30%)		90	90	60	(60)
Earnings after tax		$210	$110	$140	$140

* Assuming (for simplicity) all transactions are in cash

First, it illustrates the difference in the bottom line that results solely from the choice of a different accounting method. Assumptions relative to sales, beginning inventory, and purchases are the same in both cases. The only difference between the two is the inventory accounting method. Second, the exhibit provides an explanation for a common accounting change undertaken by large corporations—a switch from FIFO to LIFO inventory accounting in order to save taxes.

As Exhibit 5.3 shows, the use of FIFO results in reported earnings of $210 versus LIFO reported earnings of $140. The difference in reported earnings is solely attributable to the difference in inventory accounting. Both cases assume beginning inventory of ten units costing $5 each, one purchase of ten units at $10 each, one purchase of ten units at $15 each, and sales of twenty units at a sale price of $25 each for total sales of $500. Thus, in both cases, there are ten units left in ending inventory. Determining the value of these ten units, and therefore simultaneously determining the value of the twenty units that were sold, is the crux of the difference between FIFO and LIFO accounting.

Under FIFO accounting, it is assumed that the units acquired first were sold first. The ten units of beginning inventory plus the ten units purchased at $10 each are assumed sold, leaving an ending inventory of ten units at $15 each or $150 ending inventory value. Cost of sales (beginning inventory plus purchases less ending inventory) is therefore $150 ($50 + $250 − $150). Sales less cost of sales yields a gross profit of $350. Subtracting other expenses of $50 yields earnings before tax of $300, a $90 tax (at a 30 percent tax rate), and earnings after tax of $210.

The "phantom profit" problem is illustrated in the cash flow column of the FIFO example. It is assumed for simplicity that all transactions are in cash. It can be seen that sales less purchases, other expenses, and taxes yield cash earnings after tax of $110 versus the reported earnings of $210. The "missing" $100 is reflected in the increased value of the inventory—the ending inventory of ten units is now valued at $150 versus the beginning inventory value of $50 for ten units. The major problem with FIFO, however, is that the firm pays taxes on the reported earnings before tax of $300 rather than on its cash earnings of $200 and is thus paying a tax on the "phantom" inventory profit. Proponents of FIFO claim that this is how it should be since rising prices have made the ten units in inventory more valuable and have in fact increased the book value of the firm by $100. Opponents of FIFO obviously do not agree.

Under LIFO accounting, it is assumed that the last units acquired were sold. The ten units purchased at $15 each and the ten units purchased at $10 each are assumed sold, leaving an ending inventory of ten units at $5 each, or $50 ending inventory value. In the LIFO case, cost of sales is $250 ($50 + $250 − $50), earnings before tax are $200, and earnings after tax are $140. Examination of the LIFO cash flow column also shows cash earnings to be $140—there is no "phantom profit" in the LIFO case.

This simple and admittedly contrived example shows the impact of a change from FIFO to LIFO inventory accounting. The LIFO example results in lower reported earnings after tax than FIFO but a higher cash flow due to the lower tax burden. Thus, the switch to LIFO amounts to a bad-news, good-news joke: The bad news is that the company reports earnings lower than it would have under FIFO. The good news is that it also pays less taxes and therefore holds on to more cash.

ACCOUNTING FOR LEASES

Under generally accepted accounting principles, companies are required to classify leases as either a capital lease or an operating lease. Any lease agreement that does not meet the criteria for a capital lease must be classified as an operating lease and treated the same way as any other expense. Capital leases must be capitalized and recorded as an asset with an associated liability. A lease is considered to be a capital lease if it meets *any one* of the following four conditions:

1. Title is transferred to the lessee at the end of the lease term.
2. The lease contains a bargain purchase option.
3. The term of the lease is greater than or equal to 75 percent of the estimated economic life of the asset.
4. The present value* (current lump sum of all future payments, taking into account the rate of return that could be earned on money in hand today) of the minimum lease payments is greater than or equal to 90 percent of the fair value of the leased property.

A capital lease is recorded on a lessee firm's balance sheet as an asset entitled "capital-lease asset" and an associated liability entitled "obligation under capital lease." The amount of the asset and liability entitled "obligation under capital lease" is equal to the present value of the minimum lease payments. The asset is accounted for like any other asset account that is amortized. The liability is accounted for in the same manner as interest-bearing debt that is reduced over its term. Lease payments are treated partially as interest expense and partly as amortization of the capital-lease liability.

Present value is explained in detail in Chapter 11.

INTERCORPORATE INVESTMENTS

Many corporations have subsidiary corporations or own voting stock in other corporations. Three accounting methods are used to account for the ownership of voting stock in another corporation:

1. Consolidated financial statements
2. Equity method
3. Cost method

Consolidated financial statements are normally used when one corporation (called the parent) owns 50 percent or more of the voting stock of another corporation (called the subsidiary) or, pursuant to FIN 46, has a controlling financial interest other than equity or voting rights. In contrast, the rules for tax consolidation require more than 80 percent ownership of a subsidiary for the subsidiary to be considered part of the parent's "consolidated group." A wholly owned subsidiary is one in which the parent owns 100 percent of the voting stock of the subsidiary. Many wholly owned subsidiaries are originally founded by the parent for some special purpose. A high-technology corporation, for example, might launch a subsidiary to manufacture components for major systems produced by the parent.

Consolidated financial statements combine the accounts of the subsidiary with the accounts of the parent. Intercompany accounts (for example, a loan from the parent to the subsidiary) are eliminated from the consolidated financial statements. The resulting financial statements present the operations of the parent and subsidiary as one consolidated entity. If the subsidiary is less than 100 percent owned, a minority interest is shown. The minority interest represents subsidiary ownership held by stockholders other than the parent.

The *equity method* of accounting is generally used when from 20 to 50 percent of the subsidiary is owned by the parent. It is also used when the parent owns more than 50 percent of the subsidiary but consolidation would be considered inappropriate. Examples of this are such cases as when the parent has incomplete or temporary control of the subsidiary, when the subsidiary's operations are significantly different from those of the parent (for example, financing subsidiaries of automobile manufacturers), or when there is substantial uncertainty as to whether the subsidiary income can be remitted to the parent (as with some foreign subsidiaries).

The equity method of accounting is sometimes called *one-line consolidation*. The parent's share of the subsidiary's earnings is taken in as a single line item on the parent's income statement. The investment in the common stock of the subsidiary is shown as a single asset item on the parent's balance sheet.

The *cost method* of accounting for intercorporate ownership is generally used when less than 20 percent of the voting stock of another corporation is owned. The method may also be used when there exists considerable doubt that the equity of a subsidiary is effectively accruing to the benefit of the parent. The investment in the subsidiary is recorded at cost on the parent's balance sheet. Income is recognized on the parent's income statement only when received in the form of dividends.

SUMMARY

The majority of changes in the equity account are the end result of earning revenue or incurring expenses. Two other common changes result from owners' contributions of additional capital and owners' capital withdrawals or profit distributions. For corporations, capital contributions take the form of stock sales; withdrawals of profits are paid out in dividends to the stockholders.

Depreciation methods allocate the cost of an asset over time in an attempt to match the cost to the period in which the asset is being used up to produce revenue. Four common methods of depreciation accounting are straight-line, units-of-production, sum-of-the-years'-digits, and double-declining-balance depreciation. For financial accounting purposes, the depreciation method that most closely matches the rate at which an asset actually depreciates should be used. Depreciation for tax purposes was changed by the Tax Reform Act of 1986, which introduced the modified accelerated cost recovery system (MACRS). TRA 86, as amended, also allows up to $250,000 of the cost of an asset to be expensed in the year of acquisition. Differences between financial accounting depreciation methods and tax accounting depreciation methods result in the creation of a liability account entitled "deferred income taxes."

There are four commonly used inventory accounting methods: specific identification, weighted-average, FIFO, and LIFO. FIFO values inventory on the balance sheet at prices closer to replacement value than does LIFO, but LIFO more closely matches current inventory costs with current revenue dollars on the income statement. Switching from FIFO to LIFO inventory accounting results in decreased reported earnings but increased cash flows.

Leases must be classified as capital leases or operating leases. Capital leases are recorded on the lessee firm's balance sheet as a "capital-lease asset" and an associated liability, "obligation under capital lease." Lease payments for capital leases are treated partially as interest expense and partially as amortization of the capital-lease liability.

Intercorporate investments may be accounted for by one of three methods: consolidated financial statements, the equity method, or the cost method. The choice of method is a function of the voting control exercised by the parent corporation over the subsidiary. Tax consolidation rules differ from the accounting rules.

KEY POINTS

EQUITY CHANGES	Capital contributions (proprietorship, partnership) increase. Stock sales (corporation) increase. Drawings (proprietorship, partnership) decrease. Dividends (corporation) decrease.
DEPRECIATION	Straight line Units of production Sum of the years' digits Double declining balance Method used for financial accounting does not match that used for tax purposes. Deferred income taxes result from depreciation timing differences.

INVENTORY ACCOUNTING	Specific identification Weighted average First-in, first-out (FIFO) Last-in, first-out (LIFO) Income ≠ Cash flow FIFO may yield "phantom profits" in a period of rising prices.
CAPITAL LEASES	Capital leases capitalized on balance sheet—"capital-lease asset" and "obligation under capital lease"
INTERCORPORATE INVESTMENTS	Consolidated financial statements Equity method (one-line consolidation) Cost method (use restricted)

PART III

Financial Analysis and Control

6

Financial Statement Analysis

OBJECTIVES OF FINANCIAL STATEMENT ANALYSIS

Financial statement analysis is the art of analyzing and interpreting financial statements. One major objective of financial statement analysis is to "understand the numbers" or "get behind the figures"— that is, to employ the tools of financial analysis as an aid to understanding reported financial data and then use that understanding to better manage a business. Thus, one may develop various analytical measures to portray meaningful relationships and extract information from raw financial data.

In the final analysis, informed decision making is the overriding goal of financial statement analysis. Whether one is a potential equity investor, a potential credit grantor, or a staff analyst of the corporation under analysis, the final objective is the same: to provide a basis for rational decision making. Decisions such as whether to purchase or sell stock, to grant or deny a loan, and to continue with past practices or change to a new procedure are strongly dependent on the results of competent financial analysis. The type of decision under consideration will be the major determinant of the focus of the analysis, but the decision-making objective is a constant. Both stockholders and bank loan officers analyze financial statements as an aid to decision making, for example, but the major focus of their separate analyses will differ. The bank loan officer may be more concerned with short-term liquidity and the collateral value of liquid assets, while the potential (or current) stockholder will be more concerned with long-term profitability and capital structure. Nevertheless, in both situations, the decision-making orientation of the analyst is a common feature.

Another important objective of financial statement analysis is to develop a reasonable basis for forecasting the future. Various tools and techniques of financial statement analysis can be employed to make a reasonable assessment of the future financial condition of the firm based on an analysis of its present and past financial condition and on the best available estimate of future economic occurrences.

In many cases, one finds that a large part of financial statement analysis consists of a careful scrutiny of reported financial statements, an even more careful reading of the footnotes, and a rearrangement or restatement of the available data to meet the needs of the analyst. One might then ask why one cannot accept prepared financial statements at face value—in other words, why meddle with the figures in the first place? One obvious answer is that a bit of meddling is almost always necessary to understand the numbers. Prepared financial statements generally require some analysis as a first step toward extracting information from the data presented in the statements. Second, most decisions made on the basis of financial analysis are of sufficient importance that accepting presented financial data at face value is often a poor policy. Most financially motivated decisions demand the employment of a logical framework within which impressions and conclusions may be systematically developed and judgment applied. In the pages that follow, such a framework will be suggested.

RATIO ANALYSIS

Ratio analysis is one commonly used tool of financial statement analysis. Financial ratios can be used to develop a set of statistics that reveal key financial characteristics of a company. In almost all cases, ratios are used in two major ways. First, ratios are compared with industry standards. These industry standards may be obtained through commercial services, such as Dun and Bradstreet or Robert Morris Associates, or through industry trade associations.

When industry standards are not readily available for a given industry or a particular company is not easily grouped into one of the standard industry categories, analysts may have to develop their own standards by calculating average ratios for leading companies in the same industry. Whatever the source of the ratios, care must be taken to compare the company under analysis to standards developed for companies in the same industry and of approximately the same asset size.

The second major use of ratios is to analyze the trend over time for a particular company. For example, the trend of the after-tax profit margin for the company may be evaluated over a five- or ten-year period. It is often useful to track key ratios through the previous one or two economic recessions to determine how well the company holds up financially during periods of economic adversity.

Key financial ratios are commonly grouped into four major categories, according to the particular aspect of the company's financial condition that the ratios attempt to highlight. The four major categories, in the order in which they will be examined here, are:

1. *Profitability*: "bottom-line" ratios designed to measure the earning power and profitability record of the company.
2. *Liquidity*: ratios designed to measure the ability of the firm to meet its short-term liabilities as they come due.
3. *Operating efficiency*: measures of the efficiency with which corporate resources are employed to earn a profit.
4. *Capital structure (leverage)*: measures of the extent to which debt financing is employed by the company.

Each category of ratios is discussed below with major ratios identified within each group.

Profitability Ratios

Three commonly used measures of profitability are return on sales, return on assets, and return on equity.

Return on sales (*ROS*) is determined by dividing after-tax profits by net sales, where net sales represents the dollar volume of sales less any returns, allowances, and cash discounts:

$$ROS = \frac{\text{Earnings after tax}}{\text{Net sales}}$$

Return on assets (*ROA*) relates after-tax earnings to the corporation's total asset base:

$$ROA = \frac{\text{Earnings after tax}}{\text{Total assets}}$$

ROA is sometimes referred to as *return on total assets* (ROTA) and occasionally as *return on investment* (ROI). All three expressions have the same meaning.

Return on equity (ROE) relates after-tax earnings to stockholders' equity. Stockholders' equity normally excludes the effect of any intangible assets (for example, goodwill, trademarks, and so on) and is determined by deducting total liabilities and intangible assets from total assets. The ratio is computed as follows:

$$ROE = \frac{\text{Earnings after tax}}{\text{Stockholders' equity}}$$

Return on equity is often considered to be the most important of the profitability ratios because it measures the return to owners' invested capital. As a general guide, a return on equity of at least 15 percent is a reasonable objective to provide adequate dividends and to fund expected future growth. This 15 percent "hurdle" is approximately equal to the average industrywide ROE result reported each year in *Forbes* magazine's annual survey of American business.

Liquidity Ratios

The four most commonly used measures of liquidity are the current ratio, quick ratio, average collection period, and days sales in inventory.

The *current ratio* is designed to measure the relationship, or balance, between current assets (mainly cash, marketable securities, accounts receivable, and inventories) and current liabilities (mainly accounts payable, current notes payable, and the currently due portion of any long-term debt). The ratio is computed as follows:

$$\text{Current ratio} = \frac{\text{Current assets}}{\text{Current liabilities}}$$

The *quick ratio* is a second commonly used ratio and is related to the current ratio. This ratio, also called the "acid test," is designed to measure the relationship between so-called quick assets (assets that can be quickly converted to cash) and current liabilities. It is computed as follows:

$$\text{Quick ratio} = \frac{\text{Cash} + \text{Marketable securities} + \text{Accounts receivable}}{\text{Current liabilities}}$$

As can be seen from the above formula, the quick ratio essentially measures the relationship between current assets net of inventories (called "quick assets") and current liabilities. One common rule of thumb used by bankers and other lenders maintains that this ratio should be at least 1 to 1.

The *average collection period* measures the speed with which receivables are turned into cash:

$$\text{Average daily sales} = \frac{\text{Net sales}}{\text{365 days}}$$

$$\text{Average collection period} = \frac{\text{Accounts receivable}}{\text{Average daily sales}}$$

A common rule of thumb states that the average collection period should not exceed the net maturity indicated by the firm's selling terms by more than ten to fifteen days.

The *days sales in inventory* ratio measures the number of days of revenue that are tied up in inventories—in other words, how many days of selling it will take to completely sell out a firm's inventory:

$$\text{Days sales in inventory} = \frac{\text{Inventory}}{\text{Average daily sales}}$$

Operating Efficiency Ratios

Operating efficiency ratios measure the relationship between annual sales and investments in various classes of asset accounts. The three most common ratios used to measure operating efficiency are the cost of goods sold to inventory, sales to total assets, and sales to working capital.

The *cost of goods sold to inventory ratio* is similar to the sales to inventory ratio listed under liquidity ratios but has one very important difference. The cost of goods sold to inventory turnover ratio provides an estimate of physical turnover rates since the numerator of the ratio uses cost of goods sold and therefore measures how efficiently inventory is being managed. The days sales in inventory ratio uses net sales in the numerator, which represents cost of goods sold plus the gross profit margin. Thus, while the days sales in inventory ratio does not provide a measure of physical turnover, it does provide an important and readily available benchmark against which to compare the ratio of sales dollars to inventory stocks of one business to that of another and how efficiently management is using its inventory resources to support sales:

$$\text{Cost of sales to inventory} = \frac{\text{Cost of goods sold}}{\text{Inventory}}$$

The *sales to total assets ratio* measures the relationship between sales and the assets used to support those sales:

$$\text{Sales to total assets} = \frac{\text{Net sales}}{\text{Total assets}}$$

The *sales to working capital ratio* provides a similar measure of the relationship between sales and dollars invested in working capital (recall that working capital is defined as current assets minus current liabilities):

$$\text{Sales to working capital} = \frac{\text{Net sales}}{\text{Working capital}}$$

It is often useful to think of the operating efficiency ratios as representing the number of dollars of investment needed to support a dollar of sales. The sales to total assets ratio in particular is often used to compare the structure and capital requirements of different industries. Heavy manufacturing companies, for example, commonly have sales to asset ratios in the range of 1.5 to 1. This shows that these industries are fairly "capital intensive" in the sense that a 1 to 1 ratio indicates that an additional investment of $1.00 in assets is required to support every additional increase in sales of $1.00. Retail companies, by comparison, often show sales to asset ratios of 20 to 1 or even higher, indicating that asset investments to support new sales are very low.

Capital Structure (Leverage) Ratios

The term *leverage* refers to the extent to which a firm employs debt capital to finance its operations. The more debt employed by a firm, the more highly leveraged it is said to be. Four important ratios in this category are the debt ratio, long-term debt to total assets ratio, debt equity ratio, and times interest earned ratio.

The *debt ratio* measures the relationship between total assets and the amount of debt used to finance those assets:

$$\text{Debt ratio} = \frac{\text{Total debt}}{\text{Total assets}}$$

The *long-term debt to total assets ratio* measures the percentage of total assets that is financed by long-term debt:

$$\text{Long-term debt/Total assets ratio} = \frac{\text{Long-term debt}}{\text{Total assets}}$$

The *debt equity ratio* measures the relationship between capital supplied by lenders (debt) and capital supplied by owners (equity):

$$\text{Debt equity ratio} = \frac{\text{Total debt}}{\text{Equity}}$$

The *times interest earned ratio* measures thc number of dollars of income before interest and taxes available to meet a dollar of interest expense. The ratio is computed as the ratio of earnings before interest and taxes (EBIT) to interest expense:

$$\text{Times interest earned} = \frac{\text{Earnings before interest and taxes}}{\text{Interest expense}}$$

To compute EBIT, one need only sum up earnings after tax plus interest expense plus income tax cxpense from the income statement. This total is then divided by interest expense to obtain the times interest earned ratio. For most industrial companies, a times interest earned ratio in the 4.5 to 6.0 range is considered quite strong. A ratio in the 3 to 4 range would be considered adequate protection to allow for making interest payments during difficult economic times.

Interrelationships Among Ratios

In addition to considering the individual ratios in isolation, it is important to consider the interrelationships among the various ratios. A given firm's profitability, liquidity position, operating efficiency, and leverage position are all interrelated, and no single aspect of performance should be considered in isolation from the other three aspects. Two formulations are particularly helpful in identifying these interrelationships. The first of these formulations, which has long been known as the DuPont system of analysis, relates return on assets to a firm's profit margin and asset turnover:

$$\frac{\text{Net income}}{\text{Total assets}} = \frac{\text{Net income}}{\text{Sales}} \times \frac{\text{Sales}}{\text{Total assets}}$$

As the equation shows, ROA results from the interaction of two important components, the firm's profit margin (net income/sales) and asset turnover (sales/total assets). As a shorthand statement, one often sees the comment that ROA equals margin times turnover. This is an important relationship because it shows that ROA as an overall performance measure is a product of two factors: the firm's profitability (measured by its profit margin) and its operating efficiency (measured by its total asset turnover). In analyzing a firm's return on assets, it is not adequate to look at only one measure of performance; one must consider both. As a diagnostic aid, this formulation further shows that a potential ROA problem may be either an income statement problem (profit margin) or an asset management problem (asset turnover).

A second formulation of a similar nature provides an interesting and useful insight into the relationships among return on assets, return on equity, and the firm's leverage position:

$$\frac{\text{Net income}}{\text{Stockholders' equity}} = \frac{\text{Net income}}{\text{Total assets}} \times \frac{\text{Total assets}}{\text{Stockholders' equity}}$$

$$\text{ROE} = \text{ROA} \times \text{Equity Multiplier}$$

This equation shows the direct relationship between ROE, ROA, and leverage. The higher the firm's leverage (as measured by the ratio of total assets to stockholders' equity), the higher will be its ROE relative to ROA. The equity multiplier is a measure of leverage used to show that the use of debt (leverage) is reflected in an increasing ratio of assets to equity because the use of debt allows a firm to add assets without increasing equity. For example, two firms both have a 9 percent ROA. If Firm A has a total asset to stockholder's equity ratio of 2 to 1, while Firm B has less leverage, with a ratio of 1.5 to 1, the ROE figures for the two firms will be as follows:

$$\text{Firm A, ROE} = (9\%) \times (2.0) = 18.0\%$$
$$\text{Firm B, ROE} = (9\%) \times (1.5) = 13.5\%$$

This example shows that although the two firms are equally profitable from an operating point of view (ROA), Firm A provides a much higher return on equity solely as a result of the firm's financial structure. In return for this higher ROE, however, the equity holders must accept the much higher degree of risk associated with the added leverage.

As a final note relative to ratio analysis, it must again be stressed that the computation and display of a set of ratios for a given company in a given year is of limited usefulness by itself. Ratios must be compared to performance in other years and to appropriate standards for companies of approximately equal asset size in similar industries.

COMMON-SIZE STATEMENTS

Common-size financial statements express all accounts on the balance sheet and income statement as a percentage of some key figure. On the income statement, net sales are set equal to 100 percent, and all other items are expressed as a percentage of net sales. On the balance sheet, total assets are set equal to 100 percent on the left-hand side, while total liabilities and equities are set equal to 100 percent on the right-hand side. All asset accounts are listed as a percentage of total assets, and all liability and equity accounts are listed as a percentage of total liabilities and equities.

Preparing these types of statements facilitates analysis of significant aspects of the financial condition and operations of the firm. These statements provide a crucial supplement to the information available from the various kinds of ratios previously discussed. On the common-size balance sheet, the analytical effort focuses on the internal structure and allocation of the firm's financial resources. On the asset side, the common-size statement portrays the manner in which investments in various financial resources are distributed among the asset accounts. Of particular interest here is the choice of resource distribution between current and fixed assets and the distribution of current assets among the various categories of working capital accounts—mainly the distribution of working capital investment among cash, accounts receivable, and inventory. On the liabilities and equity side, the common-size balance sheet shows the percentage distribution of financing provided by current liabilities, long-term debt, and equity capital. Of particular interest here is the relationship between long-term debt and equity and the "split" between current liabilities and long-term sources of financing provided by debt and equity.

The second common-size statement, the common-size income statement, shows the proportion of the sales or revenue dollar absorbed by the various cost and expense items. Once again, one must caution that the relationships portrayed by common-size statements cannot be considered in isolation. The year-to-year trend for the firm must be examined, and comparisons must be made with industry standards.

SEQUENCE OF ANALYSIS

The major objective of each analysis will determine the relative degree of emphasis to place on each main area of analysis—that is, on profitability, liquidity, operating efficiency, or capital structure. But regardless of the intent of the analysis, no individual area can be safely ignored, and one logical framework can be employed to systematically explore the financial health of the organization. Step 1 in this sequence should be to specify clearly the objectives of the analysis and develop a set of key questions that should be answered to attain this objective. Step 2 then becomes the preparation of data necessary to work toward the specified goals. This step normally requires the preparation of key ratios and common-size statements.

Step 3 involves the analysis and interpretation of the numerical information developed in Step 2. It is generally useful to examine the information provided by the ratio analysis first in order to develop an overall feel for potential problem areas and then to move on to the information contained in the common-size statements. Preliminary questions and opinions developed during the analysis of the ratio data often provide valuable insights that may help focus one's efforts in examining the common-size statements.

The final step in the investigation requires the analyst to form conclusions based on the data and answer the questions posed in Step 1. Specific recommendations, backed up by the available data, are presented in Step 4, along with a brief summary of the major points developed previously. If the analysis is to be submitted for review by other interested parties, it is common practice to begin a written report with a summary of the conclusions developed in this final phase.

This allows readers to grasp the main issues of the case and then selectively read more detailed areas according to their major interest.

CASE STUDY: TECHNOSYSTEMS, INC.

The basic tools and techniques of financial statement analysis will be applied to the financial statements of Technosystems, Inc., a three-year-old, privately owned company engaged in the wholesale distribution of plumbing, heating, and air-conditioning equipment. The case is based on a real start-up company.

Technosystems was founded in 2006 by John Diamond and two business associates, David Walker and Carla Gilberti. Sales are made mainly to contractors working on commercial projects such as office buildings or warehouses. Two of the company's founders, John and David, as well as its three sales representatives, are engineers. Carla is a CPA and serves as a part-time financial adviser to Technosystems.

At the time Technosystems was started, John was employed as sales manager for Walker Equipment Company, a company owned by the Walker family. David Walker is the president of Walker Equipment, and Carla Gilberti is the company's CPA. Walker Equipment is a successful company specializing in the sale and leasing of heavy construction equipment. Through his contacts as sales manager for Walker Equipment, John became interested in the possibility of setting up a new company in the wholesale heating and air-conditioning business. Although David and Carla had no interest in operating the new company, they did agree with John's assessment of its economic potential and agreed to become equal partners in financing the new company if John would start up and manage it. John was appointed president of the new company and was an equal owner along with David and Carla.

Technosystems originally was financed with a $100,000 loan from David and Carla, payable in ten annual installments of $10,000 plus 14 percent interest on the declining balance. The 10,000 shares of stock issued upon incorporation were divided equally among the three founders, each of whom paid $0.10 per share, its par value. The last three years' balance sheets and income statements for the company are shown in Exhibits 6.1 and 6.2.

98

EXHIBIT 6.1   TECHNOSYSTEMS, INC.
CONDENSED BALANCE SHEET

	2008	2007	2006
ASSETS			
Cash	$40,400	$31,800	$60,300
Accounts receivable	114,300	200,200	126,400
Inventory	93,900	65,600	66,200
Prepaid expenses	5,000	1,800	500
Total current assets	$253,600	$299,400	$253,400
Fixed assets (net)	30,500	23,900	5,200
Total assets	$284,100	$323,300	$258,600
LIABILITIES AND EQUITY			
Accounts payable	$94,200	$124,400	$111,100
Notes payable	24,800	45,400	11,600
Accrued expenses	900	4,200	3,700
Taxes payable	11,600	9,500	0
Deferred taxes	6,700	1,100	0
Total current liabilities	$138,200	$184,600	$126,400
Long-term notes	83,200	118,500	130,000
Total liabilities	$221,400	$303,100	$256,400
Capital stock	1,000	1,000	1,000
Retained earnings	61,700	19,200	1,200
Total equity	$62,700	$20,200	$2,200
Total liabilities and equity	$284,100	$323,300	$258,600

EXHIBIT 6.2   TECHNOSYSTEMS, INC.
CONDENSED INCOME STATEMENT

	2008	2007	2006
Sales	$1,277,000	$1,159,000	$773,300
Cost of sales	952,700	900,500	627,000
Gross profit	$324,300	$258,500	$146,300
Interest income	800	200	1,000
Total income	$325,100	$258,700	$147,300
Sales salaries	96,200	90,300	42,200
Office salaries	63,300	46,900	28,200
Office equipment rental	28,200	29,800	25,500
Interest expense	15,000	20,000	17,000
General and administrative	50,500	36,900	33,300
Total expenses	$253,200	$223,900	$146,200
Income before tax	71,900	34,800	1,100
Income taxes	29,200	10,500	300
Net income	$42,700	$24,300	$800
Earnings per share (10,000 shares)	$4.27	$2.43	$0.08

**EXHIBIT 6.3   TECHNOSYSTEMS, INC.
KEY FINANCIAL RATIOS**

	2008	2007	2006	INDUSTRY AVERAGE
Profitability:				
Return on sales (percent)	3.34	2.10	0.10	3.48
Return on assets (percent)	15.03	7.52	0.31	11.21
Return on equity (percent)	68.10	120.30	36.36	16.43
Liquidity:				
Current ratio (times)	1.80	1.61	2.00	2.63
Quick ratio (times)	1.12	1.26	1.48	1.15
Average collection period (days)	33	63	60	45
Days sales in inventory (days)	27	21	31	32
Operating efficiency:				
Cost of Sales/Inventory (times)	10.1	13.7	9.5	9.7
Sales/Total assets (times)	4.5	3.6	3.0	4.2
Sales/Working capital (times)	11.6	10.3	6.1	7.5
Leverage:				
Total debt/Total assets (percent)	77.9	93.8	99.1	49.5
Long-term debt/Total assets (percent)	29.3	36.7	50.3	15.5
Debt/Equity (times)	3.5	15.0	116.5	1.0
Times interest earned	5.8	2.7	1.1	4.4

Key Financial Ratios

Key financial ratios for Technosystems, along with industry standards, are given in Exhibit 6.3. Examination of these data indicates that Technosystems suffers from a malady common to many small and rapidly growing businesses in an early stage of development—it is severely undercapitalized. Technosystems' debt ratio is extremely high, both on an absolute basis and in comparison to industry standards. Total debt is equal to almost 80 percent of total assets, compared with the industry standard of 50 percent. Long-term debt is equal to nearly 30 percent of total assets, approximately double the industry standard of 15.5 percent. On the other hand, now that the company is in its third full year of operations and has become profitable, the times interest earned ratio is at a comfortable

5.8 to 1 margin, well above the industry average of 4.4 to 1. This ratio is up from a rather meager 2.7 last year and a breakeven level of 1.1 the prior year.

On the positive side of the debt picture is the fact that the debt is private debt loaned to the company by two of its principals. In this sense, although David and Carla eventually must be repaid, they are not likely to force the corporation into liquidation if payments are late or have to be postponed.

Profitability ratios are very encouraging, with both the overall level and the trend of earnings looking positive. Return on sales is currently just below the industry average of 3.5 percent and shows a rapidly increasing trend. Return on investment is increasing quickly and is now above the industry average. Return on equity is extremely high, but this is due mainly to the extremely high debt position of Technosystems. The abnormally high return on equity is a result of the fact that the company's equity is so low relative to its debt.

Technosystems' ROA ratio has improved as the result of improvement in both the return on sales ratio and the asset turnover ratio. The interaction of these two key variables to produce return on investment can be seen as follows:

$$\text{ROA} = (\text{Profit margin}) \times (\text{Asset turnover})$$
$$\text{ROA (2008)} = (3.34\%) \times (4.5) = 15.0\%$$
$$\text{ROA (2007)} = (2.10\%) \times (3.6) = 7.5\%$$

Technosystems' extremely high rate of return on equity capital of 68.1 percent is the result of their high debt position. The relationship between return on assets, return on equity, and the use of debt financing can be seen in the following calculation:

$$\text{ROE} = (\text{ROA}) \times (\text{Total assets/Equity})$$
$$\text{ROE (2008)} = (15.03\%) \times (\$284,100/\$62,700) = (15.03\%) \times (4.53) = 68.1\%$$

This calculation measures the extent of debt financing by the ratio of total assets to equity; the higher this ratio, the more debt a company uses. The results of this calculation clearly show that Technosystems' inordinately high rate of return on equity is primarily a result of the company's extremely high usage of debt financing.

Liquidity ratios are mixed. The current ratio is below the industry average but has shown strong improvement from last year, and the quick ratio is approximately equal to the industry average. The average collection period is well below the industry average, indicating

EXHIBIT 6.4   TECHNOSYSTEMS, INC.
COMMON-SIZE BALANCE SHEET

	2003	2002	2001
ASSETS			
Cash	14.2%	9.8%	23.3%
Accounts receivable	40.2%	61.9%	48.9%
Inventory	33.1%	20.3%	25.6%
Prepaid expenses	1.8%	0.6%	0.2%
Total current assets	89.3%	92.6%	98.0%
Fixed assets (net)	10.7%	7.4%	2.0%
Total assets	100.0%	100.0%	100.0%
LIABILITIES AND EQUITY			
Accounts payable	33.2%	38.5%	43.0%
Notes payable	8.7%	14.0%	4.5%
Accrued expenses	0.3%	1.3%	1.4%
Taxes payable	4.1%	2.9%	0.0%
Deferred taxes	2.4%	0.3%	0.0%
Total current liabilities	48.6%	57.1%	48.9%
Long-term notes	29.3%	36.7%	50.3%
Total liabilities	77.9%	93.8%	99.1%
Capital stock	0.4%	0.3%	0.4%
Retained earnings	21.7%	5.9%	0.5%
Total equity	22.1%	6.2%	0.9%
Total liabilities and equity	100.0%	100.0%	100.0%

that the company is doing an excellent job of collecting its receivables. Inventory control, as measured by the below-average days sales in inventory number, also must be judged as excellent.

Operating efficiency ratios show that Technosystems runs a lean operation, with all ratios above the industry averages. Inventory turnover (the cost of sales to inventory ratio) is above average, as are the sales to total assets and sales to working capital ratios. These ratios show that Technosystems is getting a bigger bang for the buck than the average company in the industry.

Common-Size Analysis

Common-size statements for Technosystems are given in Exhibits 6.4 and 6.5. Several interesting trends are revealed by an analysis of these statements. First, from the common-size balance sheet (Exhibit 6.4),

EXHIBIT 6.5   TECHNOSYSTEMS, INC.
COMMON-SIZE INCOME STATEMENT

	2003	2002	2001
Sales	100.0%	100.0%	100.0%
Cost of sales	74.6%	77.7%	81.1%
Gross profit	25.4%	22.3%	18.9%
Interest income	0.1%	0.0%	0.1%
Total income	25.5%	22.3%	19.0%
Sales salaries	7.5%	7.8%	5.5%
Office salaries	5.0%	4.0%	3.6%
Office equipment rental	2.2%	2.6%	3.3%
Interest expense	1.2%	1.7%	2.2%
General and administrative	4.0%	3.2%	4.3%
Total expenses	19.8%	19.3%	18.9%
Income before tax	5.6%	3.0%	0.1%
Income taxes	2.3%	0.9%	0.0%
Net income	3.3%	2.1%	0.1%

we can see that fixed assets as a percentage of total assets have increased markedly since 2006. Along with the increase in the retained earnings account and hence total equity as a percent of total assets, we can see the sharp downward movement in the percentage of total assets financed by current liabilities and long-term debt. Additionally, within the working capital accounts, we note a steady decrease in total current assets as a percent of total assets.

The common-size income statement (Exhibit 6.5) shows a very encouraging pattern. The gross profit margin has increased steadily over the last three years, from 18.9 percent in 2006 to 25.4 percent in 2008. Similarly, the pretax and after-tax profit margins also have shown steady improvement over the last three years, from 0.1 to 5.6 percent and from 0.1 to 3.3 percent, respectively. Total expenses as a percent of sales have remained relatively steady as the company has grown, increasing by only 0.9 percent, to 19.8 percent in 2008 from 18.9 percent in 2006.

Technosystems Conclusions

Overall, the trend in the financial condition of Technosystems appears very encouraging. Profitability is excellent and improving. The company's liquidity position is strong and also improving. These encouraging trends are counterbalanced somewhat by the fact that Technosystems currently carries a very heavy debt load. However, this debt has been supplied by two of the founders of the company, and it is likely they will be quite patient waiting for payment. It is the founders' plan that John will eventually buy out the interests of David and Carla sometime after the initial loan is repaid. Based on the apparently sound management of the company as reflected in its operating efficiency ratios and the growing profitability of Technosystems, it is quite likely that the company will be able to repay the loans on the original terms. (In fact, the real company that provided the model for this Technosystems case did prosper, and "John" did buy out the other two founding partners with a long-term loan they made to him for the purpose of buying their stock.)

FINANCIAL ANALYSIS, FINANCIAL FRAUD, AND FINANCIAL STRESS

In late 2002, Enron and Worldcom filed two of the largest corporate bankruptcies in history, and amid allegations of fraud and criminal conspiracy related to the failure of Enron, the once venerable accounting firm of Arthur Andersen and Company disintegrated after being convicted of criminal behavior related to its audits of Enron. Andersen, a nearly hundred-year-old firm founded in Chicago at the turn of the last century, was the fifth largest of the world's "Big Five" accounting firms. A key assistant to the former chief financial officer of Enron pleaded guilty to charges of conspiracy to commit wire fraud and money laundering. The assistant arranged a plea bargain with federal prosecutors and testified against the former CFO and CEO of Enron in exchange for a more lenient sentence.

Enron and Worldcom were two of the largest corporate bankruptcies related to allegations of widespread fraud, cover-ups, and criminal behavior by senior executives and their auditors. However, as major public corporations have come under increased public scrutiny in the years since Enron, massive fraud on the scale of the Enron case is being shown to be the exception and not the rule. Although interpretations of accounting standards are often subject to differences of opinion, the vast majority of public corporations do not "cook the books" to mislead the public. From 2003 to October

2007, the stock markets shook off the Enron and Worldcom frauds and had a significant bull market, with the Dow Jones Industrials rising to over 14,000.

Nevertheless, in the years since the Enron and WorldCom scandals, a different set of issues emerged that has created even more risk than those earlier problems. Since October 2007, Washington Mutual, Bear Stearns, Merrill Lynch, Lehman Brothers, Fannie Mae, AIG, Wachovia, and IndyMAC, among others, have either failed or been forced to sell at fire-sale prices because of a combination of excessive leverage, bad real estate deals, underprovisioning for loan losses, derivative losses, and bad management. Time and investigations will reveal whether fraud was a significant component of any or all of these failures, but the key point for the student is that the analytical techniques set forth in this chapter did allow a few brave financial analysts (such as Meredith Whitney while at Oppenheimer) and hedge fund operators (such as John Paulson) to identify the problems early on and either make their reputations or make their fortunes by acting accordingly. In Paulson's case, he bet heavily against the overleveraged companies' stocks and bonds and reaped large gains when the prices of those securities fell sharply in 2008.

New regulation will likely prohibit the leverage ratios of 30 to 1 or more that existed at Bear Stearns and others and the ability of homeowners to borrow all or more than all of the value of the equity in their homes. New regulations also will likely prohibit the unregulated writing of credit default swaps without appropriate insurance reserves (accounting for concentration of risk) that existed at AIG as a result of a decision made in 2000 by the New York State Department of Insurance. While such limitations may cap the potential ROE for financial companies (by limiting the extent of financial leverage such companies can employ) and may also, for a time, reduce home ownership rates, they are also likely to reduce the probability of a systemic meltdown such as what occurred in late 2008.

SUMMARY

Financial statement analysis is the art of translating data from financial statements into information that is useful for informed decision making. Two commonly used tools of financial statement analysis are ratio analysis and common-size statements. Major areas of emphasis include profitability, liquidity, operating efficiency, and capital structure. One logical sequence of analysis consists of first, specifying one's objectives; second, developing key ratios and common-size statements; third, analyzing and interpreting the data; and finally, developing a set of conclusions and recommendations backed up by the data. Good financial analysis can translate into real-world results.

KEY POINTS

OBJECTIVES
Understand the numbers
Provide basis for financial forecasting
Ultimate goal of informed decision making

RATIO ANALYSIS
Profitability:
    Return on sales
    Return on assets
    Return on equity
Liquidity:
    Current ratio
    Quick ratio
    Average collection period
    Days sales in inventory
Operating efficiency:
    Cost of sales to inventory
    Sales to total assets
    Sales to working capital
Capital structure (leverage):
    Total debt to total assets
      (debt ratio)
    Long-term debt to total assets
    Debt equity
    Times interest earned

RELATIONS AMONG RATIOS
$ROA = Margin \times Turnover$
$ROE = ROA \times Assets/Equity$

COMMON-SIZE STATEMENTS
Balance sheet as a percentage of total assets

Income statement as a percentage
of net sales

COMMON-SIZE ANALYSIS   Balance sheet:
Distribution of assets in working
capital accounts
Distribution of assets between
current and long-term
Distribution of liabilities between
current and long-term
Choice between debt and equity
financing
Overall trend in all accounts
Income statement:
Absorption of revenue dollars by
cost and expense items
Trend of costs and expenses

ANALYTICAL SEQUENCE   Establish objectives
Prepare numerical data
Analyze data
Form conclusions targeted to
objectives

7

Financial Forecasting and Cash Budgeting

OBJECTIVES OF FINANCIAL FORECASTING

Adequate financial planning is a key element in the success of any business venture. Conversely, the lack of adequate financial planning is a key element in the failure of many business enterprises. In this chapter, we will examine commonly used techniques for both short-term and long-term financial forecasting and budgeting. The objectives for both short-term and long-term planning are the same, and the techniques employed differ primarily in the degree of detail developed in the analysis. Both types of planning have as their overriding objective the development of a financial planning and control system to guide the financial future of the firm. Short-term forecasts tend to focus closely on cash budgeting and cash flow planning, while long-term forecasts tend to focus more on planning for future growth in sales and assets and for the financing of this growth.

SHORT-TERM FORECASTS AND CASH BUDGETING

A *short-term forecast and cash budget* is simply a plan for the near future expressed in monetary terms. The objective of this plan is to provide a planning and control system to guide the next few months or quarters of the company's operations. Use of the cash budget as a control system highlights the key role of the financial plan in guiding a company's fiscal course. It is obviously unreasonable to expect a monthly budget to be 100 percent accurate over a planning period of six to twelve months. This, of course, is not the intent of the budget. The intent of the budget is to lay out a plan, and the guidelines provided by the budget should be used to control the operations of the firm according to the plan. Thus, rather than look at the budget as simply a device for controlling expenditures, one should see it as a dynamic financial planning and control tool to guide the financial future of the firm. As general economic conditions and business opportunities change, the budget also must change. As actual operations deviate from the plan, the financial manager can use the cash budget to assess the reason for the variation and take corrective action where appropriate.

The Cutler Toy Company will be used to illustrate the use of a short-term financial planning and control system. The system illustrated here follows a logical sequence of development resulting in a short-term financial planning and cash budgeting system. This particular application illustrates the use of this system to set up and monitor a line of credit to be established for a seasonal inventory buildup. The general procedure can be used for a variety of planning needs and follows these logical steps:

1. Develop sales forecast for upcoming year.
2. Develop estimates of next year's expected profitability.
3. Develop forecasted (pro forma) income statement for upcoming year.
4. Estimate cash payment and collection lags.
5. Develop detailed cash collections and payments forecast.
6. Construct cash budget.
7. Develop forecasted (pro forma) balance sheet for end of next year.

FINANCIAL FORECAST FOR THE CUTLER TOY COMPANY

The Cutler Toy Company was founded in 1999 by William Cutler, a mathematician who began devising intricate toys as a hobby while a graduate student in the early 1990s. From 1999 through the 2007 Christmas season, Cutler Toy had been run as a "seat-of-the-pants" operation by William and two part-time employees. William performed all management functions for the company when he was not busy teaching at the local university, where he was employed as an assistant professor of applied mathematics. By the early spring of 2008, it was evident that the company had become too large to be run by William alone, so he asked Neville Hook, a young finance professor at the university, to help him plan the financial future of the company in return for a share of ownership in the company.

Neville and William agreed that if the past successful growth of the company were to continue into the future, a formal financial planning system would have to be implemented as soon as possible. As the first step in setting up a planning and control system, Neville requested and received a sales forecast for the next ten months from William. On the basis of this forecast, which is shown in Exhibit 7.1, and an analysis of the previous year's financial statements, Neville next planned to construct a cash payments and collections forecast, a cash budget, and a pro forma balance sheet for December 2008.

EXHIBIT 7.1 CUTLER TOY COMPANY
MONTHLY SALES FORECAST, MAY 2008–FEBRUARY 2009

January–April (actual sales)	$35,000
May	10,000
June	10,000
July	15,000
August	20,000
September	30,000
October	40,000
November	60,000
December	<u>30,000</u>
Total calendar year 2003	<u>$250,000</u>
January 2004	$25,000
February 2004	7,000

Note from Cutler:
This forecast is based on my survey of the stores we are now supplying and the assumption that our fixed assets (building and fixtures) will have to be expanded by 25 percent with a corresponding increase in the long-term bank loan to $15,000.

As with any financial planning system, the first area of concern is the revenue forecast—in this case, William's sales forecast. The entire planning and budgeting effort is based on this sales forecast; the end product can be only as good as this key cornerstone. As can be seen from Exhibit 7.1, William is planning a major expansion of Cutler Toy's operations and is forecasting a total 2008 sales volume of $250,000, an increase of 150 percent over 2007. This sales increase is a result of William's decision to make the transition to a full-time operation under the control of his new general manager.

The note at the bottom of Exhibit 7.1 indicates that the sales forecast is based on William's personal survey of his present customers and thus represents these customers' forecasted purchases, assuming William goes ahead with his expansion plans. Since William has been in business many years and presumably has a great deal of experience in dealing with these customers, it seems reasonable to accept his forecast at face value. William's note to Exhibit 7.1 also indicates that his building and fixtures will have to be expanded by 25 percent ($5,000) and that this expansion will be financed by an increase in the long-term bank loan to $15,000 from its current level of $10,000.

As a baseline for her 2008 forecasts, Neville will use the actual income statement and balance sheet for Cutler Toy for the calendar year 2007. These statements are shown in Exhibits 7.2 and 7.3.

EXHIBIT 7.2   CUTLER TOY COMPANY
INCOME STATEMENT, 2007

Sales		$100,000
Cost of goods sold		75,000
Gross margin		$25,000
Expenses:		
Depreciation	$2,400	
Employee wages	10,000	
Other expenses	1,000	
Interest	1,200	
Total expenses		14,600
Net income before tax		10,400
Taxes		2,300
Net profit		$8,100

**EXHIBIT 7.3   CUTLER TOY COMPANY
BALANCE SHEET, DECEMBER 31, 2007**

ASSETS

Cash		$10,500
Accounts receivable		10,000
Inventory		16,000
Building and fixtures	$20,000	
Less: Accumulated depreciation	6,000	14,000
Total assets		$50,500

LIABILITIES AND EQUITY

Liabilities:		
Accounts payable	8,000	
Long-term bank loan*	10,000	$18,000
Equity:		
Common stock		17,500
Retained earnings		15,000
Total liabilities and equity		$50,500

*Interest payable quarterly at the rate of 3%, or $300, per quarter.

The next logical step in our planning system is to develop a fore-casted, or pro forma, income statement for calendar year 2008. To develop this statement, Neville must first develop a set of profitability estimates for this year's operations. Several estimates based on past performance and expected future operating characteristics must be made at this point. One of the most important and most sensitive variables to be estimated is the gross profit margin. It is generally best to develop a relatively conservative estimate here, as fairly small percentage changes in the gross margin often result in fairly large percentage changes in the bottom line. On the basis of past experience (see the actual 2007 income statement in Exhibit 7.2), the gross profit margin for 2008 is estimated at 25 percent.

Three other key variables—depreciation, employee wages, and other expenses—can be estimated from William's projections of the upcoming year's operations. Depreciation, which is essentially a policy variable determined by William's choice of depreciation methods, is fixed at $3,400, an increase of $1,000 over last year. Employee wages for the year are estimated at $22,000 and other expenses at

$1,800. For purposes of developing the cash budget, it is further estimated that remaining wages to be paid in 2008 ($4,400 has been paid so far) will be paid at the rate of $2,200 per month and that other expenses will occur evenly at the rate of $150 per month. Finally, interest expense on the long-term bank loan is payable quarterly at the rate of 12 percent per year. Total payments of $1,500 will be made, with $300 due at the end of March and June and $450 due at the end of September and December. The $150 quarterly increase reflects the increase in size of the loan due to the fixed asset expansion. The end result of all of these estimates is the pro forma income statement for calendar year 2008, shown in Exhibit 7.4. A gross margin of $62,500 is anticipated on $250,000 in sales. Deducting depreciation expenses, employee wages, interest, and other expenses yields income before tax of $33,800. Deducting taxes of $7,400 leaves an after-tax profit of $26,400.

**EXHIBIT 7.4   CUTLER TOY COMPANY
PRO FORMA INCOME STATEMENT, 2008**

Sales		$250,000
Cost of goods sold		187,500
Gross margin		$62,500
Expenses:		
Depreciation	$3,400	
Employee wages	22,000	
Other expenses	1,800	
Interest	1,500	
Total expenses		28,700
Income before tax		$33,800
Taxes		7,400
Net profit		$26,400

Now that we have an estimate of the year's profitability and income tax expense, we may move ahead to the next three steps, which involve estimating cash payment and collection lags, developing cash payment and collection forecasts, and constructing the cash budget. These three steps are actually undertaken simultaneously because they are largely interdependent and will collectively culminate in the cash budget. First, the cash collections forecast is developed. In William's case, this is a relatively simple task, since he deals mainly with department stores, toy specialty shops, and discount chains, all of which customarily pay him no later than the month following the sale. Thus, the cash collections forecast is a simple matter of "lagging sales" one month: Cash collections in one month will be equal to sales from the previous month. Exhibit 7.5 shows the result of this process.

EXHIBIT 7.5   CUTLER TOY COMPANY
CASH COLLECTIONS FORECAST, 2008

	SALES	CASH COLLECTIONS
April	$ 8,000	n.a.
May	10,000	$ 8,000
June	10,000	10,000
July	15,000	10,000
August	20,000	15,000
September	30,000	20,000
October	40,000	30,000
November	60,000	40,000
December	30,000	60,000

The next step, estimating expected cash payments over the next year, is a bit more complex, mainly because of the need to estimate future inventory purchases. As a first step, a decision must be made to establish an inventory policy—that is, to determine how much inventory should normally be carried. In Cutler Toy's case, the inventory policy is that the dollar value of inventory on hand at the end of each month should be approximately equal to the next two months' expected sales at cost. Using cost values will result in the physical volume of inventory being approximately equal to the upcoming two months' physical sales volume. Since the gross profit margin is 25 percent, this policy results in a target ending inventory approximately equal to 75 percent of the next two months' sales at retail.

Given an estimate of required ending inventory and the known quantity of inventory on hand at the beginning of the month, we need consider only one more variable in determining the current month's purchases. This last variable is the amount of inventory expected to be used up during the month to support the current month's sales. Since the gross margin is 25 percent, inventory used up in any one month will be equal to 75 percent of the current month's sales at sales prices. Now to estimate the required monthly purchases, we need only add the required ending inventory to the inventory expected to be used up during the month and deduct beginning inventory. Required ending inventory for each month moves ahead to become the estimate of beginning inventory for the following month, and the process is repeated.

Exhibit 7.6 illustrates the overall process. Required ending inventory for May is equal to $18,750, which is 75 percent of forecasted sales during June and July ($25,000). Expected sales during May of $10,000 (at sales prices) will use up $7,500 of inventory (at cost) during the month of May. Thus, total inventory requirements for May are $26,250. Subtracting beginning inventory of $15,000 results in purchases of $11,250. Assuming that Cutler Toy normally pays for purchases during the month following the purchase, the $11,250 cash outflow will occur during June. May's cash outflow will be equal to the accounts payable balance on April 30 of $12,000. Finally, required ending inventory at the end of May is moved forward to become our estimate of beginning inventory for June, and the process is repeated. Exhibit 7.6 traces the process through the end of the calendar year. Note that required ending inventory and purchases peak in September, while cash payments on purchases peak in October.

Only a few remaining items are necessary to develop the cash budget. First we must consider the impact of tax payments. Cutler Toy's total tax bill of $7,400 is payable in quarterly installments of $1,850 on April 15, June 30, September 30, and December 31. The April 15 payment has already been made, so the next payment is due on June 30. Second, we know from developing the pro forma income statement that wages of $2,200 per month and other expenses of $150 per month must be paid. Third, as a policy matter, normal prudence suggests that some minimum level of cash on hand should be maintained. In fact, since bank borrowing is anticipated to support seasonal inventory needs, it is highly likely that the bank supplying the loan will require some minimal balance in the form of a compensating balance. In Cutler Toy's case, a minimum balance of $2,000 is specified.

Finally, in constructing the cash budget, we are assuming that if a cash shortage is indicated for any month, bank credit will be available. Thus, the cash budget assumes approval of a credit line and is designed as a planning and control technique to monitor the credit

EXHIBIT 7.6 CUTLER TOY COMPANY
PURCHASES AND PURCHASES PAYMENTS FORECAST, 2008

	MAY	JUNE	JULY	AUG	SEPT	OCT	NOV	DEC
Required ending inventory*	$18,750	$26,250	$37,500	$52,500	$75,000	$67,500	$41,250	$24,000
Expected sales at cost~	7,500	7,500	11,250	15,000	22,500	30,000	45,000	22,500
Total	$26,250	$33,750	$48,750	$67,500	$97,500	$97,500	$86,250	$46,500
Less: Beginning inventory#	15,000	18,750	26,250	37,500	52,500	75,000	67,500	41,250
Purchases	$11,250	$15,000	$22,500	$30,000	$45,000	$22,500	$18,750	$5,250
Purchases payments^	$12,000	$11,250	$15,000	$22,500	$30,000	$45,000	$22,500	$18,750

* Next two months' estimated sales × 75% = Next two months' sales at cost
~ Estimated current month's sales × 75% = Inventory required at cost to support current month's sales
# May figure equals April 30 inventory balance
^ May figure equals April 30 accounts payable balance

line. If the credit line is not already approved, then the cash budget will become a key document in supporting the credit application.

Exhibit 7.7 presents the finished product—the cash budget for May through December 2008. The top line—cash collections from sales—comes directly from Exhibit 7.5, the cash collections forecast. Cash outflows are also straightforward. Purchases are as developed in Exhibit 7.6, while wages, other expenses, and interest are as previously specified. Taxes represent the three quarterly payments remaining on Cutler Toy's 2008 tax liability. Total inflows minus total outflows results in the predicted net cash gain or loss during the month. Deducting the loss from (or adding the gain to) the cash balance at the beginning of the month yields Cutler Toy's cumulative end-of-month cash balance if no outside financing is obtained.

At this point, following the cash budget becomes slightly more complicated. The cumulative cash if no financing account represents Cutler Toy's projected levels of cash if outside financing (in this case, bank financing) were not available. If the cash outflow continues to exceed inflows, then this account will eventually become negative, indicating a need for external financing. In addition to this financing need, the desired minimum level of $2,000 must also be considered. Thus, in May, a cash balance of $12,750 is indicated. Deducting the desired minimum level of $2,000 shows that William expects to have on hand $10,750 in excess of his desired minimum level. If this indicated balance were negative, a need for cash would be indicated.

Cutler Toy's first external financing needs are indicated in July. At the end of July, a cash loss of $7,350 subtracted from beginning cash of $7,000 results in cumulative cash without financing of a negative $350. Deducting the $2,000 minimum cash level from this cumulative balance shows total financing needs of $2,350—$350 to cover the operating deficit and $2,000 to maintain the required minimum level of cash. Additional cash loans will be required in August ($9,850), September ($14,650), and October ($17,350), so that the cumulative loan balance at the end of October will stand at $44,200. Finally, in November, cash inflows begin to exceed outflows following the seasonal sales peak (that is, cash collections begin to accelerate while purchases slow down), and a net cash gain of $15,150 is realized. This gain is applied to the outstanding loan balance, reducing it to $29,050. The remainder of the loan is then paid off in December.

**EXHIBIT 7.7 CUTLER TOY COMPANY
CASH BUDGET, 2008**

	MAY	JUNE	JULY	AUG	SEPT	OCT	NOV	DEC
Cash collections:								
Collection from sales	$8,000	$10,000	$10,000	$15,000	$20,000	$30,000	$40,000	$60,000
Cash outflows:								
Purchases	12,000	11,250	15,000	22,500	30,000	45,000	22,500	18,750
Wages	2,200	2,200	2,200	2,200	2,200	2,200	2,200	2,200
Other expenses	150	150	150	150	150	150	150	150
Interest	0	300	0	0	450	0	0	450
Taxes	0	1,850	0	0	1,850	0	0	1,850
Total outflows	$14,350	$15,750	$17,350	$24,850	$34,650	$47,350	$24,850	$23,400
Net cash gain (loss) during month	(6,350)	(5,750)	(7,350)	(9,850)	(14,650)	(17,350)	15,150	36,600
Cash beginning of month*	19,100	12,750	7,000	(350)	(10,200)	(24,850)	(42,200)	(27,050)
Cumulative cash if no financing	$12,750	$7,000	($350)	($10,200)	($24,850)	($42,200)	($27,050)	$9,550
Desired minimum cash level	2,000	2,000	2,000	2,000	2,000	2,000	2,000	2,000
Cumulative cash above minimum needs (or financing needs)	$10,750	$5,000	($2,350)	($12,200)	($26,850)	($44,200)	($29,050)	$7,550

* May figure is April 30 cash balance.

118

EXHIBIT 7.8 CUTLER TOY COMPANY
SCHEDULE OF CASH AND LOAN BALANCES, 2008

	(1) BEGINNING CASH	(2) BANK BORROWINGS	(3) TOTAL (1+2)	(4) NET CASH GAIN (LOSS)	(5) BANK REPAYMENTS	(6) LOAN BALANCE	(7) ENDING CASH (3+4−5)
May	$19,100	0	$19,100	($6,350)	0	0	$12,750
June	12,750	0	12,750	(5,750)	0	0	7,000
July	7,000	$2,350	9,350	(7,350)	0	$2,350	2,000
August	2,000	9,850	11,850	(9,850)	0	12,200	2,000
September	2,000	14,650	16,650	(14,650)	0	26,850	2,000
October	2,000	17,350	19,350	(17,350)	0	44,200	2,000
November	2,000	0	2,000	15,150	$15,150	29,050	2,000
December	2,000	0	2,000	36,600	29,050	0	9,550

Exhibit 7.8 provides a schedule of Cutler Toy's cash and loan balances for the period covered by the cash budget. This schedule simply lists the beginning cash, required bank borrowing, net cash gain or loss, repayments (when possible), ending loan balance, and ending cash balance. The usefulness of this type of schedule lies primarily in its explicit listing of the amount and timing of loan requirements and repayments.

The final exhibit of the forecasting package, Exhibit 7.9, is Cutler Toy's pro forma balance sheet for the year ending December 31, 2008. All accounts from the balance sheet follow directly from the previous exhibits, thus providing a convenient computational check on the internal consistency of the set of forecasts. As can be seen from the balance sheet, Cutler Toy's total assets are expected to be $79,150, with liabilities of $20,250 and equity of $58,900.

EXHIBIT 7.9 CUTLER TOY COMPANY
PRO FORMA BALANCE SHEET, DECEMBER 31, 2008

ASSETS

Cash (Exhibit 7.7)		$9,550
Accounts receivable (December sales)		30,000
Inventory (Exhibit 7.6)		24,000
Building and fixtures*	$25,000	
Less: Accumulated depreciation~	9,400	15,600
Total assets		$79,150

LIABILITIES AND EQUITY

Liabilities:		
Accounts payable (Exhibit 7.6)	5,250	
Long-term bank loan^	15,000	$20,250
Equity:		
Common stock		17,500
Retained earnings#		41,400
Total equity		58,900
Total liabilities and equity		$79,150

* Beginning balance of $20,000 + $5,000 addition
~ Beginning balance of $6,000 + $3,400 2008 depreciation expense
^ Beginning balance of $10,000 + $5,000 addition
# Beginning balance of $15,000 + $26,400 2008 earnings

At this point, one important observation is worth repeating. It must be stressed that the foregoing budgeting system must be viewed as dynamic rather than static in nature. Certainly, one cannot expect the forecasted figures to be completely accurate for each month. The most important use of the budget is as a planning and control device. A budget is simply a plan in dollar terms. As the future planning period becomes the current operating period, the budget becomes the basic document for checking operations against plans and taking corrective action where appropriate—either revising the plan or controlling operations to agree with the plan. In this regard, the observant reader will note that the plan contains no provision for interest payments on the credit line. To allow for interest, one may wish to go back and revise the budget to allow for the interest payments or, if the interest amount appears relatively small, simply adjust the budget for interest expense as the planning period unfolds.

Before moving to the topic of long-term forecasting, a final caveat is necessary. The cash budget developed for Cutler Toy focuses on the firm's financial position as of the last day of each month and implicitly assumes that cash inflows and outflows occur at a fairly uniform rate during the month. If this is not the case—for example, if most expenses are paid early in the month while most cash collections come in late in the month—it will be necessary to shift the date of the cash budget from the end of the month to the point at which peak cash needs may be anticipated. In the case of early outflows and late inflows, the fifteenth of the month may be the most appropriate date. The final cash position at the end of the planning period will be the same, of course, but greater loan needs during individual months will be shown.

Having examined short-term financial planning techniques, it is now appropriate to examine long-term financial planning techniques. As previously noted, long-term forecasts differ from short-term forecasts primarily in the level of detail required. The major objective remains the development of financial planning and control systems, but we will now shift our attention toward planning for future growth in sales and assets and the financing of this growth.

LONG-TERM FINANCIAL PLANNING

In developing long-term financial plans, one is most often concerned with planning for future sales growth and devising plans to finance this growth. Probably the most common approach to this makes use of the *percentage of sales* technique. The essential logic of this technique is that, as future sales grow, assets will also have to increase to support the sales increases. These increased assets will be financed partially by reinvested earnings and partially by increases in so-called spontaneous liabilities such as accounts payable. Some short-term notes payable may also be available. Any shortages of financing sources (overages are not usually a problem!) will have to be provided for from external financing sources, usually long-term debt or additional equity. The nature of this forecasting technique will be illustrated by a continuation of the Cutler Toy Company example.

Suppose that following the 2008 planning period, William Cutler believes that sales can be expanded by an additional 25 percent in 2009 and 2010, by 15 percent in 2011, and by 10 percent in 2012, with this growth leveling off to approximately 5 percent per year thereafter. If we wish to develop a five-year financial plan for Cutler Toy, the percentage of sales technique requires that we first develop a five-year profit forecast.

Devising the five-year forecast requires several key estimates. First, it is estimated that cost of sales will remain at 75 percent of sales as in the past. Second, although expenses in the past have been approximately 11.5 percent of sales, allowance must now be made for hiring additional workers, a few of whom may be full-time. According to Neville's estimates, expenses may be expected to increase to 16 percent of sales. Finally, although William and Neville have been reinvesting all profits for the past two years in order to provide funds for growth, in the future, they plan to draw a small salary from the expanded company. The total of their two salaries is shown as a separate line in the forecast. The five-year profit forecast (to the nearest thousand dollars) is now as shown in Exhibit 7.10.

**EXHIBIT 7.10   CUTLER TOY COMPANY
FIVE-YEAR PROFIT FORECAST**

	2009	2010	2011	2012	2013
Sales	$313,000	$391,000	$450,000	$495,000	$520,000
Cost of sales (75%)	234,750	293,250	337,500	371,250	390,000
Gross profit	$78,250	$97,750	$112,500	$123,750	$130,000
Expenses (16%)	50,080	62,560	72,000	79,200	83,200
Cutler and Hook salary	20,000	20,000	25,000	25,000	25,000
Income before tax	$8,170	$15,190	$15,500	$19,550	$21,800
Taxes	2,170	3,190	3,500	3,550	4,800
Net profit	$6,000	$12,000	$12,000	$16,000	$17,000

The next step is to forecast Cutler Toy's balance sheet position at the end of each year. The objective here is to determine how much— if any—external financing will be required to support the expected sales levels. All asset and liability accounts that are expected to increase with sales are estimated as a percentage of sales, with the appropriate percentage determined according to the account's past relationship to sales. In William's case, if we assume that his year-end balance sheet accounts for 2008 as a percentage of 2008 sales are reasonably representative, then we can estimate cash at 4 percent of sales, accounts receivable at 12 percent, inventory at 10 percent, net fixed assets at 6 percent, and accounts payable at 5 percent. The long-term bank loan and equity accounts, which are not expected to maintain a constant relationship to sales, must be treated separately. In this case, the principal amount due on the long-term bank loan is payable at the rate of $5,000 per year for the next three years. The equity amount, of course, is straightforward. In the absence of any stock sales or redemptions, the common stock account will remain constant. The retained earnings account will increase by the amount of after-tax profit earned each year (if dividends were paid, they would be deducted from the retained earnings account). Finally, in order to force the total of liabilities and equity to equal total assets, a "force," or "plug," figure is used to bring liabilities and equity up to total assets. This figure represents Cutler Toy's external financing requirements— that is, the amount of money required over and above current liabilities and reinvested earnings to finance expected future growth. The five-year plan for Cutler Toy is shown in Exhibit 7.11.

EXHIBIT 7.11   CUTLER TOY COMPANY
FIVE-YEAR PRO-FORMA BALANCE SHEET

	2009	2010	2011	2012	2013
ASSETS					
Cash (4%)	$12,520	$15,640	$18,000	$19,800	$20,800
Accounts receivable (12%)	37,560	46,920	54,000	59,400	62,400
Inventory (10%)	31,300	39,100	45,000	49,500	52,000
Net fixed assets (6%)	18,780	23,460	27,000	29,700	31,200
Total assets	$100,160	$125,120	$144,000	$158,400	$166,400
LIABILITIES AND EQUITY					
Accounts payable (5%)	$15,650	$19,550	$22,500	$24,750	$26,000
Long-term bank loan	10,000	5,000	0	0	0
Required external financing	17,110	31,170	40,100	36,250	26,000
Common stock	10,000	10,000	10,000	10,000	10,000
Retained earnings	47,400	59,400	71,400	87,400	104,400
Total liabilities and equity	$100,160	$125,120	$144,000	$158,400	$166,400

This analysis indicates that Cutler Toy's external financing needs will grow during the high growth years 2009–2010 and then begin to decline as growth tapers off in 2011–2013. It must be noted that these external financing requirements are in addition to the normal seasonal fund requirements indicated on the one-year cash budget illustrated for 2008. Thus, the external requirements indicated represent a permanent need for funds that will not begin to decline until over three years from now.

At this point, William must assess his financing options. The most obvious source of financing would be a long-term loan, with principal repayments beginning in 2012. A bank or potential private financing source may be approached in this regard. Failing a loan, William and Neville can finance growth by giving up their salaries and reinvesting more earnings in the company. Bearing in mind that the external financing needs indicated on the balance sheet represent cumulative needs at year end, it can be seen that each year's incremental need through 2011 can be covered by William and Neville's salaries. If they are unwilling to give up their salaries, a private equity investment might be possible. In any event, it appears that adequate financing can be arranged.

SUMMARY

The objective of a short-term forecast and cash budget is to provide a formal planning and control system to guide a company's operations. Developing a short-term forecast and cash budget follows a logical, seven-step procedure: (1) develop a sales forecast for the upcoming year, (2) develop estimates of next year's expected profitability, (3) develop a pro forma income statement, (4) estimate cash payment and collection lags, (5) develop a detailed cash collections and payments forecast, (6) construct a cash budget, and (7) develop a pro forma balance sheet. A budget system should be used as a dynamic planning and control device that is revised as the future planning period becomes the current operating period, and the budget is used to check operations against plans.

Long-term financial planning centers on planning for the future growth of the company and devising plans to finance this growth. Long-term plans differ from short-term plans primarily in the level of detail required. Long-term plans require the development of pro forma income statements and balance sheets for a three- to five-year period; detailed cash budget forecasts are not required. The percentage of sales method is commonly used to determine the future external financing requirements of a growing business organization.

The cash budgeting and financial forecasting system illustrated here highlights the importance of an adequate financial planning and control system to guide a company's fiscal course. The system is useful both as an explicit statement of management's future goals and as a control device to chart the firm's progress toward these goals. In evaluating the quality of an overall management system, the existence of an explicit financial plan is a key prerequisite for a favorable assessment.

KEY POINTS	
OBJECTIVES	Planning seasonal fund needs Planning financing needs for growth Controlling to plan
SHORT-TERM FORECAST	Monthly sales forecasts Pro forma income statement Monthly cash budget Pro forma balance sheet
LONG-TERM FORECAST	Annual sales forecasts Annual pro forma income statements Annual pro forma balance sheets Identification of long-term financing requirements

8

Breakeven Analysis for Profit Planning

Breakeven analysis is a simple yet powerful approach to profit planning that illuminates the relationships among sales, fixed costs, and variable costs. The technique is also commonly referred to as *cost-volume-profit analysis*. As its name implies, breakeven analysis requires the derivation of various relationships among revenue, fixed costs, and variable costs in order to determine the units of production or volume of sales dollars at which the firm breaks even—that is, where total revenues are exactly equal to the total of fixed and variable costs.

ASSUMPTIONS OF BREAKEVEN ANALYSIS

Application of linear (straight-line) breakeven analysis requires the acceptance of three major assumptions:

1. Costs can be reasonably subdivided into fixed and variable components.
2. All cost-volume-profit relationships are linear.
3. Sales prices will not change with changes in volume.

It will be shown later that the technique can be adapted so that the linearity assumption may be relaxed. For now, however, the reasonableness of the above assumptions should be closely examined.

The first assumption seems quite reasonable. Fixed costs such as depreciation expenses, salaries, rental expenses, and so forth normally can be easily identified. Similarly, variable costs, such as the cost of direct labor and materials used, can also be identified clearly in most cases. Some problems may be encountered in identifying so-called semivariable expenses, but these expense items can normally be separated into fixed and variable components for analysis purposes. The cost of heating a factory in winter is a good example of this type of cost. Some heat expense will be incurred even when the factory is closed because some minimal level of heat is always necessary if only to prevent the water pipes from bursting. When the factory is in operation, heat expense will rise to a level adequate to maintain reasonable comfort, and this increment may be treated as a variable component of the expense. The expense of maintaining the minimal heat level would then be considered a fixed expense.

The second assumption is also valid if we confine the analysis to a reasonable range of operations. If we are dealing with a volume change of plus or minus 10 percent, for example, we would normally expect the relevant cost-volume-profit relationships to remain the same. If, on the other hand, we wish to examine the effect of doubling the level of operations, new relationships will probably have to be developed. These relationships may be linear or nonlinear.

The final assumption, which is actually a subcategory of the second assumption, may be a bit more tenuous. Economic theory tells us that one would normally expect a price increase (after adjusting for general inflation effects) to be accompanied by a decrease in sales volume and vice versa. This assumption will later be relaxed when the nonlinear breakeven case is examined. For the present, it may be noted that if we confine our attention to a reasonable range of prices, the practical effect of this assumption is not severe.

BREAKEVEN APPLICATIONS

There are four major (and related) applications of breakeven analysis:

1. *New product decisions.* Breakeven analysis may be used to determine the sales volume required for a firm (or an individual product) to break even, given expected sales prices and expected costs.
2. *Pricing decisions.* Breakeven analysis may be used to study the effect of changing price and volume relationships on total profits.

3. *Modernization or automation decisions.* Breakeven analysis may be used to analyze the profit implications of a modernization or automation program. In this case a firm is normally substituting fixed costs (such as capital equipment costs) for variable costs (such as direct labor).
4. *Expansion decisions.* Breakeven analysis may be used to study the aggregate effect of a general expansion in production and sales. In this case the relationships between total dollar sales for all products and total dollar costs for all products are examined in order to identify potential changes in these relationships.

THE BREAKEVEN TECHNIQUE

Application of breakeven analysis is quite straightforward and will be illustrated with a simplified example based on an actual case. Peter Porter, a successful young entrepreneur, spends his free time racing Porsche cars. On the basis of his racing experience plus a degree in mechanical engineering, Peter believes that he can assemble and market an improved racing suspension for Porsches. He intends to start up a small business in his garage called Peter Porter's Porsche Plant.

Peter feels he can identify the expected cost and revenue items for his planned racing suspensions. Fixed costs for the first year are estimated at $1,650, with variable costs estimated at $350 for each suspension package. A quick check with several potential customers indicates that a selling price of $500 per package will be reasonable. In order to determine the point at which the new product will break even, one need only solve for the following simple relationship:

$$\text{Revenue} = \text{Fixed costs} + \text{Variable costs}$$

Solving this equation requires determining the quantity of items to be produced and sold so that the above relationship is true. Letting X be equal to the unknown breakeven quantity, the equation becomes:

where: $500X$ = total revenue produced by selling X items,
$1,650$ = total fixed costs, and
$350X$ = total variable costs incurred by producing X items.

Solving the equation is quite simple:

$$\$500X = \$1,650 + \$350X$$
$$\$150X = \$1,650$$
$$X = 11 \text{ units}$$

Thus, eleven units is the breakeven point for this product. As a computational check, one need only substitute $X = 11$ into the breakeven equation:

$$\$500\,(11) = \$1,650 + \$350\,(11)$$
$$\$5,500 \quad = \$1,650 + \$3,850$$
$$\$5,500 \quad = \$5,500$$

Operating Leverage

We can see from the solution to the equation that the difference between the selling price and the variable cost ($150) is the key to the breakeven problem. This difference is called the contribution margin and represents the contribution made by each unit sold toward covering fixed costs and making a profit. Once enough units are sold to cover fixed costs (in this case, eleven units), each unit then makes a direct contribution to profits. Once above the breakeven point, a fairly small percentage increase in the number of units sold will produce a relatively large percentage increase in profit. For example, if the firm produces twelve units, it will then earn $150 in profit ($500[12] – $350[12] – $1,650). An increase in production of one unit, or 8.3 percent (1/12 = 8.3 percent), will result in a profit of $300, an increase of 100 percent. An additional increase of one unit will increase profits to $450, a 50 percent increase. This leverage effect is called operating leverage. As production moves further and further above the breakeven point, the operating leverage effect becomes less dramatic in terms of the percentage increases in profits generated.

The major practical implication of the operating leverage concept is that it illustrates the leverage effect of incurring various levels of fixed costs. In general, as a firm incurs higher levels of fixed costs due to the use of more capital equipment—in other words, becomes more capital intensive—it normally incurs lower levels of variable costs, becoming less labor intensive. Once the fixed costs are covered, the beneficial side of operating leverage shows that any available contribution margin will make a direct contribution to profit. On the other hand, if the firm falls short of covering its fixed costs, a loss will be incurred. For a given production process, the higher the degree of operating leverage, the higher the probability that a loss may be incurred, and the higher the risk.

Additional Breakeven Applications

The breakeven concept is also very useful in determining the breakeven point in terms of aggregate sales dollars for a multiproduct operation. In this case, the breakeven equation is set up in terms of percentage relationships. For example, if Peter decides to expand his operation to a full-time business carrying a full line of specialized racing equipment, he would have to estimate his fixed costs in dollars and variable costs as a percentage of revenue for the entire product line. If he determines that variable costs for the entire product line will maintain the same percentage relationship to revenue as for the racing suspensions, then variable cost will be estimated at 70 percent of sales ($350/$500 = 70 percent). The contribution margin per unit will then be 30 percent ($150/$500 = 30 percent). If fixed costs of the new operation are estimated at $30,000, the new breakeven point may be determined by solving the following equation to determine the revenue dollars required to break even:

$$\text{Revenue } (R) = \text{Fixed costs} + \text{Variable costs}$$
$$R = \$30,000 + 0.7R$$
$$0.3R = \$30,000$$
$$R = \$100,000$$

Thus, the new operation will break even at a sales level of $100,000.

Another useful application of the breakeven technique is in determining the sales dollars (or units) required to earn a given level of profit. Returning to the original example, Peter Porter was concerned with the sales volume required to earn $3,000 in profit. (A profit of $3,000 was specified because this was the amount of money required to finance a trip to enter a race on the West Coast.) To determine the required sales volume, one need only add the required profit to the right-hand side of the original equation (X will now equal the number of units required to earn a $3,000 profit):

Revenue = Fixed costs + Variable costs + Required profit
$500X = $1,650 + $350X + $3,000
$150X = $4,650
X = 31 units

Thus, Peter must sell thirty-one units, or $15,500 worth of suspensions ($500 x 31 = $15,500), in order to finance his trip.

A final interesting use of the breakeven technique is in the area of pricing decisions. Peter was interested in determining what price he would have to charge for a given number of orders and a predetermined level of profit. Specifically, Peter felt certain that he could sell twenty units and wanted to know what price he should charge in order to earn his $3,000 profit for the West Coast trip. To solve this problem, he needed only to solve the breakeven equation in terms of selling price (X = sales price):

Revenue = Fixed costs + Variable costs + Required profit
$20X = $1,650 + $350 (20) + $3,000
$20X = $1,650 + $7,000 + $3,000
$20X = $11,650
X = $582.50

Thus, we can see that a selling price of $582.50 will yield the required profit. A simple computational check confirms that this is so:

Profit = Revenue – Fixed costs – Variable costs
= (20) ($582.50) – $1,650 – (20) ($350)
= $11,650 – $1,650 – $7,000
= $3,000

BREAKEVEN CHARTS

Exhibit 8.1 presents a graphic representation of the breakeven problem posed by Peter Porter's Porsche Plant. The horizontal line at $1,650 represents fixed costs (*FC*), and the upward-sloping line beginning at $1,650 represents total cost (*TC*), which is equal to the sum of fixed plus variable costs (*VC*). This line has a slope equal to $350— every unit increase in production results in a $350 increase in the total cost. The upward-sloping line beginning at the origin represents

EXHIBIT 8.1   PETER PORTER'S PORSCHE PLANT BREAKEVEN CHART

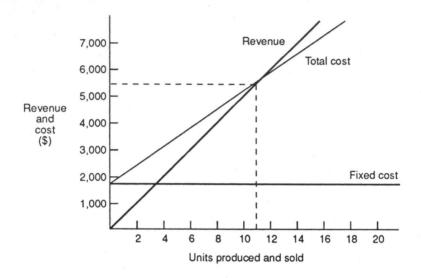

revenue (R) and has a slope of $500—every unit increase in sales produces a $500 increase in revenue. The distance between the revenue line and the total-cost line represents dollars of profit (above the breakeven point) or loss (below the breakeven point).

The graph is useful for two reasons. First, it illustrates the key assumptions of breakeven analysis discussed earlier. It clearly shows that revenue and total cost are treated as simple linear functions of the number of units produced and sold. Profit or loss is thus simply the difference between revenue and total cost, and the breakeven point occurs where revenue is exactly equal to total cost.

The second use of the graph is that it provides a simple visual interpretation of the effect of changing cost-volume-profit relationships. For example, it can be seen that the effect of incurring additional fixed costs is to shift the horizontal fixed-cost line upward, thus raising the total-cost line parallel to itself and causing the breakeven point to rise. The graph also illustrates the effect of "substituting" additional fixed costs (such as additional depreciation for improved capital equipment) for lower levels of variable cost (such as less direct labor and material waste). In this case the horizontal fixed-cost line will move upward but the total-cost line will become less steep due to lower levels of variable cost. The usual net effect of this process is that the firm will now operate at a higher breakeven level but will also have a higher contribution margin (revenue per unit less variable cost per unit). Thus, at levels of operation suffi-ciently above the breakeven point, profits are much higher, while near or below the breakeven, profits are less, or losses are greater.

To illustrate this point, assume that Peter Porter buys additional capital equipment to produce racing suspensions, causing his annual fixed costs to rise to $1,920. At the same time, assume that variable costs per unit decline to $340. The new contribution margin is thus $160 per unit, and the new breakeven point is found as follows:

$$\text{Revenue} = \text{Fixed cost} + \text{Variable costs}$$
$$\$500X = \$1,920 + \$340X$$
$$\$160X = \$1,920$$
$$X = 12 \text{ units}$$

This new breakeven level is shown graphically in Exhibit 8.2. At the new level of operations, the breakeven point is one unit higher than the old level. At high levels of operations—say, production of thirty units—profits under the new cost-volume-profit relationships would be $2,880, versus $2,850 according to the old relationships. At lower levels, however—say, twenty units—profits for the new system would be only $1,280 versus $1,350 for the old system. At loss levels of operations—say, five units—the new relationships would produce a loss of $1,120 versus a loss of only $900 under the old relationships.

EXHIBIT 8.2 PETER PORTER'S PORSCHE PLANT REVISED BREAKEVEN CHART

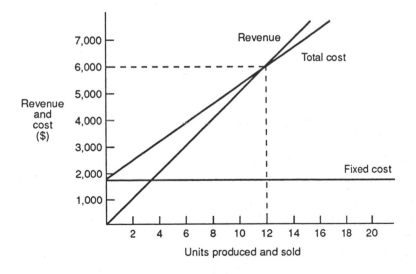

In general, even this very simple illustration shows that an increase in the level of fixed costs must be justified by the expectation of a level of operations substantially in excess of the breakeven level. An extended application of the breakeven concept may also be used to determine the point at which the new relationships produce the same profit as the old relationships. Letting FC' equal the new fixed costs, VC' equal the new variable costs, and R equal revenue in both cases, one need only solve the following simple equation:

$$R - FC - VC = R - FC' - VC'$$
$$\$500X - \$1{,}650 - \$350X = \$500X - \$1{,}920 - \$340X$$
$$\$150X - \$1{,}650 = \$160X - \$1{,}920$$
$$\$270 = \$10X$$
$$X = 27 \text{ units}$$

Thus, at twenty-seven units of production, profits are the same under either alternative. Under the first alternative, profits will be $2,400, computed as follows:

$$\begin{aligned} \text{Profit} &= (\$500)\,(27) - \$1{,}650 - (\$350)\,(27) \\ &= \$13{,}500 - \$1{,}650 - \$9{,}450 \\ &= \$2{,}400 \end{aligned}$$

Under the revised alternative, profits will also be $2,400, computed as follows:

$$\begin{aligned} \text{Profit} &= (\$500)\,(27) - \$1{,}920 - (\$340)\,(27) \\ &= \$13{,}500 - \$1{,}920 - \$9{,}180 \\ &= \$2{,}400 \end{aligned}$$

At all levels of production above twenty-seven units, the second alternative will produce larger profits than the first alternative. Below twenty-seven units, the first alternative will produce higher profits (in the profit zone) or lower losses (in the loss zone) than the second alternative. These relationships are illustrated graphically in Exhibit 8.3, where profit as a function of units produced and sold is graphed for each alternative.

EXHIBIT 8.3 PETER PORTER'S PORSCHE PLANT PROFITABILITY ALTERNATIVES

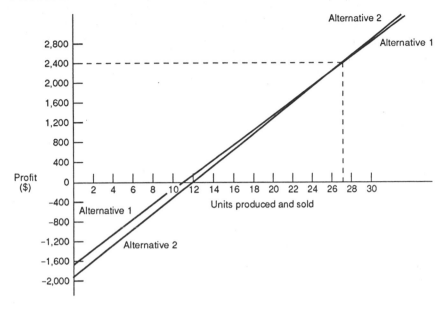

NONLINEAR BREAKEVEN ANALYSIS

As mentioned earlier, the linearity assumptions of breakeven analysis are generally quite useful if one restricts attention to a limited range of production and sales. However, when attempting to analyze the cost-volume-profit relationships over a very wide range of output—for example, in planning the plant size for a new production plant—the linearity assumptions must be relaxed. Empirical studies of cost behavior over wide ranges of output suggest that the average variable cost per unit declines over some range and then begins to increase. Thus, for wide ranges of output the total cost function looks like the curve shown in Exhibit 8.4. The total cost curve increases at a decreasing rate over some range and then begins to increase at an increasing rate.

The revenue function also more nearly resembles a curve than a straight line over wide ranges of output. Economic theory (and common sense) suggests that if sales volume continues to expand over a very wide range, the sales price per unit must eventually decline in order to achieve ever-increasing sales. Thus, the revenue function is best represented by the curve shown in Exhibit 8.4.

EXHIBIT 8.4   SAMPLE NONLINEAR BREAKEVEN ANALYSIS

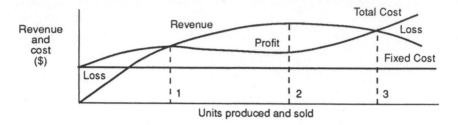

A detailed discussion of how the curves in Exhibit 8.4 are derived and how one determines the maximum profit level indicated requires some background in calculus and is beyond the scope of this book. However, two key factors may be noted from this graph. First, there are two breakeven points in the nonlinear case. The first one, the lower breakeven point in the graph, occurs at the point where the rising revenue curve crosses the rising total cost curve. The second breakeven point, the upper breakeven point in the graph, occurs at a very high output level where the declining revenue curve crosses the now rapidly increasing total cost curve.

The second major point of interest is of particular relevance to the case mentioned earlier concerning planning plant capacity. The point denoted as the maximum profit point in the graph represents the point of maximum separation of the revenue and cost curves. This point is thus the optimal production level for the plant since production at either higher or lower levels of output will result in lower profits.

In reality the mathematics required to develop these relationships is actually quite elementary. The most difficult part of the job lies in developing reasonable estimates of the equations for the curves. Developing these required equations is at best difficult and at worst nearly impossible. Given the equations, the necessary mathematical manipulation is almost trivial. In any event, for a wide array of applications the linearity assumptions are quite reasonable, and the possibility of nonlinear functions may be ignored for practical purposes.

SUMMARY

Breakeven analysis is a simple yet useful and powerful technique for profit planning. Cost-volume-profit relationships may be studied under a variety of conditions to aid in profit planning, pricing, and planning for modernization, expansion, or automation. Linear breakeven analysis assumes that costs can be reasonably subdivided into fixed and variable components, that all cost-volume-profit relationships are linear, and that sales prices will not change with changes in volume. Nonlinear breakeven analysis does not require that these assumptions be met. There are four major and related applications of breakeven analysis: new product decisions, pricing decisions, modernization or automation decisions, and expansion decisions. The essence of the breakeven technique is to find the level of production and sales at which revenue is equal to the total of fixed plus variable costs. Operating leverage measures the percentage increase in profits resulting from a given percentage increase in sales. Operating leverage is very high near the breakeven point and decreases as the level of production increases above the breakeven point. Breakeven charts provide a visual interpretation of the effect of changing cost-volume-profit relationships.

KEY POINTS
ASSUMPTIONS Costs may be subdivided into fixed and variable components. Cost-volume-profit relationships are linear (may be relaxed).
APPLICATIONS New product decision Pricing decisions Modernization or automation Expansion New plant construction
TECHNIQUE Revenue = Fixed cost + Variable cost
NONLINEAR BREAKEVEN Two breakeven points Maximum profit point

PART IV

Working Capital Decisions

9

Working Capital Policy

IMPORTANT OF WORKING CAPITAL POLICY

The term *working capital* refers to a firm's investment in current assets. *Net working capital* refers to the excess of current assets over current liabilities and can be thought of as the circulating capital of a business. Effective control of this circulating capital is one of the most important functions of financial management.

There are a number of reasons for the importance of working capital management. One major reason stems from the relative urgency of working capital decisions. There is a very close relationship between sales growth and growth of current assets. Current assets tend to grow spontaneously with increases in sales, and the growth of these assets must be controlled effectively if a financial manager is to maintain control of the firm's asset structure. As current assets grow, they must also be financed. Part of this financing will come from current liabilities, part from other external sources of capital, and part from reinvested earnings. Control of the portion of current asset financing that comes from current liabilities is an important aspect of working capital management.

A second major reason for the importance of working capital management is the size of the working capital accounts. Current assets, particularly accounts receivable and inventory, often represent the largest single category of asset investment for many firms. This is particularly true for small and rapidly growing businesses.

If we look to the right-hand side of the balance sheet, current liabilities often provide a major source of financing for a firm. For small businesses in particular, where long-term debt is often unavailable

141

at any cost, current liabilities may represent the firm's largest single source of financing. A new firm may find it impossible to obtain a long-term loan but relatively easy to establish an open account with a major supplier. Similarly, a short-term bank loan, collateralized by accounts receivable or inventory, is much easier for a new firm to obtain than long-term debt.

A third reason for the importance of working capital management is that it represents a firm's first line of defense against recessionary downturns in sales. In the face of sales declines, a financial manager can do little about fixed asset commitments or long-term debt arrangements. However, a manager can do a great deal relative to the firm's credit policy, inventory control policy, and accounts payable policy. If the firm is facing a credit crunch, inventory may be reduced or accounts receivable tightened up to provide increased liquidity. On the other side of the balance sheet, accounts payable payments may be slowed to provide an additional source of financing.

A fourth and final reason for the importance of working capital management lies in the relationship of effective management to the survival of the firm. As noted, working capital accounts tend to grow spontaneously with growth in sales. The inability to control this growth is a major cause of business failures. Once again, control is particularly important for the small, rapidly growing firm.

SHORT-TERM VERSUS LONG-TERM FINANCING

One important working capital policy issue deals with the use of short-term versus long-term financing. The selection of short-term or long-term financing requires the consideration of a very definite risk-return tradeoff. As a general rule, short-term financing is normally a riskier form of financing than long-term financing, but it is also normally less costly. It is less costly because short-term interest rates are normally lower than long-term interest rates. It is riskier because future short-term interest rates cannot be known with certainty, whereas the cost of long-term debt is fixed in advance for the life of the loan. Short-term debt is also riskier because there is always the possibility that a firm may not be able to renew a short-term debt obligation when it comes due. Thus, the use of short-term debt exposes a firm to two distinct types of risk: interest rate risk and renewal risk. These two types of risk are the price the firm pays for the lower cost of short-term financing.

In addition to its lower cost, short-term debt offers one other advantage over long-term debt: added flexibility. Once a long-term loan is negotiated or a bond issue is sold, the firm is locked in to the terms of the note over its life span (unless the note is callable). If the firm has a short-term or cyclical need for funds, a long-term obligation may be highly undesirable. If the need for funds is a seasonal one, such as the need to finance a seasonal inventory buildup, long-term debt may be particularly inappropriate.

In general, firms strive to match their loan maturities with their asset maturities. Short-term fund requirements, such as seasonal buildups of inventory and growth of accounts receivable, should be financed with short-term financing sources, such as accounts payable and short-term loans. Long-term fund requirements, such as new plant and equipment, should be financed from long-term financing sources, such as long-term loans, leases, and equity capital. In this regard, it is instructive to note the classic rule for going broke: "Borrow short, and invest long." This old saying refers to the fact that using short-term financing sources to fund long-term needs is the fastest known route to financial insolvency. When the short-term note comes due, the funds are still needed and therefore unavailable to repay the note. Bear Stearns and Lehman Brothers both relearned this old lesson (to their detriment) in 2008.

In managing working capital needs, it is important to recognize that listing an asset as "current" on the balance sheet does not necessarily mean the need to finance this asset is short-term. As current assets grow with sales, for example, the overall level of current assets will increase permanently. Part of this increase will be financed by a permanent increase in the level of accounts payable, part by other permanent increases in other short-term liabilities, and part by permanent sources of capital (long-term debt, reinvested earnings, and new equity capital). As a firm grows, current assets will generally grow faster than current liabilities. The difference between the two— net working capital—will also grow. This permanent growth in net working capital requires a source of permanent financing.

Term Structure of Interest Rates

Effective management of financing sources requires an understanding of the relationship between short-term and long-term interest rates. Interest rates normally are measured by the yield to maturity of a debt agreement. The yield to maturity is simply the average annual compound rate of return earned by the lender. For a short-term loan, the debt agreement is usually evidenced by a written loan agreement between the borrower and the bank or other source of funds. For long-term loans the agreement may be a publicly or privately placed bond issue or a long-term loan agreement between the borrower and a bank or other supplier of long-term capital.

The number of years over which debt is to be repaid is referred to as the *term to maturity* of the debt. The term structure of interest rates describes the relationship between the yield to maturity and the term to maturity of debt issues.

The term structure of interest rates can be represented by a graph showing yield to maturity as a function of term to maturity. Such a graph is called a *yield curve*. Since there are many different categories of debt issues, there are many different possible types of yield curves. The yield curve for corporate bonds, for example, will look quite different from the yield curve for municipal bonds or U.S. government securities. Each category of debt will have its own yield curve relationships.

Exhibit 9.1 shows the so-called normal yield curve, where long-term rates are higher than short-term rates. Such a curve is described as an upward-sloping, or "positive," yield curve. A positive yield curve

EXHIBIT 9.1   POSITIVE YIELD CURVE

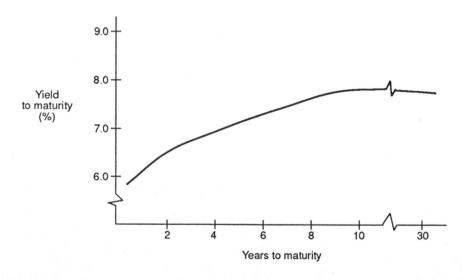

EXHIBIT 9.2   NEGATIVE YIELD CURVE

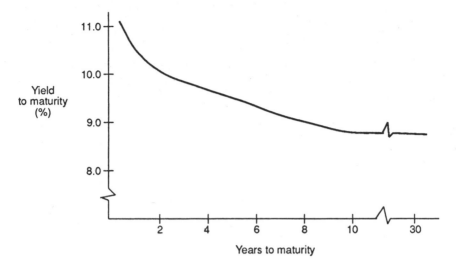

represents the normal condition of the capital markets. This curve presents borrowers with the risk-return trade-off described in the previous section: Short-term debt is less costly than long-term debt but is riskier due to the interest rate risk and the renewal risk.

As with most situations in life, however, the yield curve is not always "normal." The yield curve is sometimes downward sloping, or "negative." In this case, short-term rates are higher than long-term rates. Such conditions generally occur during periods of very high interest rates. Exhibit 9.2 shows a negative yield curve.

There are a number of theoretical explanations for the term structure of interest rates. The *liquidity preference theory* states that long-term interest rates should be higher than short-term interest rates due to the liquidity preferences of lenders and borrowers. In an uncertain world, lenders normally prefer to lend short-term rather than long-term because of the greater liquidity of short-term debt. Lenders may get locked into long-term debt agreements during periods of rising interest rates, suffering losses as their cost of funds rises but their loan portfolios continue to provide relatively low rates of return. From a bond investor's point of view, short-term debt is subject to less fluctuation in principal value as interest rates fluctuate. Investors holding ninety-day Treasury bills experience very small changes in the value of those bills as interest rates fluctuate. Since long-term debt is riskier than short-term debt from the perspective of lenders and investors, suppliers of long-term debt demand higher interest rates on long-term debt than on short-term debt. The additional interest charged on long-term debt is a premium for lack of liquidity.

On the other side of the transaction, borrowers will normally prefer to avoid the renewal and interest-rate risk and therefore will prefer to borrow long-term rather than short-term. Thus, borrowers are willing to pay higher interest rates for long-term debt than for short-term debt. The interaction of borrowers' and lenders' liquidity preferences normally results in an upward-sloping yield curve.

Since the yield curve is not always positive, there must be forces other than liquidity preference at work. The *expectations hypothesis* provides a convincing explanation of the effect of market participants' future expectations on the term structure of interest rates. In particular, the expectations hypothesis states that capital market competition forces long-term rates to be equal to the average annual compound rate of return that participants expect to earn on short-term debt over the life of the long-term issue. The yield to maturity on a ten-year bond, for example, should be equal to the yield investors expect to earn by continually investing and reinvesting in one-year bonds over each of the next ten years. Thus, if investors expect future one-year interest rates to rise, they would expect to reinvest in one-year bonds at higher and higher interest rates over the next ten years. Hence, the current ten-year rate would be higher than the current one-year rate. This expectation would result in a normal, positive yield curve.

During periods of high interest rates, investors expect to see future short-term rates declining. They would therefore anticipate reinvesting in one-year bonds at lower and lower interest rates over the next ten years. They would also expect long-term rates to decline in the future and would be anxious to lock in the current high rates available on long-term bonds. Hence, long-term rates would be lower than short-term rates, and the yield curve would be negative.

It is easy to see that the expectations hypothesis is quite versatile. If investors anticipate stable future interest rates, then the yield curve will be flat. If they expect to see future interest rates rising and then falling or falling and then rising, the yield curve will have one or more "humps" in it. All these shapes—rising, falling, flat, and humped—have been observed in the yield curve in the past. The expectations hypothesis provides a convenient and intuitively appealing explanation for these shapes.

The *market-segmentation theory*, also known as the *institutional* or *hedging-pressure theory*, provides the final theoretical explanation for the term structure of interest rates. This theory states that various market participants have distinct maturity preferences. Pension funds and insurance companies, for example, normally prefer to invest in long-term securities. The federal government, through the Federal Reserve, may seek to purchase long-term bonds to put downward pressure on long-term interest rates. Commercial banks, on the other hand, normally prefer to invest in short-term loans. Borrowers also have distinct maturity preferences according to the needs they are attempting to finance. Interest rates are determined by the supply of and demand for money in each market segment, where a market segment is defined by debt maturities. Hence, the yield curve may assume any shape, depending on supply and demand conditions.

The available empirical evidence indicates that all three explanations have some validity. The term structure of interest rates is affected by liquidity preferences, future expectations, and supply and demand conditions. The shape of the yield curve is the result of the interaction of all three forces, any one of which may be primary at any given time.

RELATIVE MAGNITUDE OF WORKING CAPITAL INVESTMENT

A second important working capital policy issue concerns the relative magnitude of a firm's investment in working capital. A firm may choose to have an aggressive policy or a conservative policy. An aggressive policy implies that the firm maintains relatively low levels of current assets and relatively high levels of current liabilities. A firm following such a policy would be very aggressive in attempting to minimize its cash balances, maximize inventory turnover, and minimize the level of investment in accounts receivable. At the same time, an aggressive firm would make maximum use of trade credit and short-term debt financing. The net effect of an aggressive policy is to minimize the firm's overall investment in working capital.

Minimizing the investment in net working capital has important implications for the sales and profitability of the firm. Although minimizing cash balances is almost always desirable, problems may arise as a result of accounts receivable and inventory control policy decisions. An aggressive accounts receivable collection policy, for example, may cause lost sales to customers who find a competitor's credit terms more agreeable. Sales may also be lost because the aggressive firm is more selective in granting credit than its competitors. In a similar vein, a high level of inventory turnover may result in lost sales because desired items are out of stock. On the liabilities side of the balance sheet, the extensive use of trade credit may result in missed discounts (discounts from the face amount of the invoice are commonly allowed for prompt payment). Similarly, extensive use of short-term credit may result in incurring relatively high interest costs, as well as subjecting the firm to renewal and interest rate risk.

There are two major benefits corresponding to the cost of an aggressive working capital policy. First, the firm's investment in current assets is minimized under an aggressive policy. If net income levels can be maintained, return on assets (ROA) can be increased through a reduction in the firm's total asset base. Second, as previously noted, short-term debt is less expensive than long-term debt when the yield curve is positive. Hence, overall financing costs are reduced in two ways: first, a lower level of assets requires less financing to begin with, and second, the cost of short-term debt may be lower than long-term debt.

A conservative policy implies that the firm is less aggressive in minimizing current assets and employing short-term debt. A simple computational example will serve to highlight the differences. Suppose the Kyle Manufacturing Company follows a fairly conservative working capital policy. The company has total assets of $2,700,000 and expects to earn $425,000 after-tax on sales of $5,000,000 this year. Return on assets (ROA) is thus projected at 15.7 percent ($425,000/$2,700,000) and return on sales at 8.5 percent ($425,000/$5,000,000). Tom Kyle is considering shifting to a more aggressive working capital policy. It is estimated that total assets can be reduced to $2,200,000 but that sales will drop to $4,500,000. Savings in interest expenses are expected to increase return on sales to 8.7 percent. Should the company make the switch?

In this case, the decision seems relatively straightforward. Net income with the more aggressive policy is expected to be $391,500 (8.7 percent times $4,500,000). With assets reduced to $2,200,000, ROA will increase to 17.8 percent—a substantial increase over the current level of 15.7 percent. If the assets freed up by the shift can be employed elsewhere at a comparable ROA, the increase in ROA would argue strongly in favor of changing to a more aggressive policy. Nevertheless, a number of additional factors require careful consideration before making such a change. All these factors are related to the existence of uncertainty and may be summarized by the following questions:

1. How accurate are the revised sales, earnings, and asset estimates?
2. What is the probable impact of the shift to more short-term financing on the riskiness of the firm?
3. What is the likely impact of this shift on the long-term growth and profitability of the company?
4. Can the assets freed up by this change be employed elsewhere at a comparable ROA?

Obviously these questions are much easier to pose than they are to answer. A number of analytical techniques may be used to quantify these problems. However, in the final analysis, answering these questions is a matter of judgment. There is no pat answer or mechanical algorithm available to make these kinds of decisions. The usefulness of financial analysis lies in answering the "what if" questions: "What if assets do this and sales and earnings do that? What will be the impact on the bottom line?" These "what if" exercises are extremely important because they can turn expectations and speculations into dollars and percentages, but the final decision requires a judgment as to the likely occurrence of each outcome. The next chapter will explore some of the analytical techniques that are commonly employed in working capital management.

INVENTORY CONTROL POLICY

Inventory control is a third important issue in working capital policy. As noted, a firm may have an aggressive or a conservative inventory control policy. A manufacturing firm, for example, may carry fairly high levels of raw materials inventory in order to minimize the probability of production slowdowns due to inventory shortages. Finished goods inventory may be held at fairly high levels, also to minimize lost sales due to stockouts. Wholesalers and retailers, who do not face production problems, are concerned primarily with potential lost sales due to stockouts. An aggressive inventory policy may be decided on by management in order to improve ROA, even though such a policy increases the risk of lost sales. An aggressive policy may also be dictated by economic circumstances. A company with severe cash flow problems may have no choice but to run a lean inventory operation.

Within the context of an overall inventory control policy, each item in inventory normally is assigned a high limit (maximum quantity that should be held in inventory), low limit (minimum quantity that should be held), reorder point (quantity at which a replenishment order should be placed), and a reorder quantity (quantity that should be ordered when the reorder point is reached). A mathematical model is available to aid in establishing these key decision points. This model, called the *economic order quantity model* (EOQ), determines the optimal average inventory level that should be carried and the optimal quantity that should be ordered each time an order is placed. The model will be examined in detail in the next chapter, which deals with working capital management techniques.

CREDIT POLICY

A fourth important working capital policy issue deals with establishing a firm's credit policy. Credit policy requires the establishment of the major policy variables within which accounts receivable will be managed. These variables include deciding to whom credit should be extended, the length of time to be allowed for payment of invoices, and whether discounts will be offered for prompt payment.

Conceptually, accounts receivable management has two separate aspects. First, the firm must establish the terms under which credit will be granted and to whom credit will be offered. Making this decision requires an analysis of the potential impact of credit policy terms on sales and profits. Second, the firm must consider the relationship of accounts receivable to the short-term liability structure. It is possible to use accounts receivable as collateral for short-term loans. It is even possible, under an arrangement known as factoring, to sell accounts receivable at a discount to a commercial bank or a commercial factor. This type of arrangement relieves the firm of the need to make additional credit policy decisions. Once the policy of factoring is established, the factor will dictate credit terms.

The techniques of accounts receivable management will be discussed in the next chapter. Management techniques and the role of accounts receivable in short-term financing will also be discussed.

ACCOUNTS PAYABLE PAYMENT POLICY

The fifth and final working capital policy issue deals with the establishment of an accounts payable payment policy. Suppliers commonly offer discounts on accounts payable to induce prompt payment by customers. Typical terms might be expressed as "2/10, net 60." These terms mean that a 2 percent discount off the face amount of the invoice is allowed if payment is made within ten days of receipt of the invoice. If the discount is not taken, then the total amount is due within sixty days.

There are two major concerns in establishing a firm's payment policy. First is the cost and availability of money. The cost of missing the discount can be translated easily into an approximate annual percentage rate of interest.* In the preceding example, the approximate annual percentage rate is 14.6 percent. This percentage cost is called the imputed interest rate on missed discounts. The rate is determined by considering the discount terms as if they were simple loan terms (which, of course, they are). The discount terms allow a 2 percent reduction in the amount payable if payment is made within 10 days but require the full amount to be paid if payment is not made until 60 days have passed. In effect, then, missing the discount results in a 50-day loan from the supplier to the purchaser. The cost of this loan is approximately 2 percent for the 50-day period.** The annual cost of the loan is thus 2 percent per period for 7.3 periods per year (365 days divided by 50 days), or approximately 14.6 percent (2 percent times 7.3 periods, ignoring compounding). If the firm's cost of money is less than 14.6 percent, then the discount terms are financially attractive.

The availability of money is also a key consideration. If a firm's cash flow or credit capacity is strained, then it may not be possible

---

*See Chapter 11 for a detailed discussion of the mathematics of compound interest.

**Since the face amount of the loan is actually the invoice amount less the 2 percent discount, the exact cost of the loan is slightly above 2 percent.

to take advantage of the discounts even if the terms are financially attractive. Actually, if a firm is unable to obtain the funds necessary to take discounts, its cost of money may be considered infinite: Money is unavailable at any cost. If funds can be obtained only at a relatively high cost, this would make the discount terms unattractive.

It should be noted that the shorter the lending period, the higher the cost of missed discounts. Terms of "2/10, net 30," for example, increase the cost of missed discounts to 36.5 percent per year (2 percent times 365/20). These high short-term financing costs dictate that, once the discount is missed, payment should be delayed until the latest allowable payment date. Considering an extreme example, if the discount is missed and full payment is made on the eleventh day, then the loan period is reduced to one day. At a 2 percent discount rate, the approximate annual cost of missed discounts for payment on the eleventh day is 730 percent (2 percent times 365 days). As a general rule a firm should not make an early payment after the discount is missed or if no discount is allowed.

A second major concern in establishing an accounts payable payment policy is the impact of the policy on the firm's credit rating. Some firms will pay their payables promptly and take discounts even though the discounts are not particularly attractive strictly on a cost basis. They do this because they believe (usually correctly) that a record of prompt payment enhances the credit reputation of the firm. It may seem that taking discounts that are not attractive "on the numbers" is economically irrational. However, considering that maintenance of a good credit rating improves the firm's future access to and cost of external financing, such a policy might be quite rational, even if difficult to quantify.

SUMMARY

Effective working capital management is one of the most important functions of financial management. It is important because of the size of the investment in these accounts, the urgency of working capital decisions, and the relationship of effective management to the survival of the firm. Working capital management represents the firm's first line of defense against recessionary downturns in sales.

The selection of short-term or long-term financing is one important working capital policy issue. Short-term debt is generally less costly than long-term debt but is also riskier. As a general rule, firms should strive to match their loan maturities with their asset maturities. Effective management of debt financing requires an understanding of the term structure of interest rates—in other words, the relationship between the yield to maturity and the term to maturity of debt. This relationship is portrayed by a yield curve, which may be positively or negatively sloped. There are three major theoretical explanations for the term structure of interest rates: liquidity preference, the expectations hypothesis, and the market segmentation theory.

Establishing the relative magnitude of a firm's investment in working capital is a second major policy issue. An aggressive policy implies that a firm maintains a relatively low level of current assets and employs a relatively high level of current debt. Additional important working capital policy issues include inventory control policy, credit policy, and accounts payable payment policy.

KEY POINTS

IMPORTANCE OF WORKING CAPITAL	Urgency of decisions
	Size of investment
	Response to recession
	Relationship to business failures
MAJOR POLICY ISSUES	Short-term versus long-term financing
	Relative magnitude of investment
	Inventory control policy
	Credit policy
	Accounts payable payment policy
TERM STRUCTURE OF INTEREST RATES	Liquidity preference theory
	Expectations hypothesis
	Market segmentation (institutional or hedging-pressure) theory

---

10

Working Capital Management

Most firms have four major categories of current assets to manage: cash, marketable securities, accounts receivable, and inventory. On the current liabilities side of the balance sheet, most firms use two major sources of short-term financing: trade credit (accounts payable) and short-term bank loans. A third major source of short-term financing, commercial paper, is available to large firms with high-quality credit ratings. Commercial paper is a short-term (generally fewer than 270 days at the time of issue) corporate IOU sold through commercial-paper dealers to other corporations, banks, money market funds, and individuals. In recent years, the use of commercial paper has become much more common, and commercial paper has replaced short-term bank financing to a great extent for large corporations. This chapter deals with the management of these major components of net working capital.

MANAGEMENT OF CASH AND MARKETABLE SECURITIES

Firms generally hold cash balances in checking accounts for four major reasons. The first three of these reasons are commonly identified by economists as the transactions motive, the precautionary motive, and the speculative motive. The *transactions motive* simply means that firms must hold cash in order to conduct normal business transactions. The payroll has to be met, supplies and inventory purchases must be paid, trade discounts should be taken if financially attractive, and so forth. The firm must have enough money available in its checking account to meet the day-to-day expenses of being in business.

The *precautionary motive* states that firms maintain cash balances to meet precautionary liquidity needs. There are two major categories of these liquidity needs. First is the need for liquidity to bridge the gaps between a firm's cash inflow and its cash outflow. The primary method of predicting these gaps is through the construction of a detailed cash budget, as was done in Chapter 7. The second liquidity need is the same liquidity need that individuals have—firms need to maintain some cash balances to meet unexpected emergencies.

The final motive for holding cash balances is the *speculative motive*. As the name implies, firms maintain cash balances in order to speculate—that is, to take advantage of unanticipated business opportunities that may come along from time to time. The nature of such opportunities varies, but they have one common feature: The firm may need ready cash to take advantage of them.

In addition to the traditional economic motives for holding cash balances, there is also a fourth reason, which overshadows the economic motives for many firms. Firms using bank debt are normally required to maintain a compensating balance with the bank from which they have borrowed the money. When a bank makes a loan to a firm, the bank often requires that the firm maintain a minimum balance in a non–interest-earning checking account equal to a specified percentage of the amount borrowed. This minimum balance that the firm is required to maintain is referred to as a *compensating balance*. A compensating balance equal to 5 to 10 percent of the amount of the loan is a common arrangement. A firm with a $250,000 credit line, for example, might be required to maintain a compensating balance of $12,500 to $25,000.

The obvious effect of a compensating balance is to raise the effective interest rate on a loan. Suppose a bank charges 14 percent interest (annual percentage rate) on the $250,000 loan but requires a $25,000 compensating balance. The loan amount available to the borrowers is only $225,000 ($250,000 minus $25,000), but interest is charged on the entire $250,000. Assuming the interest is paid monthly at 1.167 percent per month (14 percent divided by 12 months), the monthly interest cost would be $2,917.50 (0.01167 times $250,000). The effective monthly interest rate is then 1.297 percent ($2,917.50 divided by $225,000) for an annual percentage rate of 15.56 percent (1.297 times 12 months). Some bankers maintain that the existence of a compensating balance prevents firms from overextending their cash flow position because it forces them to maintain a reasonable minimum cash balance. However, to a rational observer, having

$25,000 that cannot be withdrawn does not seem to leave the firm much better off than having nothing at all.

Most firms meet some of their anticipated cash needs, particularly those arising from the precautionary and speculative motives, in the form of marketable securities. *Marketable securities* are short-term, high-quality debt instruments that can be easily converted into cash. There are three primary criteria for selecting appropriate marketable securities to meet a firm's anticipated short-term cash needs. In order of priority, these criteria are safety, liquidity, and yield. A high degree of *safety* implies that there is a negligible risk of default of the securities purchased. Safety also implies that marketable securities will not be subject to excessive market fluctuations due to fluctuations in interest rates. The *liquidity* criterion requires that marketable securities can be sold quickly and easily with no loss in principal value due to an inability to readily locate a purchaser for the securities. The *yield* criterion requires that the highest possible yield be earned that is consistent with the safety and liquidity criteria. In structuring a marketable securities portfolio, yield is generally considered far less important than safety and liquidity.

Satisfying the safety, liquidity, and yield criteria severely restricts the range of securities acceptable as marketable securities—and justifiably so. Most major corporations meet their marketable securities needs with U.S. Treasury bills or with corporate commercial paper carrying the highest credit rating. These securities are short-term, highly liquid securities with reasonably high yields. Treasury bills are default-free, and high-quality commercial paper carries a minuscule default risk. Those firms that, in recent years, have stretched to achieve higher potential yields via money market funds invested in asset-backed securities have learned that those higher potential yields did indeed carry higher risk.

Improving Cash Flow

There are a number of actions a firm may take to improve its cash flow pattern. One common action, particularly taken by large corporations, is to attempt to synchronize cash inflows and cash outflows. A firm may, for example, bill customers on a regular schedule throughout the month and also pay its own bills according to a regular monthly schedule. Adhering to a regular monthly schedule enables a firm to match cash receipts with cash disbursements and synchronize cash inflow and outflow patterns.

Corporate treasurers also devote a good deal of time to expediting the check-clearing process, slowing disbursements of cash, and maximizing the use of "float" in their corporate checking accounts.* In recent years, however, three developments in the financial services industry have changed the nature of the cash management process for corporate treasurers. The first development is the impact of electronic funds transfer systems (EFTS) including so-called remote capture technology for quickly depositing checks without visiting a bank branch. The ability of the banking system to clear checks and transfer funds electronically has radically reduced the amount of time necessary to turn a customer's check into an available cash balance on the corporate books. It has also sharply reduced the amount of float available, as the corporation's own checks clear more rapidly. For very large corporations, however, the use of even a one- or two-day float may justify the expenditure of a good bit of time and effort on these kinds of activities.

The second development is the expanded use of money market mutual funds. Individuals and business firms have turned to money market mutual funds as a substitute for conventional checking accounts. A money market mutual fund is conceptually simple. The funds sell shares at a constant price of $1.00 per share. The proceeds of sales are invested in short-term money market instruments, primarily U.S. Treasury bills, short-term obligations of U.S. government corporations and agencies, bank and corporate commercial paper, bank certificates of deposit, bankers' acceptances, and sometimes asset-backed securities. Interest earned is credited daily, and fluctuations in market values are credited or debited daily. Since large funds hold a broadly diversified portfolio of short-term securities, market-value fluctuations of the overall portfolio normally are small relative to interest earned.

Checks written** against money market funds continue to earn interest until the check clears the fund. Hence, available float in a

---

Float is the difference between the cash balance shown in the firm's checkbook and the cash balance shown in the bank's records.

**Technically, money market fund checks are not the exact equivalent of commercial bank checks, but they are close enough for all practical corporate needs.

money market fund is continually earning interest for the account. In this sense, the use of float is automatically optimized on a continuous basis. For small to medium-size organizations, a money market mutual fund may be a particularly attractive means of managing cash and marketable securities at a very low cost. For larger corporations, direct participation in the money market may still be cost effective.

The third development is the growth in cash management services offered by commercial banks. Nearly all large commercial banks now offer highly sophisticated cash management systems for their commercial accounts. These systems efficiently handle a firm's cash management needs at a competitive price. Even small firms that bank with small commercial banks can use such systems through established arrangements among the banks.

ACCOUNTS RECEIVABLE MANAGEMENT

In general, management of accounts receivable requires that the financial manager balance the cost of extending credit with the benefit received from extending credit. Since each firm has unique operating characteristics that affect its credit policy, there is no universal optimization model to determine the correct credit policy for all firms. Here we will review a number of general techniques for credit management.

The decision whether to offer credit terms is generally dictated by industry conditions. For manufacturing firms and wholesalers, extension of credit terms is generally taken for granted. Retailers also commonly extend consumer credit, either through a store-sponsored charge plan or acceptance of external credit cards, such as Visa, MasterCard, or American Express. Small retailers generally cannot afford the cost of maintaining a credit department and thus generally do not offer store-sponsored charge plans.

In deciding whether or not to extend credit to a particular customer, commercial credit managers commonly analyze what are known as the "five Cs" of credit analysis: character, capacity, capital, collateral, and conditions. *Character* refers to the moral integrity of the credit applicant and whether the borrower is likely to give his or her best efforts to honoring the credit obligation. Experienced credit analysts emphasize that the applicant's character is one of the most important concerns in making a credit decision. *Capacity* refers to whether the borrowing firm has the financial capacity to meet required account payments. Even the best intentions cannot compensate for the lack of financial ability. *Capital* refers to the general financial condition of the firm as judged by an analysis of the firm's financial statements. *Collateral* refers to the existence of assets, such as inventory or accounts receivable, that may be pledged by the borrowing firm as security for the credit extended. *Conditions* refers to the operating and financial condition of the firm.

Judging the character, capacity, and collateral of a particular firm is aided greatly by the use of commercial credit services. National credit services, such as Dun and Bradstreet, provide credit reports on potential new accounts that summarize a firm's financial condition, past credit history, and other key business information. There are also local credit associations that exchange credit information. Granting credit generally entails three types of costs: the cost of financing accounts receivable, the cost of offering discounts, and the cost of bad-debt losses. Establishing or changing an existing credit policy requires analyzing the relationship of these costs to the profitability of the firm. The marginal cost of credit must be compared to the expected marginal profit resulting from the firm's credit terms. This type of analysis is best illustrated by a specific example.

Credit policy analysis is exactly analogous to the logic used in establishing an overall working capital policy, as developed in the previous chapter. Exhibit 10.1 shows one possible credit policy, identified as Credit Policy A, for the Cahill Manufacturing Company. Current credit terms are 2/10, net 60, and the average collection period is fifty days. On expected sales of $75,000,000, income after tax is $8,700,000 for a return on sales of 11.6 percent. Return on assets is 17.3 percent, and return on equity is 34.4 percent. A second possible credit policy, Credit Policy B, is shown in Exhibit 10.2. This policy offers a tighter collection policy and shorter payment terms (2/10, net 30). Sales are expected to be lower under this policy and are projected at $70,000,000. However, a tighter policy should result in higher quality of accounts receivable and hence reduce bad-debt losses. Interest expense will also be reduced, since there will be a lower level of accounts receivable to finance. It is therefore projected that operating expenses will be reduced from 15.7 percent of sales to 15.2 percent of sales. The net result of this change is that return on sales will increase to 11.9 percent. Return on assets will increase to

EXHIBIT 10.1   CAHILL MANUFACTURING COMPANY CREDIT POLICY A

CONDENSED INCOME STATEMENT

Sales	$75,000
Cost of goods sold (65% of sales)	48,750
Gross margin	26,250
Operating expenses (15.7% of sales)	11,750
Income before tax	14,500
Income taxes (40% of income before tax)	5,800
Income after tax	$8,700

CONDENSED BALANCE SHEET

Cash	$2,000	Accounts payable	$6,000
Accounts receivable	10,300	Bank loan	7,000
Inventory	12,000	Total current liabilities	13,000
Total current assets	24,300	Long-term debt	12,000
Fixed assets	26,000	Stockholders' equity	25,300
Total assets	$50,300	Total liabilities and equity	$50,300

Current Credit Terms: 2/10, net 60
Average collection period = 50 days
Profitability Ratios: Return on sales = 11.6%
Return on assets = 17.3%
Return on equity = 34.4%

19.0 percent, and return on equity will increase to 37.3 percent. Assuming that all estimates are reasonably accurate and that funds released by Policy B can be invested profitably elsewhere, Policy B would be preferable to Policy A.

In addition to deciding to whom credit should be extended and analyzing potential changes in credit terms, the credit manager is also responsible for supervising the collection of accounts receivable. Supervising collections requires that the manager closely monitor the firm's average collection period and aging schedule. The aging schedule groups accounts by age and then identifies the quantity of past due accounts. Since these accounts are good candidates for bad-debt losses, it is important that the manager follow up on them. In performing this function, the manager needs to develop some skills of

EXHIBIT 10.2 CAHILL MANUFACTURING COMPANY CREDIT POLICY B

CONDENSED INCOME STATEMENT

Sales	$70,000
Cost of goods sold (65% of sales)	45,500
Gross margin	24,500
Operating expenses (15.2% of sales)	10,650
Income before tax	13,850
Income taxes (40% of income before taxes)	5,540
Income after tax	$8,310

CONDENSED BALANCE SHEET

Cash	$2,000	Accounts payable	$6,000
Accounts receivable	3,800	Bank loan	3,500
Inventory	12,000	Total current liabilities	9,500
Total current assets	17,800	Long-term debt	12,000
Fixed assets	26,000	Stockholders' equity	22,300
Total assets	$43,800	Total liabilities and equity	$43,800

Proposed Credit Terms: 2/10, net 30
Average collection period = 20 days
Profitability Ratios: Return on sales = 11.9%
Return on assets = 19.0%
Return on equity = 37.3%

diplomacy. It is necessary to balance the need to collect the account with the need to maintain customer goodwill. Of course, if all efforts fail and the account cannot pay, then goodwill is not particularly important. Terms of cash on delivery or advance payment should be instituted for future sales to consistently delinquent accounts.

INVENTORY MANAGEMENT

One widely used inventory management technique is the *economic order quantity* (EOQ) model. This is a mathematical model designed to determine the optimal amount of inventory that a firm should carry. The model is actually quite simple in concept and easily applied in practice. A look at the EOQ concept provides an excellent explanation of the inventory control problem in general. Readers interested in the mathematical derivation of the EOQ model may consult Appendix 10.1 at the end of this chapter.

The cost to a firm of maintaining inventory has two major components: carrying costs and ordering costs. Carrying costs include all costs associated with carrying inventory such as storage, handling, loss in value due to obsolescence and physical deterioration, taxes, insurance, and financing. Ordering costs represent the cost of placing orders for new inventory and the cost of shipping and receiving new inventory. The cost of placing an order is a fixed cost—that is, it is the same dollar amount regardless of the quantity ordered. Shipping and receiving costs, on the other hand, are variable costs. These costs increase with increases in quantity ordered.

The two components of total inventory maintenance costs— carrying costs plus ordering costs—vary inversely. Carrying costs increase with increases in average inventory levels. If a firm carries high levels of average inventory, the cost of carrying this inventory is high. Thus, carrying costs argue in favor of carrying low levels of inventory in order to hold these costs down. In contrast to carrying costs, ordering costs decrease with increases in average inventory level. If a firm carries high levels of average inventory, the firm does not have to re-order inventory as often as it would if it carried low levels of inventory.

The EOQ model attempts to minimize total cost by finding the optimal level of average inventory that should be maintained to minimize the sum of carrying costs plus ordering costs. Exhibit 10.3 graphically illustrates the cost behavior of inventory costs. The EOQ model simply determines the equation of the total cost curve and finds the minimum point on this curve. This minimum point determines the optimal average inventory. The optimal average inventory level, in turn, dictates how much inventory should be ordered on each order to maintain the average inventory level. This quantity is the EOQ and is determined as follows (see Appendix 10.1 for proof):

$$EOQ = \sqrt{\frac{2FS}{CP}}$$

where F = fixed cost per order
S = annual sales, in units
C = carrying costs as a percentage of
average inventory level
P = price (at cost) per unit

EXHIBIT 10.3   INVENTORY COSTS

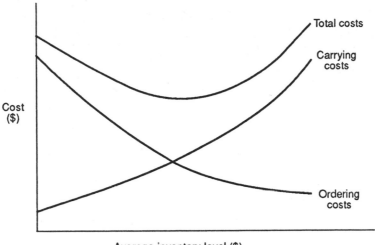

Average inventory level ($)

The basic EOQ model assumes that inventory is used up uniformly and that there are no delivery lags—that is, that inventory is delivered instantaneously. Since neither of the assumptions is normally valid, two minor modifications of the basic model are required. The first modification requires that a reorder point be established that allows for delivery lead times. If 2,700 units are ordered every three months, for example, and the normal delivery time is one month after the order is placed, then the EOQ should be ordered when the on-hand amount drops to 900 units (one month's usage).

The second modification of the basic model is required to allow for uncertainty of the estimates used in the model and the possibility of nonuniform usage. Since it is highly probable that inventory will not be used up at a uniform rate and that there will be some errors in input assumptions, a quantity of safety stock is normally added to the base average inventory. The quantity of the safety stock added is dependent on such factors as the degree of uncertainty of demand, the costs of stockouts, the level of carrying costs, and the probability of shipping delays. To continue the previous example, suppose that 500 units was determined to be an adequate level of safety stock. The reorder point would be increased to 1,400 units (900 plus 500), and a new order would be placed each time the on-hand quantity reached 1,400.

The application of the EOQ model may be illustrated by a simple example. Widget Wholesalers, Inc., sells 240,000 widgets per year. Its cost price per widget is $2, and inventory carrying costs are 20 percent of average inventory level. The fixed cost of ordering is $30 per order. Widget's EOQ may be calculated as follows:

$$
\begin{aligned}
EOQ &= \sqrt{\frac{2FS}{CP}} \\
&= \sqrt{\frac{(2)(\$30)(240,000)}{(0.20)(\$2)}} \\
&= \sqrt{\frac{14,400,000}{0.4}} \\
&= \sqrt{36,000,000} \\
&= 6,000
\end{aligned}
$$

Thus, Widget should order 6,000 units per order. If Widget allows a 10-day supply as a safety stock, the reorder point would be at 6,575 units (10 days divided by 365 days times 240,000). At 6,000 units per order, Widget would place forty orders per year (240,000/6,000).

The EOQ model has been widely applied in current asset management. Other types of "inventories," such as cash and accounts receivable, can also be managed using the EOQ approach. The cost of maintaining these assets can be segregated into "ordering" and "carrying" costs, and optimal assets levels can be determined. Thus, the EOQ model has been extended beyond its original inventory control objective.

SOURCES OF SHORT-TERM FINANCING

The three major sources of short-term financing for most firms are trade credit (accounts payable), commercial bank loans, and commercial paper. *Trade credit* is often referred to as "spontaneous financing" because accounts payable arise spontaneously during the normal course of business. Commercial firms seldom pay cash for purchases of such items as inventory and supplies. Instead, they buy these items on open account from their suppliers on whatever credit terms are available. For new or small firms, accounts payable may be the only available form of credit. Bank financing is often difficult to obtain in the early years of a new business.

Trade credit is a form of "free" financing in the sense that no explicit interest rate is charged on outstanding accounts payable. However, there are two costs associated with trade credit. One is the cost of missed discounts. If discounts are offered but not taken, accounts payable have a very definite cost. Calculation of this cost was addressed in the previous chapter. The second cost of trade credit is more subtle. Firms that offer trade credit must finance their outstanding accounts receivable. The cost of this financing increases the cost of doing business over what it would be if the firm sold on cash terms only.

The second major source of short-term financing is *commercial bank loans*. Short-term loans are commonly employed to finance inventory and accounts receivable. They may also be used as a source of funds to enable the firm to take discounts on accounts payable when the cost of missed discounts exceeds the interest cost of bank debt.

Short-term bank debt typically is structured in one of two ways. A note for a fixed period of time is one common form. The bank may lend money on a short-term note at a fixed interest rate. At the end of the note term (the maturity date), the face amount of the note must be repaid, or the note must be renewed ("rolled over"). In many cases, the bank and the borrower will enter into a formal or informal agreement to renew the note at maturity at a specified rate. The rate specified is normally tied to the prime interest rate—the rate charged to the bank's best corporate customers. Typical terms might establish the interest rate at prime plus some percentage over prime, such as "prime plus 2 percent." The size of the premium above the prime rate is determined by the bank's assessment of the risk involved in making the loan. The higher the risk, the higher will be the premium. As the prime rate changes, the bank's cost of obtaining funds changes, so requiring the firm to roll over its notes allows the bank to change the interest rate on the note.

A short-term loan also may be obtained in the form of a line of credit (sometimes called a "revolver"). In this case, the bank establishes an upper limit on the amount the firm may borrow, and the firm draws whatever money it needs against the credit line up to the maximum. The interest rate may be fixed, or it may float with the prime rate. Interest is charged only on the amount actually borrowed, not on the total amount available. Commercial credit lines are similar to consumer credit lines, with which most individuals are familiar.

Bank debt may be secured or unsecured. If unsecured, no specific assets are pledged as collateral for the loan. An unsecured loan is a "full faith and credit" obligation of the borrowing firm, and the bank has a general claim against the firm's assets if the firm defaults on the loan. If the firm pledges some specific asset as collateral for the loan—usually accounts receivable or inventory—it is a secured loan. If default occurs, the bank has a claim on the asset pledged as collateral. The asset may be seized by the bank and liquidated to satisfy the loan balance. Any excess the bank receives above the amount of the principal and interest due on the loan must be returned to the borrower.

Commercial paper is the third major form of short-term financing. As noted in the previous chapter, commercial paper is a short-term corporate IOU that is sold in large dollar amounts by large corporations, generally through commercial paper dealers. Most commercial paper is purchased by other corporations, as an outlet for marketable securities, or by financial institutions, such as banks or money market mutual funds. Commercial paper is not an available means of financing for small business organizations.

Financing Accounts Receivable

Accounts receivable often are used as collateral for short-term loans. There are three commonly used methods of accounts receivable financing: pledging, assigning, and factoring. Pledging and assigning are conceptually similar in that both methods use accounts receivable as collateral for a loan. The difference between the two methods lies in how the receivables loan is collateralized.

A *pledging* transaction is structured as its name implies. Receivables are pledged as general collateral for a loan in the same manner that inventory might be pledged. The bank or other lender makes a loan of some percentage of the value of the receivables but does not take physical possession of them. The receivables merely serve as collateral in the event of default. If the loan is not paid on time, the bank has the right to take possession of the receivables and collect the amount necessary to satisfy the loan principal and interest due. Any excess money collected above the amount owed the bank must be returned to the borrower. With a pledging arrangement, banks commonly loan 50 to 75 percent of the face amount of the receivables. The amount loaned depends mainly on the credit reputation of the borrower and the quality of the receivables pledged. The quality of the receivables, in turn, is a function of the credit rating of the customer accounts and the age of the receivables. Old and past-due accounts are obviously less valuable as collateral than the account of a customer with a reputation for prompt payment.

Assigning accounts receivable requires that the borrowing firm sign over its right to collect the account to the lender. The lender advances money to the borrower up to some predetermined percentage of accounts receivable and then collects directly from the customer account. The lender notifies the customer that the account has been assigned and that payment should be made directly to the lender. Payments received in excess of the amount loaned are the property of the borrower. As a practical matter, however, such amounts are routinely treated as part of a "circulating pot" of money from which the borrower may draw funds as needed. Lenders commonly lend from 75 to 90 percent of the face value of the receivables assigned. The percentage loaned is again a function of the credit rating of the borrower and the quality of the accounts receivable.

When accounts receivable are pledged or assigned, the lender has recourse to the borrower if an account fails to pay. In the event that an account defaults, the borrower suffers the bad-debt loss, not the lender. The lender is only acting as a supplier of funds and does not assume the risk of bad-debt losses.

A *factoring* arrangement goes one step beyond a pledging or assignment arrangement. With a factoring agreement, the lender actually buys accounts receivable outright from a borrower. The receivables are purchased at a discount from face value from the borrowing firm, and the lender then assumes the burden of collecting the receivables. This burden includes the assumption of bad-debt losses. If an account does not pay, the lender has no recourse to the borrowing firm.

Lenders actually provide a total of three services in a factoring arrangement. First, they provide financing of accounts receivable for borrowing firms. Second, they act as the borrowing firm's credit department. Normally, a firm that enters into a factoring arrangement with a bank or commercial factor will extend credit only to customers approved by the factor. If the factor will not accept the account, then the firm will not allow the customer to buy on credit terms. Thus, the borrowing firm has no need to maintain a credit department of its own and can rely on the factor to investigate potential customers.

The third important function provided by the factor is the assumption of risk of bad-debt losses. Factoring transfers this risk from the borrowing firm to the factor. As one might expect, any time risk is transferred, some cost is assessed to the party transferring the risk. Commercial factoring is no exception. Because of this, factoring is the most expensive form of accounts receivable financing. The implicit interest rate involved in the discount from face value at which receivables are purchased is almost always higher than that which could be obtained under a pledging or assignment arrangement. As a general rule, the costs of pledging and assigning are about equal.

Inventory Financing

Inventory financing is commonly arranged through blanket liens, trust receipts, or field-warehousing arrangements. A blanket lien is the least complex arrangement and is comparable to pledging accounts receivable. The firm pledges its inventory as collateral for a short-term loan, but the lender has no physical control over the inventory. If the borrower defaults on the loan, the lender has the right to seize the inventory and sell it to pay off the loan principal and interest. Any funds realized in excess of the amount owed must be returned to the borrower.

A *trust receipt* is a legal document that creates a lien on some specific item of inventory. This type of financing is commonly arranged for "big ticket" inventory items, such as inventory held by automobile dealers, jewelers, or heavy equipment dealers. Each inventory item is financed individually by a trust receipt. When the item is sold, the amount loaned against the item must be remitted to the lender. As new inventory items are received, new loans are created.

A *field-warehousing* arrangement is one in which the inventory pledged as collateral is physically maintained on the premises of the borrower but is under the control of the lender. The warehouse may be a conventional warehouse or may simply be a fenced-off area somewhere on the borrower's premises. Physical movement of inventory items into or out of the warehouse is supervised by an independent third party employed by the lender. The third party is normally an agent of an independent field-warehousing company. As inventory items are moved into the warehouse, loans are made to the borrower. As items are released from the warehouse and sold, the loans are paid off.

A field-warehousing arrangement is particularly appropriate for financing seasonal inventory buildups. Field warehousing is commonly used to finance the canning of agriculture products. As the crop is harvested and canned, the canned products are moved into a field warehouse. The lender releases money to the borrower, who then uses the money to pay wages and other expenses of the harvest. After canning is completed, the borrower sells off the canned product and pays off the loan as products are sold and released from the warehouse.

SUMMARY

Working capital management encompasses the management of current assets and current liabilities. The four major categories of current assets held by most firms are cash, marketable securities, accounts receivable, and inventory. The three main sources of short-term financing are trade credit, short-term commercial bank loans, and commercial paper. The growth of EFTS, money market mutual funds, and commercial bank cash management systems has dramatically altered the nature of cash and marketable securities management. Accounts receivable management requires striking a balance between the cost of extending credit and the benefit received from extending credit. Inventory control is commonly enhanced through the use of economic order quantity (EOQ) models to balance carrying costs and ordering costs. Accounts receivable may be pledged, assigned, or factored as a means of obtaining short-term loans. Inventory is typically financed through blanket liens, trust receipts, or field-warehousing arrangements.

APPENDIX 10.1:
MATHEMATICAL DERIVATION OF ECONOMIC ORDER QUANTITY

Definition of Variables

A = average inventory level
C = carrying costs as a percentage of average inventory level
F = fixed component of ordering costs
K = carrying costs
N = number of orders placed in one year
P = price per unit (at cost)
Q = quantity of goods ordered on each order
R = ordering costs
S = total annual sales in units and total annual quantity ordered
T = total costs
V = variable component of ordering costs

In general:

1. As Q increases, N decreases; therefore, R decreases, but K increases;

2. As Q decreases, N increases; therefore, R increases, but K decreases.

The general nature of the problem is to find the economic order quantity (EOQ) such that total cost, T, is minimized, where $T = K + R$.

Derivation

1. Carrying costs can be expressed as a percentage of average inventory level, A (assuming no order lags and uniform usage):

$$A = \frac{Q}{2} \qquad (1)$$

2. N is a function of total annual sales, S, and the quantity ordered on each order, Q:

$$N = \frac{S}{Q} \qquad (2)$$

3. Generalized expressions for K and R are:

$$K = CPA \tag{3}$$
$$R = FN + VS \tag{4}$$

4. Total cost is given by:

$$T = K + R = CPA + FN + VS \tag{5}$$

5. Substituting Equations 1 and 2 into Equation 5 allows total cost to be expressed as a function of Q:

$$T = CP\left(\frac{Q}{2}\right) + F\left(\frac{S}{Q}\right) + VS \tag{6}$$

6. The EOQ (denoted Q^*) may now be found by differentiating Equation 6 with respect to Q, setting the differential equal to zero, and solving for Q:

$$\frac{dT}{dQ} = \frac{CP}{2} - \frac{FS}{Q^2}$$
$$\frac{CP}{2} - \frac{FS}{Q^2} = 0$$
$$Q^2 = \frac{2FS}{CP}$$
$$Q^* = \sqrt{\frac{2FS}{CP}}$$
$$\text{Hence, EOQ} = \sqrt{\frac{2FS}{CP}}$$

KEY POINTS

CASH BALANCES	Compensating balances Transactions motive Precautionary motive Speculative motive
CASH MANAGEMENT	Electronic funds transfer systems (EFTS) Money market mutual funds Commercial bank cash management systems
MARKETABLE SECURITIES	Safety Liquidity Yield
ACCOUNTS RECEIVABLE	Five Cs of credit analysis Financing costs Discounts Bad-debt losses
INVENTORY MANAGEMENT	Carrying costs Ordering costs Economic order quantity (EOQ)
SHORT-TERM FINANCING	Trade credit Commercial bank loans Commercial paper
ACCOUNTS RECEIVABLE FINANCING	Pledging Assigning Factoring
INVENTORY FINANCING	Blanket lien Trust receipt Field warehousing

PART V
Long-Term
Investment Decisions

11

Mathematics of
Compound Interest

In the next two chapters, we will explore various techniques employed in making long-term investment decisions. This area of financial management is referred to as *capital budgeting*—the process of determining the amount of money to be budgeted for capital expenditure projects. In order to understand and use these techniques, it is first necessary to master the mathematics of compound interest. This chapter will discuss the mathematics necessary to deal with compound interest and the time value of money.

COMPOUND INTEREST

The familiar compound interest formula is the basis for all time value of money calculations. This equation expresses the value of a principal sum of money left on deposit (or invested) for a given number of years at a given rate of interest. The formula is as follows:

$$V_n = P(1 + i)^n$$

where V_n = value at the end of n years
 P = principal amount deposited or invested
 i = interest rate per year
 n = number of years

The derivation of the compound interest formula is actually quite simple. Exhibit 11.1 shows the value of $100, invested at the beginning of year 1 earning interest at 6 percent compounded annually, at the end of each year for four years. As can be seen from the exhibit, the

EXHIBIT 11.1   INVESTMENT GROWTH AT 6 PERCENT

YEAR	BEGINNING VALUE	INTEREST	ENDING VALUE	COMPOUND INTEREST FACTOR
1	$100.00	$6.00	$106.00	($100)(1.06) = $106.00
				($100)(1.06)(1.06) =
2	$106.00	$6.36	$112.36	($100)(1.06)^2 = $112.36
				($100)(1.06)(1.06)(1.06) =
3	$112.36	$6.74	$119.10	($100)(1.06)^3 = $119.10
				($100)(1.06)(1.06)(1.06)(1.06) =
4	$119.10	$7.15	$126.25	($100)(1.06)^4 = $126.25

value of the $100 investment at the end of year 1 is equal to $100 multiplied by 1.06 (1 plus the interest rate = 1 + 6% = 1 + 0.06 = 1.06). The quantity 1.06 is equal to 1 plus the interest rate to the first power. At the beginning of the second year, $106 is available to earn interest at 6 percent, so the ending value of the $100 investment at the end of the second year is ($106)(1.06), which is the same as ($100)(1.06)(1.06), which equals ($100)(1.06)^2, or $112.36. This process continues through the fourth year, when the ending value of the $100 investment is $126.25, which is equal to $100 times 1.06 to the fourth power: ($100)(1.06)(1.06)(1.06)(1.06) = ($100)(1.06)^4 = $100 = 1.2625.

In the general case, if interest compounds for n years, the $100 investment will grow to ($100)(1.06)^n at the end of n years. For example, if the investment is left to compound for twelve years, its ending value will be $100 x (1.06)^{12} = ($100)(2.012) = $201.20, or approximately double the amount originally invested. This example illustrates the so-called rule of 72, which states that by dividing the rate of compound interest into 72, one may estimate the number of years required to double the original investment. In this case, 6 percent divided into 72 indicates that it takes approximately twelve years for an investment to double in value if it earns interest at 6 percent compounded annually.

Compound Interest Tables

To simplify calculations of compound interest, compound interest tables are commonly available. Exhibit 11.2 presents some sample entries from such a table. One may use the table to find a given compound interest factor—that is, the amount to which $1 will grow at the end of n years at an interest rate of i percent. For example, if one wanted to find the amount to which $1,500 would grow if invested

**EXHIBIT 11.2   SAMPLE COMPOUND INTEREST FACTORS,
COMPOUND VALUE OF $1.00**

PERIOD	\multicolumn{7}{c}{INTEREST RATE (i)}
	2%	4%	6%	8%	10%	12%	14%
1	1.020	1.040	1.060	1.080	1.100	1.120	1.140
2	1.040	1.082	1.124	1.166	1.210	1.254	1.300
3	1.061	1.125	1.191	1.260	1.331	1.405	1.482
4	1.082	1.170	1.262	1.360	1.464	1.574	1.689
5	1.104	1.217	1.338	1.469	1.611	1.762	1.925
6	1.126	1.265	1.419	1.587	1.772	1.974	2.195
7	1.149	1.316	1.504	1.714	1.949	2.211	2.502
8	1.172	1.369	1.594	1.851	2.144	2.476	2.853
9	1.195	1.423	1.689	1.999	2.358	2.773	3.252
10	1.219	1.480	1.791	2.159	2.594	3.106	3.707
11	1.243	1.539	1.898	2.332	2.853	3.479	4.226
12	1.268	1.601	2.012	2.518	3.138	3.896	4.818
13	1.294	1.665	2.133	2.720	3.452	4.363	5.492
14	1.319	1.732	2.261	2.937	3.797	4.887	6.261
15	1.346	1.801	2.397	3.172	4.177	5.474	7.138
16	1.373	1.873	2.540	3.426	4.595	6.130	8.137
17	1.400	1.948	2.693	3.700	5.054	6.866	9.276
18	1.428	2.026	2.854	3.996	5.560	7.690	10.575
19	1.457	2.107	3.026	4.316	6.116	8.613	12.056
20	1.486	2.191	3.207	4.661	6.728	9.646	13.743

now at 8 percent and left to compound for twelve years, one would first look up the appropriate compound interest factor in the table and then multiply that factor times $1,500 to find the answer. In this case, ($1,500)(2.518) = $3,777 shows that $1,500 would grow to $3,777 if invested at 8 percent for twelve years.

Semiannual and Other Compounding Periods

If interest is compounded more than once a year—say, semiannually, quarterly, monthly, or even daily—then a simple adjustment to the compound interest formula introduced earlier may be made as follows:

$$V_n = P\left[\left(1+\frac{i}{m}\right)^{nm}\right]$$

where m = number of times per year that interest is compounded
$V, P, i,$ and n are as previously defined

As this formula indicates, if interest is compounded more often than annually, one need only divide the interest rate by the number of times per year that interest is compounded (m) and then raise the interest factor to the power nm, determined by multiplying the number of years interest will compound (n) times the number of annual periods (m). For example, if the interest rate is 8 percent per year compounded semiannually, the value of $100 left to compound for two years is:

$$V_n = P\left[\left(1 + \frac{i}{m}\right)^{nm}\right]$$

$$V_2 = (\$100)\left[\left(1 + \frac{0.08}{2}\right)^{(2)(2)}\right]$$

$$V_2 = (\$100)(1 + 0.04)^4$$

$$V_2 = (\$100)(1.04)^4 = (\$100)(1.170)$$

$$V_2 = \$117.00$$

If compounded quarterly:

$$V_2 = (\$100)\left[\left(1 + \frac{0.08}{4}\right)^{(2)(4)}\right]$$

$$V_2 = (\$100)(1 + 0.02)^8$$

$$V_2 = (\$100)(1.02)^8 = (\$100)(1.172)$$

$$V_2 = \$117.20$$

If compounded monthly:

$$V_2 = (\$100)\left[\left(1 + \frac{0.08}{12}\right)^{(2)(12)}\right]$$

$$V_2 = (\$100)(1.00667)^{24} = (\$100)(1.181)$$

$$V_2 = \$118.10$$

Note, of course, that as interest is compounded more often, the ending value (or terminal value) of the investment becomes larger. In all cases, the ending value is higher than that which would be obtained by earning interest at 8 percent compounded annually:

$$V_2 = (\$100)(1.08)^2$$
$$V_2 = (\$100)(1.166)$$
$$V_2 = \$116.60$$

Note also that it is a simple matter to accommodate the tables for use when the compounding periods occur more often than annually. One simply uses the compound interest factor for the relevant total number of periods and the interest rate per period. For example, if $100 is to compound for two years at 8 percent per year, compounded quarterly, the appropriate interest factor is for eight periods (four times per year times two years) at 2 percent (8 percent annually divided by four compounding periods). This factor, according to Exhibit 11.2, is 1.172—the same factor calculated earlier for this problem. Thus, $100 will grow to $117.20 over the two-year period.

Let us extend this example to introduce the concept of an effective annual interest rate. As noted, if interest is compounded quarterly, a higher terminal value of the investment results; that is, the effective rate of interest earned is higher. Since interest is calculated and compounded more often, the original investment earns interest on interest more often. Hence, the effective rate of return is higher. To calculate the effective rate of interest, one need only calculate the one-year compound interest factor for a given annual interest rate and number of compounding periods per year. The effective annual rate of interest for the preceding problem can be calculated by finding the one-year compound interest factor for 2 percent per period over four periods and then subtracting 1 (for return of principal) from it, as follows:

$$i_E = (1 + 0.02)^4 - 1$$
$$i_E = (1.082) - 1$$
$$i_E = 0.0824 = 8.24\%$$

where i_E = effective annual interest rate

Thus, the effective annual interest rate when 8 percent per year is compounded quarterly is 8.24 percent. In other words, 8 percent per year compounded quarterly provides the same return as 8.24 percent per year compounded annually (assuming, of course, that all principal plus interest is left to compound for the entire year). In general, the effective annual interest rate is found as follows:

$$i_E = \left(1 + \frac{i}{m}\right)^{mn} - 1$$

PRESENT VALUE

Present value is a key concept in finance and is closely related to the concept of compound interest. The present value of a dollar represents today's value of a sum of money to be received in the future, if money in hand today can be invested at a given interest rate. In short, a dollar received in the future is less valuable than a dollar in hand today because a dollar in hand today can be invested to grow to more than a dollar in the future. Present-value calculations provide a simple means of quantifying this time value of money by using the reciprocal of the compound interest formula.

The present-value formula may be derived directly from the compound interest formula. If we let r equal the rate at which money currently in hand may be invested (directly comparable to i in the compound interest formula), the present value of a dollar may be found as follows:

$$V_n = PV(1 + r)^n$$

$$PV = \frac{V_n}{(1 + r)^n}$$

$$PV = V_n\left[\frac{1}{(1 + r)^n}\right]$$

Note that the rate at which money currently in hand may be invested, r, is referred to as a *discount rate* rather than as an interest rate. The reason for this is that the present-value formula uses the rate of return available in order to "discount" future dollars to current (and lower) present values. Hence, one often hears terms such as *discounted present value* or *discounted cash flow* in reference to sums of cash to be received in the future.

A simple example will make the concept clearer. The present-value formula may be used to answer a question such as, "What is the present value of $1,500 to be received eight years from now if money in hand can be invested at 10 percent?" Answering this question from the present-value formula requires solving the following equation:

$$PV = V_n \left[\frac{1}{(1+r)^n} \right]$$

$$PV = (\$1,500) \left[\frac{1}{(1.10)^8} \right]$$

$$PV = (\$1,500)(0.467)$$

$$PV = \$700.50$$

The answer indicates that the present value of $1,500 to be received eight years from now given a 10 percent discount rate is $700.50. Stated alternatively, $700.50 invested today at an interest rate of 10 percent will grow to be $1,500 at the end of eight years. This answer may be confirmed by reference to the compound interest table in Exhibit 11.2 (with due allowance for rounding off):

$$V_n = P(1+i)^n$$
$$V_n = (\$700.50)(1.10)^8$$
$$V_n = (\$700.50)(2.144)$$
$$V_n = \$1501.87$$

Tables containing present-value factors are also commonly available. As previously indicated, the present-value factors are nothing more than the reciprocal of the compound interest factors introduced earlier. A sample of these present-value factors is presented in Exhibit 11.3.

PRESENT VALUE OF AN ANNUITY

The *present value of an annuity* is a financial concept that is very closely related to the concept of the present value of a dollar. In finance, an annuity is a series of constant receipts (or payments) that are received (or paid) at the end of each year for some number of years into the future. The present value of an annuity (An), then, is the present value of a stream of future cash receipts of a fixed amount received at the end of each year for some number of years into the future, given a discount rate, r. For example, the present value of a future stream of receipts of $100 per year to be received at the end of each year for the next three years given a discount rate of

EXHIBIT 11.3 SAMPLE PRESENT-VALUE FACTORS, PRESENT VALUE OF $1.00

PERIOD	DISCOUNT RATE (r)						
	2%	**4%**	**6%**	**8%**	**10%**	**12%**	**14%**
1	0.980	0.962	0.943	0.926	0.909	0.893	0.877
2	0.961	0.925	0.890	0.857	0.826	0.797	0.769
3	0.942	0.889	0.840	0.794	0.751	0.712	0.675
4	0.924	0.855	0.792	0.735	0.683	0.636	0.592
5	0.906	0.822	0.747	0.681	0.621	0.567	0.519
6	0.888	0.790	0.705	0.630	0.564	0.507	0.456
7	0.871	0.760	0.665	0.583	0.513	0.452	0.400
8	0.853	0.731	0.627	0.540	0.467	0.404	0.351
9	0.837	0.703	0.592	0.500	0.424	0.361	0.308
10	0.820	0.676	0.558	0.463	0.386	0.322	0.270
11	0.804	0.650	0.527	0.429	0.350	0.287	0.237
12	0.788	0.625	0.497	0.397	0.319	0.257	0.208
13	0.773	0.601	0.469	0.368	0.290	0.229	0.182
14	0.758	0.577	0.442	0.340	0.263	0.205	0.160
15	0.743	0.555	0.417	0.315	0.239	0.183	0.140
16	0.728	0.534	0.394	0.292	0.218	0.163	0.123
17	0.714	0.513	0.371	0.270	0.198	0.146	0.108
18	0.700	0.494	0.350	0.250	0.180	0.130	0.095
19	0.686	0.475	0.331	0.232	0.164	0.116	0.083
20	0.673	0.456	0.312	0.215	0.149	0.104	0.073

$r = 6\%$ is as follows (using Exhibit 11.3 to find the appropriate discount factors):

$$A_n = (\$100)(0.943) + (\$100)(0.890) + (\$100)(0.840)$$
$$A_n = (\$100)(0.943 + 0.890 + 0.840)$$
$$A_n = (\$100)(2.673)$$
$$A_n = \$267.30$$

In other words, the present value of an annuity of $100 per year for three years is equal to the present value of $100 received one year from now plus the present value of $100 received two years from now plus the present value of $100 received three years from now. Note that in this calculation, the present-value factors for each of the three years are simply added together and then multiplied by the constant annual receipt. Once again, tables of present-value annuity factors are readily available. These tables simply add together the individual year's present-value factors for the number of years the annuity is to run. Some sample present-value annuity factors are shown in Exhibit 11.4. To calculate these factors directly, one may use the following equation:

$$A_n = R\left[\frac{1}{(1+r)}\right] + R\left[\frac{1}{(1+r)^2}\right] + K + R\left[\frac{1}{(1+r)^n}\right]$$

$$A_n = R\left[\frac{1}{(1+r)} + \frac{1}{(1+r)^2} + K + \frac{1}{(1+r)^n}\right]$$

$$A_n = R\left[\frac{1 - 1/(1+r)^n}{r}\right]$$

where A = present value of an annuity

         R = amount of future receipts

         r = discount rate

         n = number of years

The expression within the brackets gives the present-value annuity factors presented in Exhibit 11.4.

In the simple computational example at the beginning of this section, the sum of a three-year annuity of $100 was found to be $267.30, given a 6 percent discount rate. One way to interpret this result is to note that $267.30 represents the amount of money that would have to be invested today at 6 percent so that one would withdraw $100 at the end of each year for the next three years before exhausting the investment. Exhibit 11.5 illustrates this process.

COMPOUND VALUE OF AN ANNUITY

The *compound value* (sometimes called the *future value*) of an annuity (S_n) is the "flip side" of the present value of an annuity. The compound value of an annuity is the ending value of a series of constant payments made at the end of each year for a specified number of years that earn a given rate of interest per year. In general terms, the compound value of an annuity may be found as follows:

EXHIBIT 11.4   SAMPLE PRESENT-VALUE ANNUITY FACTORS, PRES-ENT VALUE OF AN ANNUITY OF $1.00 PER PERIOD

PERIOD	DISCOUNT RATE (r)						
	2%	**4%**	**6%**	**8%**	**10%**	**12%**	**14%**
1	0.980	0.962	0.943	0.926	0.909	0.893	0.877
2	1.942	1.886	1.833	1.783	1.736	1.690	1.647
3	2.884	2.775	2.673	2.577	2.487	2.402	2.322
4	3.808	3.630	3.465	3.312	3.170	3.037	2.914
5	4.713	4.452	4.212	3.993	3.791	3.605	3.433
6	5.601	5.242	4.917	4.623	4.355	4.111	3.889
7	6.472	6.002	5.582	5.206	4.868	4.564	4.288
8	7.325	6.733	6.210	5.747	5.335	4.968	4.639
9	8.162	7.435	6.802	6.247	5.759	5.328	4.946
10	8.983	8.111	7.360	6.710	6.145	5.650	5.216
11	9.787	8.760	7.887	7.139	6.495	5.938	5.453
12	10.575	9.385	8.384	7.536	6.814	6.194	5.660
13	11.348	9.986	8.853	7.904	7.103	6.424	5.842
14	12.106	10.563	9.295	8.244	7.367	6.628	6.002
15	12.849	11.118	9.712	8.559	7.606	6.811	6.142
16	13.578	11.652	10.106	8.851	7.824	6.974	6.265
17	14.292	12.166	10.477	9.122	8.022	7.120	6.373
18	14.992	12.659	10.828	9.372	8.201	7.250	6.467
19	15.678	13.134	11.158	9.604	8.365	7.366	6.550
20	16.351	13.590	11.470	9.818	8.514	7.469	6.623

EXHIBIT 11.5   SAMPLE ANNUITY SCHEDULE

	YEAR		
	1	**2**	**3**
Beginning balance	$267.30	$183.34	$94.34
Annual interest @ 6%	16.04	11.00	5.66
Subtotal	$283.34	$194.34	$100.00
Annual withdrawal	(100.00)	(100.00)	(100.00)
Ending balance	$183.34	$ 94.34	$0.

$$S_n = P\left(1 + i\right)^{n-1} + P\left(1 + i\right)^{n-2} + K + P\left(1 + i\right) + P(1)$$

$$S_n = P\left[\left(1 + i\right)^{n-1} + \left(1 + i\right)^{n-2} + K + \left(1 + i\right) + 1\right]$$

$$S_n = P\left[\frac{\left(1 + i\right)^n - 1}{i}\right]$$

where S_n = compound sum
       P = principal amount deposited each year
       i = interest rate
       n = number of years

Note from this formula that each deposit compounds for one year less than the total number of years the annuity runs. The first deposit earns interest for $n - 1$ years, the second deposit for $n - 2$ years, and so forth. The last deposit earns no interest at all. The reason for this is that the annuity formula is set up so that deposits are made at the end of each year. For example, if $100 is invested at the end of each year for four years, the ending value of the investment will be as follows:

S_4 = ($100)(1 + i)$^{n-1}$ + ($100)(1 + i)$^{n-2}$ + ($100)(1 + i)$^{n-3}$ + ($100)(1 + i)$^{n-4}$
S_4 = ($100)(1.06)^3 + ($100)(1.06)^2 + ($100)(1.06)^1 + ($100)(1.06)^0
S_4 = ($100)(1.191) + ($100)(1.124) + ($100)(1.06) + ($100)(1)
S_4 = ($100)(1.191 + 1.124 + 1.060 + 1.000)
S_4 = ($100)(4.375)
S_4 – $437.50

In sum, the compound value of an annuity formulation addresses the question, "If I invest a constant amount of money per year at the end of each year at a given interest rate, what will be the total sum accumulated at the end of a given number of years?" Once again, tables containing compound-value annuity factors are commonly available as a computational aid. Some sample entries from such a table are shown in Exhibit 11.6.

Calculators and Personal Computers

Very few people actually use compound interest and present-value tables to solve time value of money problems. Even relatively inexpensive

EXHIBIT 11.6   SAMPLE COMPOUND-VALUE ANNUITY FACTORS, SUM OF AN ANNUITY OF $1.00 PER PERIOD

PERIOD	INTEREST RATE (*i*)						
	2%	**4%**	**6%**	**8%**	**10%**	**12%**	**14%**
1	1.000	1.000	1.000	1.000	1.000	1.000	1.000
2	2.020	2.040	2.060	2.080	2.100	2.120	2.140
3	3.060	3.122	3.184	3.246	3.310	3.374	3.440
4	4.122	4.246	4.375	4.506	4.641	4.770	4.921
5	5.204	5.416	5.637	5.867	6.105	6.353	6.610
6	6.308	6.633	6.975	7.336	7.716	8.115	8.536
7	7.434	7.898	8.394	8.923	9.487	10.089	10.730
8	8.583	9.214	9.897	10.637	11.436	12.300	13.233
9	9.755	10.583	11.491	12.488	13.579	14.776	16.085
10	10.950	12.006	13.181	14.487	15.937	17.549	19.337
11	12.169	13.486	14.972	16.645	18.531	20.655	23.044
12	13.412	15.026	16.870	18.977	21.384	24.133	27.271
13	14.680	16.627	18.882	21.495	24.523	28.029	32.089
14	15.974	18.292	21.051	24.215	27.975	32.393	37.531
15	17.293	20.024	23.276	27.152	31.772	37.280	43.842
16	18.639	21.825	25.673	30.324	35.950	42.753	50.980
17	20.012	23.698	28.213	33.750	40.545	48.884	59.118
18	21.412	25.645	30.906	37.450	45.599	55.750	68.394
19	22.841	27.671	33.760	41.446	51.159	63.440	78.969
20	24.297	29.778	36.786	45.762	57.275	72.052	91.025

handheld calculators solve most compound interest and present-value problems quickly and easily. More complex annuity problems can also be programmed on nearly all business and scientific calculators rather easily. Spreadsheet software for personal computers can be used to solve any class of time value of money problem without much difficulty. Compound interest and present-value tables have rapidly become anachronisms. They are shown here for illustrative purposes to illustrate the time value of money concept.

APPLICATION TO PERSONAL DECISION MAKING

A useful personal application of the techniques just described is in planning for a child's college expenses. Assume that a parent wishes to provide $50,000 per year for four years for an infant's college tuition eighteen years from now. (Given current college tuition levels and current rates of inflation, $50,000 seems a reasonable or even low estimate.) Assume further that the parent wishes to accumulate a lump sum sufficient to pay out $50,000 per year beginning eighteen years from now by making annual installment payments at the end of each of the next seventeen years and then making the first withdrawal at the end of the eighteenth year. Finally, assume that the annual payment is invested to earn an average effective annual rate of return equal to 8 percent.

The parent now faces two simple problems that can be solved using the formulations for the sum of annuity and present value of annuity just described. First, he or she must determine how much of a lump sum is needed to pay out $50,000 per year for four years. Second, the parent must then determine how much money must be deposited each year for the next seventeen years in order to accumulate this lump sum. The first problem may be solved by referring to the present-value-of-annuity formula to solve the following problem (using the present-value-of-annuity factor from Exhibit 11.4):

$$A_n = R\left[\frac{1 - 1/(1 + r)^n}{r}\right]$$

$$A_4 = \$50,000\left[\frac{1 - 1/(1.08)^4}{0.08}\right]$$

$$A_4 = (\$50,000)(3.312)$$

$$A_4 = \$165,600$$

The solution shows that a lump sum of $165,600 is required in order to pay out $50,000 per year for four years. A quick computational check shows why this is so (with due allowance for rounding error):

	YEAR			
	1	**2**	**3**	**4**
Beginning balance	$165,600	$128,848	$89,156	$46,288
Interest at 8 percent	13,248	10,308	7,132	3,703
Subtotal	$178,848	$139,156	$96,288	$49,991
Annual withdrawal	(50,000)	(50,000)	(50,000)	(49,991)
Ending balance	$128,848	$89,156	$46,288	$0

The second part of the problem is, "Given that $165,600 must be accumulated over the next seventeen years, what annual investment to the fund is required to accumulate this lump sum?" To answer this question, the compound-value-of-an-annuity formulation must be used as follows (using the sum of an annuity factor from the table in Exhibit 11.6):

$$S_n = P\left[\frac{(1+i)^n - 1}{i}\right]$$

$$\$165,600 = P\left[\frac{(1.08)^{17} - 1}{0.08}\right]$$

$$P = \$165,600 / 33.750$$
$$P = \$4,906$$

The parent must therefore invest $4,906 at the end of each year for the next seventeen years in order to accumulate a lump sum of $165,600 from which $50,000 may be withdrawn each year for four consecutive years. It should be noted that using a different interest rate will result in a different answer. Specifically, a lower interest rate will require a larger lump sum to be accumulated and larger annual deposits. A higher interest rate will allow a smaller lump sum and lower annual deposits.

The second part of this type of problem is often of interest in a corporate setting, when a corporation sets up a sinking fund of some type. Such funds may be set up to retire a bond issue. Thus, for example, if a company issues bonds worth $100,000,000 that must be redeemed at par (paid off at face value) twenty years from the date of issue, the company may set aside a fixed annual contribution to a sinking fund to redeem the issue. The calculations illustrated in the first part of the problem may be used to determine the amount of money that must be contributed to the sinking fund each year in order to retire the issue. In this case, if the annual deposit could be invested at 8 percent, an annual payment of $100,000,000/(45.762) = $2,182,213 would be required.

SUMMARY

The compound interest formula expresses the value of a principal sum of money left on deposit or invested for a given number of years at a given rate of interest. This formula is the basis for all time value of money calculations. The present-value formula is simply the reciprocal of the compound interest formula: The present value of a dollar is the current worth of a sum of money to be received in the future if money in hand today can be invested at a given interest rate. Present-value calculations quantify the concept that time is money and that money to be received in the future is less valuable than money in hand today, assuming that money in hand today will be invested at some positive rate of return. An annuity is a series of constant receipts (or payments) of cash received (or paid) at the end of each year for some number of years into the future. The present value of an annuity is the present value of a stream of future cash receipts of a fixed amount received at the end of each year for some number of years into the future, given a discount rate. The compound sum of an annuity is the "flip side" of the present value of an annuity: It is the ending value of a series of constant payments, made at the end of each year for a specified number of years, that earn a given rate of interest per year.

The mathematics underlying the compound interest calculations in this chapter will be applied within a corporate capital budgeting framework in the next chapter. It is very important to acquire a firm grasp of the basics presented in this chapter before moving on to the next chapter.

KEY POINTS

COMPOUND INTEREST

$$V_n = P(1 + i)^n$$

PRESENT VALUE

$$PV = V_n\left[\frac{1}{(1 + r)^n}\right]$$

PRESENT VALUE OF ANNUITY

$$A_n = R\left[\frac{1 - 1/(1 + r)^n}{r}\right]$$

COMPOUND SUM OF AN ANNUITY

$$S_n = P\left[\frac{(1 + i)^n - 1}{i}\right]$$

12

Capital Budgeting

Capital budgeting is the process by which an organization evaluates and selects long-term investment projects. An organization's capital budget represents its expected commitments to long-term investments, such as investments in capital equipment, purchase or lease of buildings, purchase or lease of vehicles, and so forth. In this chapter, we will explore the various techniques used to make capital budgeting decisions and apply the mathematics of compound interest introduced in the previous chapter.

PAYBACK

One capital budgeting technique that is widely used by small businesses but seldom employed in large corporations is the payback method. This method is popular because of the simplicity of its decision rule and its sensitivity to the scarcity of capital—an important factor in many small businesses. It requires calculation of the number of years required to pay back the original investment. If a choice must be made between two mutually exclusive investment projects, one simply chooses the project with the shortest payback period. If a "go–no go" decision is to be made, one simply compares the project's payback with some predetermined standard. In this case, a simple decision rule such as "accept all projects with a payback of less than five years, and reject all others" may be used.

Although payback is a simple rule to apply, it is a poor method on which to rely for the allocation of a firm's scarce capital resources—for two major reasons. First, payback ignores the time value of money. Second, it ignores expected cash flows beyond the payback period. For example, consider the comparison shown in Exhibit 12.1. Project B would be ranked higher than Project A because its payback

EXHIBIT 12.1   SAMPLE PAYBACK DECISION RULE, MUTUALLY EX-CLUSIVE PROJECTS

PROJECT A	PROJECT B
Cost = $100,000	Cost = $100,000
Expected future cash flow:	Expected future cash flow:
Year 1 $ 50,000	Year 1 $100,000
Year 2 $ 50,000	Year 2 $ 5,000
Year 3 $110,000	Year 3 $ 5,000
Years 4 and thereafter: None	Years 4 and thereafter: None
Total = $210,000	Total = $110,000
Payback = 2 years	Payback = 1 year

is shorter, even though Project A obviously provides a much higher return to the company and is clearly a superior investment project. Although this example is admittedly extreme and the better selection is fairly obvious, the example does highlight a crucial flaw of the payback technique. To overcome this flaw, the net-present-value and internal-rate-of-return techniques have become standard practice for the evaluation of capital budgeting projects.

NET PRESENT VALUE

The *net-present-value* (NPV) method of selecting capital budgeting projects is also commonly referred to as *discounted cash flow, DCF analysis, discounted present value,* and *present-value analysis.* But whatever name is used, the nature of the technique is the same and is actually quite simple in concept. The net-present-value method compares the present value of the expected future benefits of a project to the present value of the expected cost of the project. The net present value of the project is simply the difference between the present value of the benefits and the present value of the costs. If the net present value is positive—that is, if the present value of the benefits exceeds the present value of the cost—then the project is accepted. If the reverse is true and the net present value is negative, the project is rejected. In sum:

$$NPV = PVB - PVC$$

where *NPV* = net present value
PVB = present value of benefits
PVC = present value of costs

If *NPV* positive, accept.
If *NPV* negative, reject.

If a choice must be made between two mutually exclusive projects, the project with the highest net present value should be selected. Continuing the previous example, if a choice must be made between Projects A and B and a 12 percent discount rate is used, the present value of the benefits of the two projects would be calculated as follows:

$$PVBA = (\$50,000)(0.893) + (\$50,000)(0.797) + (\$110,000)(0.712)$$
$$PVBA = \$44,650 + \$39,850 + \$78,320$$
$$PVBA = \$162,820$$

$$PVBB = (\$100,000)(0.893) + (\$5,000)(0.792) + (\$5,000)(0.712)$$
$$PVBB = \$89,300 + \$3,960 + \$3,560$$
$$PVBB = \$96,820$$

Since both projects cost $100,000 and the cost is incurred immediately, the present value of the costs in both cases is $100,000:

$$PVCA = PVCB = \$100,000$$

The net present value of the two projects would then be determined as follows:

$$NPVA = \$162,800 - \$100,000 = \$62,800$$
$$NPVB = \$96,820 - \$100,000 = (\$3,180)$$

It is now clear that Project A is superior to Project B. The present value of the benefits for A exceeds the present value of the cost by $62,800. For Project B, the present value of the benefits is actually less than the present value of the costs by $3,180. Note that the negative value for Project B's net present value does not necessarily imply that Project B loses money. In this case, the total cash return over the three-year period of $110,000 exceeds the $100,000 cash cost. However, the present value of the $110,000 is less than $100,000. The net-present-value method points out the fact that the return on Project B is insufficient to justify the investment, given the firm's cost of capital.

Selection of a Discount Rate

To evaluate a capital budgeting project, one need only compare the present value of the benefits to the present value of the costs. The choice of an appropriate discount rate is a key decision in the capital budgeting process. As illustrated in the previous chapter, the choice of an appropriate discount rate for individual use in personal decision making is fairly straightforward. In order to find the discounted present value of a sum of money to be received in the future, one simply chooses the rate at which money in hand may be invested between now and the future period in which the money is to be received. In economic terms, this rate represents the individual's "opportunity cost"—that is, the cost of the individual's next-best opportunity.

For corporate financial decision making, the selection of an appropriate discount rate follows a conceptually similar process. The firm's opportunity cost is related to the cost of funds to the firm. The cost of funds to the firm is referred to as the firm's *cost of capital*, a cost treated as a "given" for present purposes. Determination of a firm's cost of capital will be discussed in detail in the next chapter. For now, however, we will treat the cost of capital as an exogenously determined variable and define *cost of capital* simply as the percentage cost of funds available to the firm.

INTERNAL RATE OF RETURN

The *internal rate of return* (IRR) is normally calculated in addition to the net-present-value calculation. The internal rate of return may be defined as the discount rate that exactly equates the present value of the expected benefits from a project to the cost of the project. Stated another way, the IRR is the discount rate that will drive the net present value of the project to zero. One normally finds this discount rate by trial and error (a computer program will usually be available to solve directly for the IRR). Continuing our previous example, we might use a discount rate of 20 percent as a first estimate of the IRR on Project A. A simple calculation may then be undertaken to determine whether a 20 percent discount rate will equate the expected future benefits of Project A to its cost of $100,000 and drive the net present value to zero:

$NPVA = PVBA - PVCA$
$NPVA = (\$50,000)(0.833) + (\$50,000)(0.694) + (\$110,000)(0.579) - \$100,000$
$NPVA = \$41,650 + \$34,700 + \$63,690 - \$100,000$
$NPVA = \$40,040$

In this case, using the appropriate present-value factors for a 20 percent discount rate still results in a high net present value. Since the net present value is too high, a higher discount rate is required to drive the net present value to zero. Use of a 40 percent discount rate yields the following result:

$NPVA = (\$50,000)(0.714) + (\$50,000)(0.510) + (\$110,000)(0.364) - \$100,000$
$NPVA = \$101,240 - \$100,000$
$NPVA = \$1,240$

Refining the calculations a bit further shows that a discount rate of 41 percent will drive the net present value very close to zero:

$NPVA = (\$50,000)(0.702) + (\$50,000)(0.503) + (\$110,000)(0.364) - \$100,000$
$NPVA = \$100,290 - \$100,000$
$NPVA = \$290$

The meaning of the 41 percent internal rate of return is that 41 percent represents the average annual compound rate of return on investment for Project A. Stated in terms of the costs and benefits associated with Project A, if one were to invest $100,000 at a 41 percent annual compound rate of return, one would be able to withdraw from that investment a cash flow of $50,000 at the end of one year, $50,000 at the end of the second year, and $110,000 at the end of the third year. Exhibit 12.2 illustrates this point (some small rounding error results in a cash outflow of $110,417 instead of $110,000 in the third year).

Application of the IRR decision rule in this case would cause Project A to be accepted. In general, the IRR decision rule states that any project with an IRR greater than or equal to the firm's cost of capital should be accepted. Any project with an IRR less than the firm's cost

EXHIBIT 12.2   PROJECT A CASH FLOW SCHEDULE

	YEAR		
	1	**2**	**3**
Beginning investment	$100,000	$91,000	$78,310
Annual earnings @ 41%	41,000	37,310	32,107
Subtotal	$141,000	$128,310	$ 110,417
Annual cash flow	(50,000)	(50,000)	(110,417)
Ending investment	$ 91,000	$ 78,310	$0

of capital would be rejected. The IRR of 41 percent on Project A, when compared with the 12 percent cost of capital, clearly indicates the acceptability of Project A.

For Project B, the internal rate of return is approximately 8.75 percent, as can be seen in the following calculation:

$NPVB$ = ($100,000)(0.920) + ($5,000)(0.846) + ($5,000)(0.778) − $100,000
$NPVB$ = $92,000 + $4,230 + $3,890 − $100,000
$NPVB$ = $100,120 − $100,000
$NPVB$ = $120

The reason that Project B has a negative present value even though its cash return is positive now becomes clearer. Although Project B does earn a respectable rate of return of 8.75 percent per year, this return is far short of our assumed cost of capital of 12 percent. The net-present-value decision rule simply shows that the achieved rate of return on Project B falls short of the attainable rate of return on other opportunities. The rate of return on Project B falls below the firm's opportunity-cost rate of return. In other words, the IRR is less than the cost of capital.

IRR of an Annuity

Neither Project A nor Project B provides benefits in the form of an annuity—that is, a constant annual cash flow. It should be noted that the IRR calculation for an annuity is much easier than for a nonannuity, since a single calculation may be used in the annuity case. If, for example, a project costing $100,000 and returning $25,000 per year for five years is available, the appropriate annuity factor may be calculated as follows:

$$\$100,000 = \$25,000X$$
$$X = 4.0$$

In this solution, X represents the annuity factor that will cause a $25,000, five-year annuity to have a present value of $100,000. We can find the discount rate that has a present value of an annuity factor equal to 4.0 after five years by referring to the table of annuity factors in Exhibit 11.4 in the previous chapter. Looking across the five-year line, an annuity factor of approximately 4.0 corresponds to a discount rate of 8 percent. We may therefore conclude that the hypothesized investment provides an IRR of approximately 8 percent.

Personal Computer Applications

Like most other time value of money problems, net-present-value and internal-rate-of-return problems need not be solved using cumbersome present-value tables. Most business calculators can be programmed to solve capital budgeting problems. Personal computers also have simplified capital budgeting software. Business-oriented spreadsheet applications can be set up to solve these problems, and special-purpose capital budgeting software packages are readily available. The calculations shown here are for illustrative purposes. In a typical real-world application, a calculator or a computer program would be used to do the actual calculations.

PROFITABILITY INDEX

The *profitability index* (PI), also called the *benefit/cost ratio*, is an additional capital budgeting measure that is closely related to the present value of an investment. The profitability index is calculated as the ratio of the present value of the benefits of an investment to the cost of the investment (or present value of the cost if any costs are incurred after the initial outlays):

$$PI = \frac{\text{NPV (benefits)}}{\text{NPV (costs)}}$$

As a general rule, all projects with a PI greater than 1.0 should be accepted. This simple measure of relative profitability is also very useful when it is necessary to make a direct comparison between two or more mutually exclusive projects having different costs. The profitability index allows a direct comparison between the projects in terms of the present value of benefit per unit cost. In most cases, the project with the highest profitability index would be selected.

When the profitability index is used as a screening device, investment decisions based on the profitability index will be the same as decisions made using net present value. All projects having a positive net present value have a profitability index larger than 1.0 and therefore are deemed acceptable. Projects with a profitability index less than 1.0 are unacceptable.

SELECTION OF METHOD

In most cases, the choice of which method to use for capital budgeting is not a problem. All three recommended methods—net present value, internal rate of return, and the profitability index—result in the same accept-reject decision for a given investment opportunity. Thus, the three methods may be viewed as mutually supportive and mutually consistent. However, there are three important circumstances under which the methods may yield conflicting decisions. These circumstances occur fairly rarely and will be discussed only briefly here.

The first circumstance arises when one must choose from among mutually exclusive investment projects with similar costs but radically differing time patterns of cash inflows. For example, one project providing large cash flows in the early years of the investment's life and small cash flows in later years may be compared with another project providing small cash flows in the early years but large cash flows in later years. In this case, the project having the highest net present value and profitability index may have the lowest internal rate of return. Exhibit 12.3 illustrates such a possible case for two mutually exclusive projects (cost of capital is assumed to be 8 percent).

As Exhibit 12.3 shows, Project B returns more total dollars than Project A, has lower cash inflows in the early years of its life, and has higher cash inflows in the later years. Project B has a higher present value and profitability index but a lower internal rate of return than Project A. Project A provides fewer total dollars but has much higher cash inflows in the early years of its life.

The choice of which method to use is actually quite simple. The answer is inherent in the mathematics of the methods. Mathematically, the net-present-value method implicitly assumes that all cash inflows are reinvested at the firm's cost of capital. The internal-rate-of-return method implicitly assumes that all cash inflows are reinvested at the IRR of the project. Therefore, the choice of method depends on which assumption is closest to reality. The choice should be based on which reinvestment rate is closest to the rate that the firm will be able to earn on the cash flows generated by the project. Thus, if cash inflows can be reinvested at the cost of capital, the project with the higher net present value should be selected. If cash inflows can be reinvested at the IRR of the project, the project with the

EXHIBIT 12.3 CONFLICTING RANKING EXAMPLE

PROJECT A		PROJECT B	
COST = $1,900		COST = $1,900	
CASH FLOWS:		CASH FLOWS:	
YEAR	CASH FLOW	YEAR	CASH FLOW
1	$800	1	$450
2	700	2	550
3	600	3	650
4	500	4	750
5	400	5	850
	$3,000		$3,250

NET PRESENT VALUE AT 8 PERCENT:	NET PRESENT VALUE AT 8 PERCENT:
($800)(0.926) + ($700)(0.857)	($450)(0.926) + ($550)(0.857)
+ ($600)(0.794) + ($500)(0.735)	+ ($650)(0.794) + ($750)(0.735)
+ ($400)(0.681) – $1,900	+ ($850)(0.681) $1,900
= $557	= $634
Profitability index = 1.29	Profitability index = 1.34
IRR = 20%	IRR = 18.5%

RANKING BY:

RANK	NET PRESENT VALUE	PROFITABILITY INDEX	IRR
1	B	B	A
2	A	A	B

higher IRR should be selected. Following this rule will result in choosing the investment that will maximize the value added to the firm.

As a general rule, the net-present-value method should be preferred if a conflict arises because projects with very high IRRs relative to the firm's cost of capital are fairly rare. Since in most cases the reinvestment rate will be closer to the cost of capital than it is to the IRR, the net-present-value method is normally preferred to the IRR method.

The general preference for the NPV method also applies in the second important circumstance in which a conflict in ranking may occur. This is the case of choosing from among mutually exclusive projects with widely differing costs. In this case, the project with the highest net present value may have the lowest profitability index and internal rate of return. Once again, in general, preference should be given to the project with the highest net present value, since this will maximize the value of the firm. In practice, however, if the project with the highest profitability index and internal rate of return is substantially less expensive than the competing project, the high PI and IRR project is often selected. This is so because the lower-cost project may be perceived as being less risky than the higher-cost project.

The final important circumstance where a problem may occur is the case of capital rationing, where insufficient capital is available to accept all projects having positive net present values. In this case, the normal procedure is to rank-order projects from the highest IRR to the lowest and select all projects that the firm has sufficient capital to accept.

Once again, the circumstances just described are fairly rare. In all cases, all three methods will provide consistent accept-reject decisions. All projects deemed acceptable according to any one method will always be found acceptable according to the other methods. It is only in the case of selecting from among mutually exclusive projects or operating under conditions of capital rationing that a potential conflict exists. On balance, there is general preference for the NPV method over the IRR or PI method.

DEALING WITH UNCERTAINTY

The outcome of almost all business decisions is surrounded by some degree of uncertainty,* and capital budgeting decisions are no exception. A large body of theory and no small degree of controversy exist relative to the treatment of uncertainty. In practice, however, uncertainty is often dealt with through the simple mechanism of assigning higher discount rates to riskier projects. Thus, for example, if Projects A and B are being evaluated and Project B is much riskier than Project A, Project B will be "charged" a higher discount rate. If Project A is of normal riskiness and the firm's normal cost of capital is, say, 10 percent, A will be evaluated using a 10 percent cost of capital, while B will be evaluated using a cost of capital higher than 10 percent. How much higher will depend on management's perception

---

*Although many authors draw a distinction between *uncertainty* and *risk*, the terms will be used synonymously for present purposes.

of the riskiness of B versus A and the additional compensation required of B because of that risk.

It is important to note here that if Project B is evaluated using a discount rate of, say, 14 percent and is found to have a higher net present value than Project A (which would be evaluated using a 10 percent cost of capital), B should be selected in preference to A. The additional return demanded by the 14 percent discount rate charged to B is to compensate for B's risk. This point is emphasized here because of the common error of selecting A over B in spite of B's higher risk-adjusted net present value on the grounds that since A is less risky than B, it should receive preference. This is an incorrect logical procedure since risk has already been compensated for through the mechanism of the increased discount rate for Project B. To further discriminate against B after the final risk-adjusted net-present-value calculations have been completed would be inappropriate.

CASE STUDY: DROPPITT PARCEL COMPANY

As an illustration of the capital budgeting techniques just described, consider the case of the Droppitt Parcel Company. Droppitt is considering purchasing some new equipment to replace existing equipment that has a book value of zero but a market value of $15,000. The new equipment costs $90,000 and is expected to provide production savings and increased profits of $20,000 per year for the next ten years. It has an expected useful life of ten years, after which its estimated salvage value would be $10,000. Assuming straight-line depreciation, a 34 percent effective tax rate, and a cost of capital of 12 percent, should Droppitt replace the current equipment?

This common type of capital budgeting problem is known as a "machinery replacement" problem. This type of problem is important because the appropriate method of solution is a general technique with wide applicability to a variety of capital budgeting problems.

Exhibit 12.4 illustrates the solution to this problem. Step 1 shows that the effective cost of the new equipment is $80,100. To arrive at this figure, the proceeds of the sale of Droppitt's current equipment, adjusted for taxes, are deducted from the cost of the new equipment. This is done because the relevant cost of the new equipment is the incremental cost of making the switch from the old equipment to the new. In

EXHIBIT 12.4 DROPPITT PARCEL COMPANY CAPITAL BUDGETING PROBLEM

1. *Effective cost of new equipment:*

a) Cost of new equipment	$90,000
b) Sale of old equipment	(15,000)
c) Tax on sale (34%)	5,100
Effective cost	$80,100

2. *Expected benefit of new equipment:*

	BEFORE TAX	AFTER TAX	YEARS	PRESENT-VALUE FACTOR	PRESENT VALUE
a) Profit increase	$20,000	$13,200*	1–10	5.650	$74,580
b) Depreciation tax benefit	8,000	2,720†	1–10	5.650	15,368
c) Salvage value of new equipment	10,000	10,000	10	0.322	3,220
					$93,168

3. *Net present value* = $93,168 − 80,100
   = $13,068

4. *Internal rate of return* (solve with calculator, personal computer, or by trial and error using present-value tables):

$$\$80,100 = (\$13,200 + \$2,720)\left[\frac{1 - \frac{1}{(1+r)^{10}}}{r}\right] + (10,000)\left[\frac{1}{(1+r)^{10}}\right]$$

$r = 15.7\%$

* ($20,000)(1 − T) = ($20,000)(1 − 0.34) = $13,200
† ($8,000)(T) = ($8,000)(.34) = $2,720

effect, Droppitt trades its old equipment in for the new equipment by selling it and applying the sale proceeds to the new equipment.

Step 2 calculates the present value of the expected benefits of the new equipment. All investment decisions must logically include the tax effect of any transactions, and all benefits have been converted to an after-tax basis before present values are calculated. Since Droppitt's effective tax rate is 34 percent, the profit increase is multiplied by 0.66 (1.00 minus the tax rate) to determine the increased profit remaining after tax. The tax benefit resulting from the effect of depreciation is calculated by multiplying the annual depreciation deduction by 0.34, the effective tax rate. Finally, the salvage value of the new equipment at the end of its expected useful life is reflected. In this case, there is no tax effect, since there is no profit or loss involved.

Step 3 shows the net present value to be $13,068. In Step 4, the internal rate of return on the equipment purchase is solved by trial and error using a calculator. The IRR is approximately 15.7 percent. In this case, then, the new machine should be purchased to replace the old machine since the net present value is positive and the IRR exceeds the cost of capital.

SUMMARY

Capital budgeting is the process by which an organization selects and evaluates long-term investment projects. The payback method of capital budgeting is widely used by small businesses but is a poor method on which to rely for the allocation of a firm's scarce capital resources. The two major weaknesses of payback are that it ignores the time value of money and it ignores cash flows beyond the payback period. The net-present-value method of capital budgeting compares the present value of the expected future benefits from a project with the present value of the expected cost of the project. Projects with a positive net present value—the difference between the benefit and cost—are accepted for investment. In addition to net present value, the internal rate of return on a capital budgeting project is also calculated. The internal rate of return measures the average annual after-tax compound rate of return expected to be earned on a project. Mathematically, the internal rate of return is the discount rate that exactly equates the present value of the expected benefits from a project with the present value of the expected cost. The profitability index is the ratio of the present value of the benefits to the present value of the costs.

The net present value, internal rate of return, and profitability index normally are mutually supportive and mutually consistent, although there are some unusual circumstances in which they may conflict. As a general rule, the net-present-value method is normally chosen when a conflict arises because its underlying assumptions are most often consistent with reality. The problem of uncertainty in a capital budgeting context is normally dealt with by assigning higher discount rates to riskier projects.

KEY POINTS

NET PRESENT VALUE $NPV = PVB - PVC$

If positive, accept.
If negative, reject.

NPV = net present value
PVB = present value of benefits
PVC = present value of costs

INTERNAL RATE OF RETURN   IRR = discount rate that will drive
NPV to zero
If IRR ≥ cost of capital, accept.
If IRR < cost of capital, reject.

PROFITABILITY INDEX $PI = PVB/PVC$
If PI ≥ 1.0, accept.
If PI < 1.0, reject.

CONFLICTING RANKING   Rare, but if conflicting ranking
occurs, NPV is generally preferred.

13

Cost of Capital

The capital budgeting and time value of money concepts presented in the two preceding chapters illustrate the key role of the cost of capital in making long-term investment decisions. This chapter will examine the techniques used to measure the cost of capital and explore the uses of the cost of capital in capital budgeting and capital structure management.

COST OF CAPITAL DEFINED

The *cost of capital* to a firm may be loosely defined as the percentage cost of permanent funds employed in the business—that is, the percentage cost of the firm's capital structure. The *capital structure* is the mix of long-term debt and equity employed by the firm for its permanent financing needs. A useful way to visualize the capital structure is to recast the traditional balance sheet format so that a firm is conceived of as having only two categories of assets—net working capital and fixed assets. Since net working capital is defined as current assets minus current liabilities, the "revised" right-hand side of the balance sheet will represent the firm's capital structure. This conception envisions a firm as having two categories of assets and two categories of financing for these assets—long-term debt and equity. Exhibit 13.1 illustrates this conception.

The right-hand side of the reconstructed balance sheet in Exhibit 13.1 represents the "mix" of a company's permanent financing. The cost of this capital structure is critically important to the firm in managing its capital structure and in making capital budgeting decisions. In general, two costs of capital are of interest to the firm. The first is the *average cost of capital* (ACC), which is defined as the weighted

EXHIBIT 13.1 SAMPLE RESTRUCTURED BALANCE SHEET

Net working capital	Long-term debt

Fixed assets	Equity

average after-tax cost of new capital raised during a given year. The cost of new capital is the relevant cost to the company because the analysis of current financial decisions requires that one focus on current costs. As will be explained in detail later in this chapter, the average cost of capital is primarily of interest for capital structure management.

The second cost of interest is the *marginal cost of capital* (MCC). The average cost is equal to the marginal cost over some range of capital raised, beyond which both costs begin to rise. This is so because the marginal cost of capital represents the incremental ACC as a function of the total dollar amount of capital raised. In other words, as more and more capital is raised, the cost of this capital begins to increase. The increased cost will occur in increments so that at the margin the cost of an additional dollar of capital will be greater than the average cost of capital. This marginal cost will, of course, also increase the average cost, but the average cost will increase more slowly. When evaluating capital budgeting decisions, it is this marginal cost that should be used as the appropriate cost of capital.

The relationship between the average and marginal costs of capital may be seen more clearly by making an analogy to average and marginal tax rates. Suppose, for example, that the corporate tax rate is set at 15 percent on the first $50,000 of income, then rises to 25 percent on the next $25,000, and is 35 percent on all income above $75,000. If a corporation earned $50,000 before taxes, a tax of $7,500 would be due. The corporation's average and marginal tax rate would be 15 percent. However, on the next dollar earned, the corporation's marginal rate would jump to 25 percent, because income above $50,000 is taxed at 25 percent. At $60,000 income, a total tax of $10,000 would be due. This is an average tax rate of 16.67 percent

EXHIBIT 13.2   COST OF CAPITAL CURVES

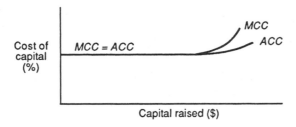

($10,000/$60,000) but a marginal rate of 25 percent (the tax rate on income above $50,000). Above $75,000, the marginal rate would jump again, to 35 percent.

The same general pattern holds for corporate cost of capital. As more capital is raised, the cost increases at the margin, increasing the marginal cost in increments. The average cost then increases at a slower rate and eventually approaches the marginal cost. Exhibit 13.2 illustrates this process. Note that the average cost is equal to the marginal cost over some range of capital raised, beyond which both costs begin to rise. This is so because capital may be raised at a constant cost over a range but then becomes more and more expensive as more and more capital is sought.

MARGINAL COST AND CAPITAL BUDGETING

The marginal cost of capital is the capital cost that should be used for making capital budgeting decisions. This leads a firm toward making capital budgeting decisions based on a comparison of the cost of each additional dollar of capital raised with the expected rate of return on each additional dollar of capital invested. In terms of internal-rate-of-return calculations, the firm should accept all available investment projects where the internal rate of return is greater than or equal to the marginal cost of capital. Such a policy will maximize the value of the firm. In economic terms, the firm will invest up to the point where the marginal rate of return (IRR on the last project selected) is equal to the marginal cost of capital.

Exhibit 13.3 illustrates the capital budgeting process. The line labeled *IRR* is the investment-opportunity schedule. This schedule represents the rank ordering of all available investment projects in

EXHIBIT 13.3   MARGINAL COST OF CAPITAL AND INTERNAL RATE OF RETURN

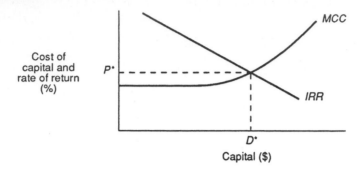

order of the magnitude of each project's IRR. The line therefore decreases as a function of the dollars of capital invested. The curve labeled *MCC* represents the firm's marginal cost of capital, an increasing function of the dollars of capital raised. The point at which the IRR and MCC intersect indicates the optimal size of the firm's capital budget (denoted $D*$ on the graph) and the firm's marginal cost of capital for that size capital budget (denoted $P*$ on the graph).

CALCULATING THE AVERAGE COST OF CAPITAL

To calculate a given company's weighted average after-tax cost of capital, one must first calculate the after-tax cost of its individual capital components. The average of the component costs, weighted by the percentage that each comprises of the total capital structure, is then calculated. The cost of debt and preferred stock is relatively easy to calculate, but estimating the cost of equity is somewhat difficult.

Cost of Debt

The before-tax cost of debt is simply the interest paid divided by the principal amount borrowed. To convert this cost to an after-tax basis, the before-tax cost is multiplied by 1 minus the firm's effective tax rate. Since every dollar of interest paid is tax deductible, 1 minus the tax rate represents the percentage of the interest that is paid by the

firm after taking into account the tax deductibility of interest payments. The tax rate multiplied by the dollars of interest paid represents the amount of interest that is "paid" through tax savings. The
effective after-tax cost of debt is thus:

$$K_d = \frac{I}{P}(1-T)$$

where K_d = after-tax cost of debt
I = interest in dollars
P = principal amount borrowed
T = effective tax rate

If a firm raises debt capital by selling bonds publicly, then some
sales costs will be incurred. Such costs may run from as little as one-
quarter of 1 percent of the amount of debt issued for a large bond
issue by a major corporation to as high as 3 percent or more for small
issues or issues of non–investment-grade debt. These costs, called
flotation costs, represent the cost of taking the issue public and include such expenses as legal research, underwriting expenses, and
salespersons' commissions. Since many flotation costs are fixed
costs, flotation costs as a percentage of the size of the issue become
larger as the issue size becomes smaller. Taking a very small issue
public can be very expensive.

A simple adjustment to the after-tax cost of debt calculation can
be made to account for flotation costs. Letting F equal the flotation
costs as a percentage of the face value of the bond issue, the revised
equation is:

$$K_d = \frac{I}{P(1-F)}(1-T)$$

In this revised equation, the principal amount on which interest is
calculated is simply reduced by the amount of the flotation costs. For
example, if flotation costs equal 1 percent, the principal amount received on a $10,000,000 bond issue would be $9,900,000 [$10,000,000
times (1 – .01)]. Much business debt is privately placed with banks,
insurance companies, or other financial institutions so that flotation
costs are not incurred. Flotation costs are only of concern for publicly marketed issues and private issues where a broker is involved.

Cost of Preferred Stock

If a firm has any preferred stock in its capital structure, calculating the cost of this preferred stock is quite simple. Since preferred stock is an equity security, dividends represent profit distributions to the owners of the corporation and are therefore not tax deductible to the corporation. Thus, the before-tax cost of preferred stock is the same as the after-tax cost and is calculated as follows:

$$K_p = \frac{D}{P}$$

where K_p = cost of preferred stock
D = dividend in dollars
P = price of preferred stock

For newly issued preferred stock that is publicly marketed, flotation costs must be considered. The adjustment is comparable to that made for the cost of debt:

$$K_p = \frac{D}{P(1 - F)}$$

Cost of Common Equity

The final cost to be calculated is the cost of common equity. Whereas the costs of debt and preferred stock may be calculated with some degree of precision, the cost of common stock must be estimated. A detailed development of the relevant financial theory is beyond the scope of this book. However, we may in general define the cost of equity as the rate of return stockholders require on equity capital— that is, the rate of return on equity that the firm must earn in order to maintain the value of its common stock. Stated alternatively, we may define the cost of equity as the expected rate of return necessary to induce investors to invest in a firm's common stock.

The stockholders' expected rate of return has two components— an expected dividend yield and an expected capital gain. If we let K_e represent the cost of equity, K_e may be defined as follows:

K_e = Expected dividend yield + Expected capital gain

Attempting to quantify this relationship, we may use a company's dividend divided by its price as the dividend yield and the expected growth rate of earnings and dividends as a measure of the expected capital gain, resulting in the following formulation:

$$K_e = \frac{D}{P} + g$$

where K_e = cost of equity
D = dividend in dollars
P = price of stock
g = expected growth rate

This formulation is adequate to measure the cost of equity capital generated by reinvested earnings. This measurement is generally accepted as the cost of the retained earnings portion of equity capital. To measure the cost of equity capital generated through new issues of common stock, the equation must be adjusted for flotation costs as follows:

$$K_e = \frac{D}{P(1-F)} + g$$

A Computational Example

To illustrate these definitions, assume that we wish to calculate the average cost of capital for a firm having a capital structure consisting of 40 percent debt, 10 percent preferred stock, and 50 percent equity. Assume further that debt bears interest at 8 percent, that preferred stock pays an $8 dividend and is priced at $100 (its par value), and that common stock sells for $55, paying a dividend of $2.20. Finally, assume that the expected growth rate of earnings and dividends is 9 percent and that the firm's effective tax rate is 34 percent. Newly issued debt and preferred stock will be privately placed. Required equity capital will be generated through reinvested earnings. Hence, no flotation costs will be incurred.

Exhibit 13.4 illustrates the required calculations. The cost of debt is 5.3 percent after tax. The cost of preferred stock is 8 percent. The cost of common equity is 13 percent—the 4 percent dividend yield plus the 9 percent growth rate. Multiplying each component cost by

EXHIBIT 13.4   COST OF CAPITAL COMPUTATIONAL EXAMPLE

1.
$$K_d = \frac{I}{P}(1 - T)$$
$$K_d = (8\%)(1 - 0.34) = 5.3\%$$

2.
$$K_p = \frac{\$8}{\$100} = 8\%$$

3.
$$K_e = \frac{D}{P} + g$$
$$= \frac{\$2.20}{\$55.00} + 9\%$$
$$= 4\% + 9\% = 13\%$$

CAPITAL COMPONENT	PERCENTAGE OF CAPITAL STRUCTURE	COST	PRODUCT (PERCENTAGE × COST)
Debt	0.40	5.3%	2.12%
Preferred stock	0.10	8.0%	0.80%
Common equity	0.50	13.0%	6.50%
	Weighted average cost		9.42%

the percentage of the capital structure it comprises and summing the results yields a weighted average cost of capital of 9.42 percent.

THE CAPITAL ASSET PRICING MODEL

The *capital asset pricing model* (CAPM) is one of the most important theoretical developments in finance during the past fifty years. Although the CAPM was originally developed in the area of investment analysis, it has been applied in the field of corporate finance. One major application has been to use the CAPM to measure the cost of equity capital.

The essential elements of the CAPM are actually quite simple and easily understood. The CAPM states that the stockholders' required rate of return on equity capital is a function of the risk-free rate of return, the rate of return earned on stocks in general (the "market return"), and the riskiness of the particular stock in which an investor may be considering investing. In particular, the CAPM states that K_e is equal to the risk-free rate plus a risk premium. The risk premium is determined by the riskiness of the particular stock relative to the market and by the difference between the market rate of return and the risk-free rate.

The riskiness of the individual stock is measured by the stock's *beta factor*, which is simply a measure of the volatility of the stock relative to the market. A beta of 1.0 would indicate that the stock has the same volatility as the market. A beta of 0.5 would indicate that the stock is about half as volatile as the market. A beta of 2.0 would indicate that the stock is approximately twice as volatile as the market. Statistically, a stock's beta is normally estimated by regressing the stock's price against the level of some broad market index, such as the Standard and Poor's Index of 500 Common Stocks (S&P 500). The beta factor is the slope of the regression line and also a measure of the company's systematic risk (risk that cannot be diversified away).

In equation form, the CAPM is as follows:

$$K_e = R_f + (R_m - R_f)B$$
where K_e = cost of equity capital
R_f = risk-free rate of return
R_m = market rate of return
B = beta

To actually measure K_e, some measure of R_f and R_m must be selected. In most cases, R_f is taken to be the rate of return on ninety-one-day Treasury bills. For all practical purposes, these securities are risk-free. The market rate of return is normally measured as the rate of return on some broad market index, such as the S&P 500. Beta is measured as previously defined.

It is important to reemphasize that K_e is an estimate, not a precise calculation. The CAPM approach to estimation may be employed as a supplement to the conventional means of estimating K_e previously described. Neither method is necessarily more accurate than the other. Taken together, they may be applied jointly to produce a better estimate of the cost of equity capital.

CAPITAL STRUCTURE MANAGEMENT

As mentioned earlier, the average cost of capital is of primary interest for capital structure management. If one is willing to accept the premise that the cost of capital may be approached from the perspective of the capital markets, it must follow that the cost of equity capital for a given corporation must be greater than the cost of debt for that corporation. The reason is quite simple: Investing in equity is riskier than investing in debt. If investors are to invest in the equity securities of a given corporation, they must demand a higher rate of return on equity than on debt because the equity investment is riskier than investment in debt securities. For example, if an investor is anticipating an investment in General Electric, GE common stock would have to offer a higher anticipated rate of return than GE bonds because the stock dividend and anticipated capital gain do not carry the guarantee that the payment on GE's bonds carries, the GE stock would bear the "first loss" in a bankruptcy, and GE's stock price tends to be more volatile than its bond prices. Thus, the stock investment is riskier. Since investors are generally averse to risk, the anticipated rate of return on the stock must exceed the rate of return on the bond.

Given that the cost of equity, K_e, is greater than the cost of debt, K_d, capital structure management focuses on finding an appropriate combination of debt and equity such that the combined weighted average cost of capital is minimized. Exhibit 13.5 illustrates the problem. If we measure the degree of leverage employed by a firm as the ratio of debt to total assets, it can be seen that both K_e and K_d vary as a function of leverage. Specifically, both costs are constant over a fairly broad range, but at some point they begin to increase as leverage gets higher. Once again, risk is the cause of the increase. As the firm becomes increasingly debt-heavy, the increased risk of insolvency drives up both the cost of debt (return to creditors) and the cost of equity (return to stockholders).

EXHIBIT 13.5   THEORY OF OPTIMAL CAPITAL STRUCTURE

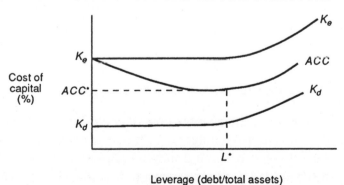

Leverage (debt/total assets)

As can be seen from the exhibit, if the firm is 100 percent equity financed (leverage = 0), its average cost of capital is at a maximum. If the firm moves from 100 percent equity financing to some usage of debt financing, it is effectively combining relatively expensive equity with relatively inexpensive debt. The result of this mix is to reduce the weighted average cost of capital. The weighted average cost of capital is shown in the exhibit as the curve labeled ACC.

The ACC curve decreases with increasing leverage up to the point at which K_e and K_d both begin to rise. After this point, the ACC curve also begins to rise. Thus, the ACC curve declines to a minimum point and then increases thereafter. The minimum point on this curve is denoted L^* on the graph. This point represents the leverage position that will minimize the firm's weighted average cost of capital, denoted ACC^* in the graph. The point at which L^* is located is known as the firm's optimal capital structure and represents the optimal mix of debt and equity.

In theory, this point may be located exactly by simply finding the equation that describes the ACC curve and locating the minimum point on the curve. In practice, however, one must realize that although the conceptual relationships portrayed in the graph are valid, the ACC curve tends to be flat over a fairly broad range. Thus, the optimal-capital-structure theory is useful primarily as a broad policy guideline. Effective capital structure management requires that the financial manager attempt to provide a capital structure mix that is within this "range of optimality."

One point of interest with respect to the optimal-capital-structure theory is that the location of the range of optimality varies with the riskiness of the particular industry within which the financial manager is operating. Thus, for example, an electrical utility can carry a much higher level of debt before its cost curves turn up than can an aerospace company. In general, the higher the business risk in the industry, the less leverage a firm may employ before the cost curves turn up. Also, riskier firms will have cost curves that are higher to begin with.

SUMMARY

A firm's capital structure is the mix of long-term debt and equity employed by the firm to meet permanent financing needs. The cost of capital is the percentage cost of these permanent funds. The average cost of capital (ACC) is defined as the weighted average after-tax cost of new capital raised in a given year. The marginal cost of capital (MCC) is the weighted average after-tax cost of the last dollar of new capital raised in a given year; the MCC is thus the ACC at the margin. The marginal cost of capital is the discount rate that should be used in making capital budgeting decisions. The average cost of capital is primarily of interest in capital structure management. Capital structure management requires the selection of the mix of debt and equity that will minimize the firm's average cost of capital.

The capital asset pricing model (CAPM) states that the rate of return on equity capital is a function of the risk-free rate of return, the rate of return earned on stocks in general, and the riskiness of an individual stock. In particular, the CAPM states that the return on equity capital is equal to the risk-free rate plus a risk premium, where the risk premium is determined by the riskiness of the stock relative to the market and by the difference between the market rate of return and the risk-free rate.

KEY POINTS

CAPITAL STRUCTURE Mix of long-term debt and equity

AVERAGE COST OF CAPITAL Weighted average after-tax cost of new capital raised during a given year

MARGINAL COST OF CAPITAL Weighted average after-tax cost of each additional dollar of new capital raised during a given year

MCC Cost of capital for capital budgeting analysis

ACC Cost of capital for capital structure management

COST OF DEBT $K_d = \frac{I}{P}(1-T)$

(no flotation costs)

$$K_d = \frac{I}{P(1-F)}(1-T)$$

(with flotation costs)

COST OF PREFERRED STOCK $K_p = \frac{D}{P}$

(no flotation costs)

$$K_p = \frac{D}{P(1-F)}$$

(with flotation costs)

COST OF EQUITY $K_e = \frac{D}{P} + g$

(retained earnings)

$$K_e = \frac{D}{P(1-F)} + g$$

(new common stock)

CAPM $K_e = R_f + (R_m - R_f)\,B$

PART VI

Long-Term Financing Decisions

14

Valuation of Financial Assets

In the last chapter, we explored how to determine a firm's cost of capital. We now apply that work to valuing financial assets.

CAPITALIZATION-OF-INCOME METHOD

A *financial asset* may be defined as a security, such as a share of stock or a bond, that establishes a claim against the future income or assets of the issuer. In financial terms, the value of any financial asset depends on the earning power of that asset. In particular, the value of a financial asset may be determined as the discounted present value of expected future cash flows earned on that asset. This widely accepted valuation method, called the *capitalization-of-income method*, is conceptually straightforward and intuitively appealing.

It is necessary to focus on two areas of concern in applying the capitalization-of-income method. The first concern is determining the appropriate earnings to be capitalized; the second is determining the appropriate capitalization rate. This chapter will address the problems of valuing bonds, preferred stock, and common stock. The valuation principles developed in this chapter also can be applied to virtually any other type of asset, including real assets such as real estate, oil and gas drilling ventures, and closely held businesses. We will explore the valuation of closely held businesses in detail in Chapter 15.

SELECTING APPROPRIATE CAPITALIZATION RATES

Selecting an appropriate capitalization rate for valuing a financial asset is analogous to selecting an appropriate discount rate for capital budgeting purposes. The first step is to define the appropriate capitalization rate (K) as the minimum rate of return necessary to induce investors to buy or hold a given financial asset. Stated alternatively (and equivalently), given the risk characteristics of a particular investment opportunity or security, K is the minimum expected rate of return required to induce investors to accept that investment.

A large body of empirical evidence supports the position that, at least for investment securities, the relationship between risk and the rate of return on financial assets is approximately linear. The capital asset pricing model (CAPM), introduced in the last chapter, is the formal statement of the body of theory known as capital asset pricing theory. According to the CAPM, the higher the risk involved in investing in an asset, the higher will be the minimum expected rate of return necessary to induce investors to invest in that asset. Thus, the appropriate capitalization rate for any financial asset is a function of the riskiness of the asset.

The details of capital asset pricing theory are well beyond the scope of this book. However, a conceptual understanding of the CAPM is not at all difficult. Risk may be measured in terms of beta risk (as was shown in Chapter 13 for equity securities) or may be more broadly defined. One widely accepted measure of risk defines risk as the standard deviation of expected future returns.* Statistically, the standard deviation measures the expected variability around the expected future rate of return: the higher the variability, the higher the standard deviation and the higher the risk. The capital market line (CML), derived from capital asset pricing theory, is a graphic representation of the risk/return trade-off line. In particular, the CAPM states that the appropriate capitalization rate (K) should be equal to the risk-free rate (R_f) plus a risk premium. The risk-free rate is by definition the intercept of the CML, since this is the return that should be earned when the standard deviation is zero—that is, when there is no risk. The risk premium is a function of the standard deviation of ex-

---

*Computational details for the standard deviation may be found in any standard statistics text.

EXHIBIT 14.1   THE CAPITAL MARKET LINE

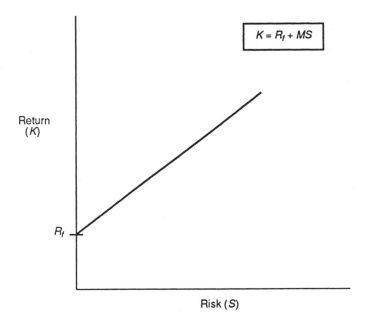

pected future returns (S). Letting M stand for the slope of the CML, we can see from Exhibit 14.1 that the equation for the line is:

$$K = R_f + MS$$

What determines the risk-free rate and the slope of the CML? As noted in Chapter 13, R_f is generally measured as the short-term Treasury bill rate. The rate of return on short-term Treasury bills is highly responsive to inflation. In fact, in the post–World War II period, the short-term T-bill rate has been very close to the rate of increase in the Consumer Price Index. Thus, increased inflation causes the intercept of the CML to shift upward, and decreased inflation causes the intercept of the CML to shift downward.

The slope of the CML reflects investors' attitudes toward risk. Increased economic uncertainty causes an increase in investors' risk aversion, which in turn causes an increase in M. Thus, greater risk aversion causes the CML curve to become steeper. A decrease in economic uncertainty allows the CML curve to become flatter.

The net result of the various forces on the CML is that the appropriate capitalization rate, K, for any particular financial asset is a dynamic concept. The capitalization rate depends on the general level of inflation and interest rates, the risk involved in the particular investment being considered, and investors' attitudes toward risk. Thus, as a theoretical proposition, K must be determined by determining the slope and intercept of the CML curve on the date the valuation is undertaken.

The CML may be estimated empirically by using regression analysis. Alternatively, one may simply accept the "going rate" for a particular asset as the appropriate K. For example, if the future cash flows from twenty-year, AAA-rated corporate bonds were to be capitalized, one might consult Standard and Poor's Bond Guide to determine the average rate of return currently being earned on such bonds. This rate could be used as the appropriate K. One might also determine K as a judgmentally derived "hurdle rate"—that is, the minimum rate of return acceptable for a particular investment as judged by the individual or organization doing the valuation.

The remainder of the valuation discussion in this chapter assumes that K has been determined in an acceptable manner. Once an appropriate K has been determined, valuation becomes a process of determining the discounted present value of expected future cash flows.

BOND VALUATION

Bond valuation is a relatively straightforward process. For regular, "bullet" bonds, there are two cash flows: the cash flow provided by the semiannual interest payments and the cash flow provided by the repayment of the bond par value at maturity. Since bond interest is almost always paid semiannually, the discount rate used in valuing a bond is one-half the appropriate annual bond-capitalization rate, and the number of discount periods used will be twice the number of years to maturity. The value of a bond is equal to the present value of the future interest payments plus the present value of the par value received at maturity. The value of any particular bond may be found by using present-value tables (such as those in Chapter 11), by using specially constructed bond-valuation tables, or by using any business calculator or spreadsheet software. If we use the notation introduced in Chapter 11, the equation for the value of a bond is as follows:

$$V = C\left[\frac{1 - 1/\left(1 + \frac{K}{2}\right)^{2n}}{\frac{K}{2}}\right] + P\left[\frac{1}{\left(1 + \frac{K}{2}\right)^{2n}}\right]$$

where V = value of bond

C = semiannual coupon interest payments

K = annual capitalization rate, compounded semiannually

n = number of years to maturity

P = par value of bond received at maturity

The first term in the equation represents the present value of an annuity of n years' duration discounted semiannually at the rate of $K/2$. This figure is the present value of the semiannual coupon-interest payments. The second term in the equation represents the present value of the par value of the bond to be received n years ($n/2$ periods) from now.

Thus, for example, suppose the appropriate capitalization rate for AAA-rated corporate bonds is 12 percent, compounded semiannually. What is the value of a seasoned AAA-rated bond with a par value of $1,000, an 8 percent coupon rate ($40 paid semiannually), and twenty years to maturity? Using the bond-valuation equation, the value is:

$$V = \$40\left[\frac{1 - 1/\left(1 + .06\right)^{40}}{.06}\right] + \$1,000\left[\frac{1}{\left(1 + .06\right)^{40}}\right]$$

$$= (\$40)(15.0463) + (\$1,000)(.0972)$$

$$= \$601.85 + \$97.20$$

$$= \$699.05$$

A more common use of the bond-valuation equation is to determine the yield to maturity on a bond that is available at a known price. In this case, the same bond-valuation equation is used, but V, C, n, and P are treated as given, and the equation is solved for K, the discount rate. The yield to maturity on the bond is then the effective annual yield at K percent, compounded semiannually. In the previous example the yield to maturity would be 12.36 percent, the effective rate of return from 12 percent compounded semiannually: $(1.06)^2 - 1$.

Since it is extremely difficult to solve for K directly using the bond-valuation equation, calculators or spreadsheet software is typically used to perform the calculations.

Zero Coupon Bonds

Zero coupon bonds began to gain popularity in the early 1980s, first through synthetically created zeros by Merrill Lynch and then Salomon Brothers and later by the U.S. Treasury directly through so-called Strips. These bonds, in contrast to bullet bonds, are originally sold at a discount from par value and pay full par value at maturity. The bonds have no coupons and pay no current interest. From an investor's point of view, zero coupon bonds offer a very attractive feature: They eliminate the reinvestment risk. The reinvestment risk is the risk that one may not be able to reinvest the coupon payments received from a conventional bond at the same rate that the bond is earning. This risk is particularly important during periods of high interest rates. An investor buying a newly issued 10 percent bond at par, for example, will not actually earn a 10 percent yield to maturity unless the future cash interest payments can be reinvested at 10 percent. Since there are no cash interest payments to be reinvested on a zero coupon bond, this risk is eliminated.

During periods of high interest rates, zero coupon bonds also offer an advantage to the issuer. Because the bond eliminates the reinvestment risk, investors will accept a lower rate of return on a zero coupon bond than they would accept on a conventional bond. A zero coupon bond therefore lowers the issuer's interest costs. Since the issuer's future repayment obligation is very large relative to the cash proceeds of a zero coupon issue, zero coupon bonds often have a sinking fund provision. In periods of low interest rates, the opposite is true, and rates on zero coupon bonds tend to be higher than bullet bonds.

Unfortunately, the Internal Revenue Service has taken the position that amortization of the discount on a zero coupon bond is taxable as if current interest were being paid. Hence, zero coupon bonds are generally suitable only for nontaxable investors such as corporate pension funds or individuals' IRA or 401(k) plans. Some municipalities issue zero coupon bonds, and these nontaxable bonds may be suitable for individuals.

Zero coupon bonds may be valued like any other financial asset. The present value of a zero coupon bond is simply the present value of the par value paid at maturity. For example, the present value of a ten-year, $1,000 par, 12 percent zero coupon bond is as follows:

$$V = (\$1,000)\left[\frac{1}{(1.12)^{10}}\right]$$

$$= (\$1,000)(0.3220)$$

$$= \$322$$

PREFERRED STOCK VALUATION

Since preferred stock has no maturity date, preferred-stock dividends go on forever—at least in theory. Thus, the value of a share of preferred stock is the present value of the dividend payment from the date of purchase to infinity. Discounting out to infinity does not seem so unreasonable when two factors are considered. First, although no corporation will exist for an infinite number of years, there are corporations that have existed for fifty or more years and can be expected to survive for another fifty or more years. Second, "economic infinity" for discounting purposes is not as far away in time as the word *infinity* implies. Assuming a 12 percent discount rate, for example, the present value of $1.00 worth of dividends to be received fifty years from now is $0.003. At sixty years, the present value of $1.00 drops to $0.001—a small enough figure to be disregarded. Thus, at a 12 percent discount rate, economic infinity occurs about fifty years into the next century.

Mathematically, assuming (for simplicity) that dividends are paid annually, the value of a share of preferred stock is:

$$V = \frac{D}{(1+K)} + \frac{D}{(1+K)^2} + \frac{D}{(1+K)^3} + \dots + \frac{D}{(1+K)^\infty}$$

where V = value of preferred stock
D = annual dividend payment
K = appropriate capitalization rate
∞ = infinity

The preferred-stock-valuation equation is an infinite series. Since the present value of each year's dividend gets smaller each year, the equation is an infinite series of decreasing numbers. Such a series may be summed mathematically by applying a technique for determining the sum of an infinite series. In this case, the sum of the preferred-stock-dividend series is:

$$V = \frac{D}{K}$$

Thus, for example, if K is 12 percent, the value of a share of preferred stock paying an $8.00 annual dividend is:

$$V = \frac{\$8.00}{0.12}$$
$$= \$66.67$$

The meaning of the $66.67 figure is that at a price of $66.67, a share of preferred stock paying an $8.00 dividend provides an annual yield of 12 percent from now to infinity.

Preferred stocks are riskier investments than bonds because, unlike bond-interest payments, preferred-stock dividends are not guaranteed and because, in a liquidation, preferred stock is junior to debt in priority. This risk differential would normally cause market-capitalization rates for preferred stock to be higher than that for bonds. However, this is not always the case: Market-capitalization rates for preferred stock are often lower than bond-capitalization rates. The reason for this stems from the tax code. Recall from Chapter 2 that 70 percent or more of stock dividends paid to a corporation are tax-free. Dividends paid by corporations that are not Real Estate Investment Trusts or other types of pass-through entities are subject to tax at the long-term capital gains rate, which, in recent years, has been significantly lower than the highest personal marginal income tax rate. Bond interest, on the other hand, is fully taxable at the highest marginal rate. Thus, a dollar's worth of preferred dividends is worth much more than a dollar's worth of bond interest to a corporation or an individual investor. As a result, investors are willing to accept a lower pretax yield on preferred stocks than on bonds. The market activities of these corporations therefore frequently result in lower pretax capitalization rates for preferred stocks than for bonds, unless the issuing company is deemed risky enough that the value of a guaranteed interest payment and priority in bankruptcy exceeds the tax benefit of the preferred dividend. Remember, however, that a company may still choose to issue debt if the after-tax rate on the debt is below the after-tax rate on the preferred stock.

COMMON STOCK VALUATION

Expected cash flows from common stocks come in two forms: dividends received over an investor's stock-holding period and the price expected to be received when the stock is sold. The nature of these cash flows presents two major concerns from a valuation standpoint. First, for most corporations, earnings and dividends per share are expected to increase over time. Hence, expected future dividends will not be a constant annual amount, as is the case with preferred-stock dividends and bond interest. It is therefore not possible to use standard annuity formulas for common-stock valuation because calculating the present value of an annuity requires that cash flows be a constant annual amount.

The second major concern stems from the uncertainty surrounding the expected future dividend payments and expected future stock price. Common-stock dividends are never guaranteed, and the price of the stock is subject to even more uncertainty than the amount of the dividend payments. As recent history has clearly shown, stock prices do fluctuate (sometimes significantly!). The price at which a share of stock will be selling in the future will depend primarily on the earning power of the corporation at that time and on the general state of the stock market and the national economy. Uncertainty is normally handled in the valuation process by assigning a higher capitalization rate to common stocks than to bonds or preferred stocks.

A number of valuation models have been developed that attempt to deal with the special valuation problems posed by common stocks. Most of the models are based on the premise that common-stock values are a function of expected future cash flows from dividends and the expected future value of the stock. One widely accepted model views the value of a share of common stock as ultimately dependent on the dividend-paying capacity of the corporation.

A simple intuitive explanation of the model begins with the observation that the present value of a share of stock (P_0) is equal to the present value of the next year's dividend (D_1) plus the present value of the stock's price at the end of the next year (P_1). However, the price of stock at the end of year 1 is equal to the present value of the dividend to be received in year 2 (D_2) plus the present value of the price at the end of year 2 (P_2). P_2 is in turn equal to the present value of D_3 plus the present value of P_3. The argument continues that the price at the end of any year is always equal to the present value of the following year's dividend and price. As the price is pushed further and further out to economic infinity, the present value of the terminal price (the price in the final year) becomes zero for valuation purposes.

Obviously, no individual investor expects to hold a stock to infinity. However, from the point of view of the value of a stock in the capital market, the time horizons of any particular investor are irrelevant. What is relevant is the fact that the value of any financial asset is equal to the present value of future cash flows. Since the stock will theoretically exist forever, and as a practical matter may well exist until economic infinity, the only cash flows that will be received from a share of common stock are the dividends. Hence, the present value of a share of common stock is equal to the present value of future expected dividends from now until infinity.

Like that of preferred stock, the value of common stock is thus the sum of an infinite series of dividends. Unlike preferred stock, however, the dividends are not constant. Two simplifying assumptions, both of which may be relaxed in applying the model, must be made in order to sum the infinite series of growing dividends. First, it must be assumed that dividends will grow at a constant rate. Second, it must be assumed that this constant growth rate will be less than the capitalization rate that will be applied to value the stream of growing dividends. Then, applying the rule for the sum of an infinite series results in the following formulation for the value of a share of common stock:

$$P_0 = \frac{D_1}{K - g}$$

where P_0 = present value of a share of common stock
D_1 = expected dividend in year 1
K = appropriate capitalization rate
g = expected future growth rate of dividends

A simple example will illustrate the application of the model. Suppose that XYZ common stock is expected to pay a dividend of $2.16 in the coming year and that this dividend is expected to increase at an average annual rate of 8 percent per year for the foreseeable future. Suppose further that the appropriate capitalization rate for stocks in XYZ's risk category is 15 percent. What is the present value of XYZ's common stock? Applying the dividend-capitalization model yields the following result:

$$
\begin{aligned}
P_0 &= \frac{\$2.16}{0.15 - 0.08} \\
&= \frac{\$2.16}{0.07} \\
&= 30.86
\end{aligned}
$$

If the expected future growth rate is not constant, then the model must be modified. In this case, each future year's expected dividend must be discounted separately out to the year for which it is estimated that dividend growth will "settle down" to some constant rate. The value of the stock at the end of the last year of irregular growth can then be determined using the dividend-capitalization model. The present value of the stock price at the end of the irregular growth period plus the present value of the dividends received during the irregular growth period will equal the present value of the stock.

If the growth rate exceeds the capitalization rate, a similar procedure is followed. Simple logic dictates that a corporation cannot be expected to grow indefinitely at a rate substantially in excess of the average growth rate of the national economy. If it did, it would eventually have to acquire all other corporations. For a corporation temporarily experiencing supernormal growth, the value of the dividends received during that period must be discounted separately. The value of the stock at the end of the supernormal growth period can then be determined using the model. The present value of the stock is then the present value of the dividends received during the supernormal growth period plus the present value of stock price at the end of the same period.

Finally, what of the case of the stock that pays no dividends? There are many such stocks selling for positive prices in the market. Capitalizing dividends obviously presents a problem. The solution to this problem is to estimate when in the future the company will be able to start paying dividends. The value of the stock at that time can then be determined using the dividend-capitalization model. This value is then discounted back to the present to determine the present value of the stock.

Exhibit 14.2 illustrates the application of the dividend-capitalization model to three cases: the no-growth stock, the normal growth stock, and the supernormal growth stock. The resulting stock values show why high-growth companies typically sell at higher multiples of earnings (price/earnings, or P/E ratios) than do lower-growth stocks: Growing dividends impart more value to the stock price. The example also shows why high-growth stocks normally have much lower dividend yields than low-growth stocks. The value of the growth potential of a high-growth stock drives up the price of the stock and thus drives down the dividend payment as a percentage of the stock price.

Intrinsic Values and Market Values

As noted, there is a wide variety of common-stock valuation models, and different investors may use different models and different sets of assumptions. The value of a share of stock as determined by a valuation model is called its *intrinsic value*. If everyone used the same model and the same set of assumptions, then all market participants would value the stock at the same price, and the market price would equal the intrinsic value. When the market price equals the intrinsic value, the stock price is said to be in *equilibrium*. Changes in market-capitalization rates used by investors or changes in the growth outlook for the stock would cause the intrinsic value and the market price to fluctuate.

The traditional approach to security analysis is for an analyst to compare his or her intrinsic value estimate to the current market price of a stock. If the market price is less than the intrinsic value, the stock is said to be *undervalued* and should be purchased. If the stock is currently priced above its intrinsic value, then it is said to be *overvalued* and should be sold (or, for the aggressive investor, sold short). If the stock is priced at its intrinsic value, it is in equilibrium and may be held or purchased.

Beginning in the 1970s, a great deal of empirical evidence was developed to support a theory known as the *efficient markets hypothesis* (EMH). The EMH states that a large number of well-educated, professional market participants have access to essentially the same databases, that all of them analyze these data in essentially the same

EXHIBIT 14.2   APPLICATION OF THE DIVIDEND-CAPITALIZATION MODEL

Assumptions: The following assumptions apply to all cases:

(a) Earnings per share = $4.00
(b) Dividends per share = $2.00
(c) Appropriate capitalization rate = 12%

Case 1: no growth ($g = 0\%$)

$$P_0 = \frac{D_1}{K - g} = \frac{\$2.00}{0.12 - 0} = \$16.67$$

Case 2: normal growth ($g = 9\%$)

$$P_0 = \frac{D_1}{K - g} = \frac{(\$2.00)(1.09)}{0.12 - 0.09} = \frac{\$2.18}{0.03} = \$72.67$$

Case 3: supernormal growth ($g = 25\%$ for three years, 9% thereafter)

$$D_1 = (\$2.00)(1.25) = \$2.50$$
$$D_2 = (\$2.00)(1.25)^2 = \$3.13$$
$$D_3 = (\$2.00)(1.25)^3 = \$3.91$$

$$P_3 = \frac{D_4}{K - g} = \frac{(\$3.91)(1.09)}{0.12 - 0.09} = \$142.06$$

Note: P_3 is the value of the stock at the *end* of year 3.

$$P_0 = \frac{D_1}{(1 + K)} + \frac{D_2}{(1 + K)^2} + \frac{D_3}{(1 + K)^3} + \frac{P_3}{(1 + K)^3}$$

$$= \frac{\$2.50}{1.12} + \frac{\$3.13}{1.12^2} + \frac{\$3.91}{1.12^3} + \frac{\$142.06}{1.12^3}$$

$$= \$2.23 + \$2.50 + \$2.78 + \$101.12 = \$108.63$$

SUMMARY:	P₀	P/E RATIO	DIVIDEND YIELD
No growth	$ 16.67	4.2	12.0%
Normal growth	$ 72.67	18.2	2.8%
Supernormal growth	$108.63	27.2	1.8%

way, and that most draw essentially the same conclusions about the intrinsic value of most stocks. The market activities of these participants cause most stocks to be priced at their intrinsic values—that is, the price at which the rate of return earned on common-stock investment is commensurate with the risk involved in the investment. Hence, it is not possible to "beat the market" in the sense of earning an above-average rate of return.

Note that the EMH does not state that it is not possible to make money in the stock market. The hypothesis only states that it is not possible to consistently earn a rate of return above that implied by the market-capitalization rate appropriate for a given class of investment. The EMH has also been extended to other markets, including the bond and preferred-stock markets.

The empirical evidence relative to the EMH is not sufficiently strong to claim "proof" or "disproof" of the theory. The theory has gained very wide support in the academic community but less enthusiastic (or even hostile) reception among professional investors such as George Soros and Warren Buffett. Security analysts and portfolio managers who make their living by claiming to provide above-average risk-adjusted rates of return have been particularly skeptical of the theory. The only thing certain about the EMH is that it will continue to be controversial.

SUMMARY

The value of a financial asset is the present value of expected future cash flows from that asset. The appropriate discount rate, or capitalization rate, is the minimum rate of return necessary to induce investors to buy or hold that asset. According to the capital asset pricing theory, the higher the risk involved in investing in an asset, the higher will be the appropriate capitalization rate. The capital market line represents the linear risk/return trade-off for investment securities. The appropriate capitalization rate is the risk-free rate of return plus a risk premium ($K = R_f + MS$). The slope and intercept of the capital-market line shift as a result of shifts in investors' expectations for inflation, future economic uncertainty, and attitudes toward risk.

The value of a bond is the present value of future interest payments plus the present value of the par value paid at maturity. The value of a share of preferred stock is the value of the constant annual dividend payment divided by the capitalization rate. The value of a share of common stock is the present value of all expected future dividends, assumed to be growing at some rate g. The efficient market hypothesis, though disputed by some market gurus, maintains that the market prices of financial assets are normally in equilibrium.

KEY POINTS

CAPITALIZATION OF INCOME Value = present value of future cash flows

CAPITAL MARKET LINE $K = R_f + MS$

BOND VALUE

$$V = C\left[\frac{1 - 1/\left(1 + \dfrac{K}{2}\right)^{2n}}{\dfrac{K}{2}}\right] + P\left[\frac{1}{\left(1 + \dfrac{K}{2}\right)^{2n}}\right]$$

PREFERRED-STOCK VALUE $V = \dfrac{D}{K}$

COMMON-STOCK VALUE $V = \dfrac{D}{K - g}$

EFFICIENT MARKET HYPOTHESIS Financial asset market prices are set such that rates of return are commensurate with risk.

15
Valuing Closely Held Businesses

VALUATION PRINCIPLES

As seen in the previous chapter, one of the most common applications of the time value of money concept is the valuation of financial assets such as stocks and bonds. Virtually all economic models that value financial assets are based on the concept of value as the discounted present value of future cash flows. Valuing other assets, such as real estate or a closely held business, is ultimately based on the same general principles as valuing financial assets. (In this context, *closely held* refers to a business that is privately owned and does not issue publicly traded stocks or bonds.)

REVENUE RULING 59–60

One commonly used source of conceptual guidance for valuing closely held companies is the Internal Revenue Service's Revenue Ruling 59–60, which was originally made to provide guidelines for estate and gift tax valuation. This ruling is the source of the classic definition of *fair market value* as the price at which a property would change hands between a willing buyer and a willing seller when the former is under no compulsion to buy and the latter is under no compulsion to sell, with both parties having reasonable knowledge of the facts.

Revenue Ruling 59–60 specifies that in the valuation of closely held corporations or valuation of the stock of corporations for which market quotations are lacking or unreliable, all available financial data as well as all relevant factors affecting fair market value should be considered. The ruling specifies that the following eight factors, although not all-inclusive, are considered to be fundamental and require careful analysis in all cases:

- Nature and history of the business
- Company and industry economic outlook
- Financial condition of the business, including book value of the stock
- Earning capacity
- Dividend payment capacity
- Whether the company has goodwill or other intangible assets
- Prior sales of stock in the company and the size of the block to be offered
- Market prices of stocks of corporations engaged in the same or similar businesses that have stocks actively traded in free and open markets

Within the broad guidelines of Revenue Ruling 59–60, many approaches to valuation may be taken, and most appraisers provide a range of values based on several methods. The most basic approach to establishing a value for a company is simply to calculate the book value of the company (assets minus liabilities). Since assets on the balance sheet are based on historical cost (less depreciation for fixed assets), the shortcomings of this method are fairly obvious. A variant that overcomes the problems of relying on historical cost is the calculation of liquidation value, which is the estimated current market value of all assets minus all liabilities. Liquidation value tells us the amount that could be obtained by selling off all the company's assets and paying off all liabilities.

Rules of thumb also may be used in businesses where an established benchmark is commonly used to determine the value at which businesses change hands. In the management training business, for example, training companies commonly sell for one to one and a half times the current year's revenue. Small investment advisory practices commonly sell for three to four times the current year's revenue. Broad rules of thumb, such as ten or fifteen times earnings, also may be used as benchmarks. These rules of thumb, although seemingly unsophisticated, often are based on many years of experience in a particular industry and ultimately are related to what is considered to be a reasonable rate of return on invested capital in that industry.

One valuation method that is almost always used is some variation of a capitalization of income method. Capitalization of income simply requires the calculation of the discounted present value of some future income stream. Even a simple rule of thumb such as "ten times earnings" is a type of discounted present value. Mathematically, ten times earnings is the discounted present value of a constant future earnings stream from now to infinity at a discount rate of 10 percent. Considering that "financial infinity" occurs in about fifty years (the present value of one dollar received fifty years from now at a 10 percent discount rate is $0.009), this rule is not as unreasonable as it may first seem.

In the general case, the present value of any constant income stream expected to be paid in perpetuity is the income amount in dollars divided by the discount rate. For example, the present value of a dollar per year paid in perpetuity (such as a dollar of dividends paid on preferred stock or a dollar of interest paid on a perpetual bond) at a 10 percent discount rate is $10.00 ($1/.10 = $10.00). Thus, a 10 percent discount rate translates into ten times income. At a 20 percent discount rate, the present value of a dollar in perpetuity is $5.00 ($1/.20 = $5.00). Applying a 20 percent discount results in a value of five times the income stream.

Of course, the most difficult issue with any discounted cash flow approach is the selection of an appropriate discount rate. For closely held businesses, experts generally select discount rates as a function of the perceived riskiness of the business. Commonly used guidelines specify a discount rate in terms of a percentage rate added to the current ninety-day Treasury bill interest rate, assuming the T-bill rate reflects the current cost of money for a short-term, risk-free loan. For well-established businesses with reasonably predictable earnings, rates in the range of 5 to 10 percent above the T-bill rate might be used. As businesses become more risky, rates as high as 20 to 25 percent above the T-bill rates (or even higher) might be appropriate. There is no hard-and-fast rule in this area; every case is unique, and selection of a discount rate is as much an art as a science.

For a growing income stream from a business, valuation becomes a bit more complicated. The most common example of valuing a growing income stream is that of valuing a share of common stock using the dividend discount valuation model explained in the previous chapter. This traditional dividend discount model forms the conceptual basis of most approaches to valuing privately held companies. In the next section, we explore the application of this approach in concrete terms through a case study on valuation.

CASE ANALYSIS: VALUING HOME MEDICAL CARE, INC.

The basic tools of valuation analysis will be used to develop a value estimate of a closely held home medical services company named Home Medical Care, Inc. (HMC). This illustration is based on actual experience in this industry. Whereas the illustration is based on the financial and operating characteristics of a typical company in this industry and on actual valuations conducted by the author, HMC is not a real company, and the financial results presented here do not represent any actual individuals or group.

HMC is a typical home health care company. Approximately 60 percent of the company's roughly $3.6 million in revenue comes from oxygen equipment rental and oxygen sales, while the other 40 percent derives from product sales. The income statement and balance sheet for HMC are shown in Exhibits 15.1 and 15.2. Key financial ratios for HMC, along with industry standards, are calculated and shown in Exhibit 15.3. Industry standards are the median ratios for a large sample of comparable companies with revenues between $1.5 and $4.0 million. These statements provide some of the information suggested by Revenue Ruling 59–60, particularly about the nature of the business, book value of the stock, financial condition of the business, and earning and dividend paying capacity of the company.

Exhibit 15.4 presents a five-year pro forma income statement for HMC. Along with information one might find about the industry in general from sources such as trade associations and economic research organizations, these statements provide some of the information needed to help judge the future financial condition of the business. The present financial condition of the business can be evaluated using the financial statements and key business ratios in the first three exhibits.

**EXHIBIT 15.1   HOME MEDICAL CARE, INC.
INCOME STATEMENT**

	2008		2007	
	($000)	%	($000)	%
Revenue:				
Rental and respiratory revenue	$2,119.3	59.1	$1,985.7	58.9
Sales revenue	1,412.9	39.4	1,335.6	39.6
Other revenue	52.2	1.5	48.7	1.4
Total revenue	3,584.4	100.0	3,370.0	100.0
Cost of goods sold:				
Cost of goods sold: rental & resp	402.6	19.0	378.6	19.1
Cost of goods sold: sales	766.9	54.3	722.7	54.1
Cost of goods sold: other	32.5	62.3	31.1	63.9
Total cost of goods sold	1,202.0	33.5	1,132.4	33.6
Gross margin	2,382.4	66.5	2,237.6	66.4
Sales and marketing expenses	230.9	6.4	211.4	6.3
General and admin expenses	1,684.5	47.0	1,592.0	47.2
Bad-debt expense	127.4	3.6	120.6	3.6
Operating income	339.6	9.5	313.6	9.3
Interest expense	52.5	1.5	50.7	1.5
Income taxes	56.3	1.6	45.2	1.3
Net income	$230.8	6.4	$217.7	6.5

Profitability

In the area of profitability, we can see that HMC is above the industry median in terms of both return on sales (ROS) and return on assets (ROA) for 2008 and 2007. In 2008, HMC's ROS of 6.4 percent is 1.8 percentage points above the industry median ratio of 4.6 percent, and its ROA is more than 3 percent above the median figure, at 11.6 percent compared to 8.4 percent for the industry. HMC's return on equity (ROE) also is above the industry median, at 23.8 percent compared to 20.6 percent for the industry. Thus, based on all three measures of profitability, HMC is significantly more profitable than the average company of comparable size in the industry.

Liquidity

In the area of liquidity, we see that the current and quick ratios for HMC are quite adequate (2.2 and 1.8, respectively) and generally in

**EXHIBIT 15.2   HOME MEDICAL CARE, INC.
BALANCE SHEET**

	2008		2007	
ASSETS	**($000)**	**%**	**($000)**	**%**
Cash	$103.7	5.2	$94.5	5.1
Accounts receivable	819.9	41.1	763.5	41.2
Inventory (sales)	247.4	12.4	227.8	12.3
Other current assets	79.8	4.0	72.3	3.9
Total current assets	1,250.8	62.8	1,158.1	62.5
Fixed assets:				
Buildings	47.9	2.4	48.1	2.6
Rental equipment inventory	464.8	23.3	431.1	23.3
Other equipment	93.8	4.7	88.8	4.8
Vehicles	79.8	4.0	74.0	4.0
Other fixed assets	55.9	2.8	51.8	2.8
Total fixed assets	742.2	37.2	693.8	37.5
Total assets	$1,993.0	100.0	$1,851.9	100.0
LIABILITIES AND EQUITY				
Accounts payable	$231.4	11.6	$216.5	11.7
Notes payable	215.5	10.8	198.7	10.7
Taxes payable	20.0	1.0	16.8	0.9
Other current liabilities	99.8	5.0	94.5	5.1
Total current liabilities	566.7	28.4	526.5	28.4
Long-term liabilities:				
Long-term debt	434.9	21.8	405.7	21.9
Deferred taxes	6.0	0.3	5.8	0.3
Other long-term liabilities	16.1	0.8	16.7	0.9
Total long-term liabilities	457.0	22.9	428.2	23.1
Equity:				
Common stockholders' equity or				
partner/proprietor capital	969.3	48.6	897.3	48.5
Total liabilities and equity	$1,993.0	100.0	$1,851.9	100.0

line with the industry medians (2.4 and 1.9, respectively). Days sales
in receivables are generally in line with the industry median, at 83
days compared to 87 days for the median company of comparable
size. Days sales in inventory also are in line with industry medians,
at 62 days for HMC compared to 55 days for the industry average.

**EXHIBIT 15.3   HOME MEDICAL CARE, INC.
KEY BUSINESS RATIOS**

	2008	2007	INDUSTRY AVERAGE
Profitability:			
Return on sales (%)	6.4	6.5	4.6
Return on assets (%)	11.6	11.8	8.4
Return on equity (%)	23.8	24.3	20.6
Liquidity:			
Current ratio (X)	2.2	2.2	2.4
Quick ratio (X)	1.8	1.8	1.9
Days sales in receivables	83	83	87
Days sales in inventory*	62	60	55
Operating efficiency:			
Sales/Receivables (X)	4.4	4.4	4.5
Sales/Inventory (X)**	5.0	5.1	5.3
Sales/Working capital (X)	5.2	5.3	4.4
Sales/Total assets (X)	1.8	1.8	1.9
Leverage:			
Total debt/Total assets (%)	51.4	51.5	51.7
Long-term debt/Total assets (%)	22.9	23.1	15.6
Total debt/Equity (X)	1.1	1.1	0.8
Total assets/Equity (X)	2.1	2.1	1.8
Times interest earned (X)	6.5	6.2	6.8

* Sales inventory reported on the balance sheet divided by average daily sales revenue reported on the income statement for sales other than rental and respiratory
** All revenue divided by sales inventory plus rental equipment inventory

$$\text{ROA} = \text{ROS} \times \text{Sales/Total assets}$$
$$\text{ROA (2008)} = 6.44\% \times 1.80 = 11.59\%$$
$$\text{ROA (2007)} = 6.46\% \times 1.82 = 11.76\%$$

$$\text{ROE} = \text{ROI} \times \text{Total assets/Equity}$$
$$\text{ROE (2008)} = 11.59\% \times 2.06) = 23.8\%$$
$$\text{ROE (2007)} = 11.76\% \times 2.06 = 24.3\%$$

Operating Efficiency

Operating efficiency for HMC, as judged mainly by the sales to total asset ratio of 1.8 compared to the industry average of 1.9, reflects the capital-intensive nature of the industry as a whole. This number indicates that an additional investment of $1.00 in assets is needed to support each additional $1.80 of sales that HMC generates as the company grows. If one compares this ratio to other types of retail operations, such as retail drugstores, the capital-intensive nature of the industry is clear. The median sales to assets ratio for retail drugstores is 3.8, indicating that $1.00 in additional assets supports sales growth of $3.80, approximately double that of the median for this industry. However, the HMC results are in line with industry standards for medical equipment rental and leasing companies, which have a median sales to asset ratio of 1.8.

Leverage

HMC's leverage position is relatively high, with total debt as a percent of total assets at 51.4 percent, but generally in line with the high use of leverage in the industry in general. The industry median ratio of debt as a percent of total assets is 51.7 percent. In comparison, the median value of debt as a percent of total assets across twenty-one broad industry groups is 31.2 percent.

HMC's (and the industry's) heavy use of debt obviously must flow through to the other leverage ratios. Long-term debt as a percent of total assets for HMC is 22.9 percent, compared to the industry median of 15.6 percent. However, in spite of the heavy use of debt, times interest earned is a healthy 6.5 for HMC, compared to an even healthier industry average ratio of 6.8.

Overall Evaluation

In summary, although Home Medical Care shares the high leverage exposure characteristic of the industry, HMC is an efficiently managed, profitable, and solvent company. The firm is quite a bit more profitable than the average company in the industry, in terms of both its 6.4 percent return on sales and a very solid 23.8 percent return on equity capital. The interaction of profit margins, asset turnover, and leverage to generate ROA and ROE results can be seen in the DuPont and ROE interaction equations described in Chapter 6. First, the interaction of profit margin and asset turnover to produce return on investment can be seen as follows:

ROA = (Profit Margin) x (Asset Turnover)
ROA = (ROS) x (Sales/Total Assets)
ROA (2008) = (6.44%) x (1.80) = 11.6%
ROA (2007) = (6.46%) x (1.82) = 11.8%

The relationship between ROA, leverage, and ROE can be seen as follows:

$$ROE = ROA \times (\text{Total Assets/Equity})$$
$$ROE (2008) = (11.59\%) \times (2.06) = 23.8\%$$
$$ROE (2007) = (11.76\%) \times (2.06) = 24.3\%$$

Overall, HMC's above-average profitability, combined with the normal debt use of the industry, results in a rate of return on equity capital that exceeds the common rule of thumb of "about 20 percent return to equity capital" for a closely held, mid-size corporation. Assuming the principals are drawing a reasonable salary from the firm, the return to their capital is very good, although the heavy debt use makes the company riskier than the average closely held corporation.

Application of Valuation Model to Home Medical Care

The pro forma income statement in Exhibit 15.4 shows the owners' forecast of expected future sales growth and profitability for HMC. Based on their expansion plans, revenues and earnings are expected to grow at 20 percent per year for the next five years. Suppose we know that the current owners of Home Medical Care are not drawing excess compensation and we can assume that the pro forma income statement in Exhibit 15.4 is a reasonable representation of the expected financial results for HMC over the next five years. Suppose further that we expect HMC's earnings to grow at 10 percent per year for all years after 2008. What is a reasonable value for Home Medical Care based on its future income stream?

The most difficult decision variable here is the selection of an appropriate capitalization rate for a potential new buyer to value HMC's future income stream. At the time this case took place, the ninety-day Treasury bill rate was approximately 5.5 percent. Given that HMC is a small company with a great deal of uncertainty as to whether its high growth expectations actually can be achieved, a fairly substantial premium above the risk-free rate certainly is in order. A rate of at least 16 percent above the risk-free rate would seem appropriate for this company. With the T-bill rate at 5.5 percent, a discount rate of 21.5 percent seems reasonable. If we round this off to 22 percent, what is the future value of HMC's income stream at a 22 percent discount rate?

EXHIBIT 15.4 HOME MEDICAL CARE, INC.
PRO FORMA INCOME STATEMENT ($000)

	ACTUAL		FORECASTED (20% GROWTH)			
	2008	2009	2010	2011	2012	2013
Revenue:						
Rental and respiratory revenue	$2,119.3	$2,543.2	$3,051.8	$3,662.2	$4,394.6	$5,273.5
Sales revenue	$1,412.9	$1,695.5	$2,034.6	$2,441.5	$2,929.8	$3,515.7
Other revenue	52.2	$62.6	$75.2	$90.2	$108.2	$129.9
Total revenue	3,584.4	4,301.3	5,161.5	6,193.8	7,432.6	8,919.1
Cost of goods sold:						
Cost of goods sold: rental & resp	402.6	483.1	579.7	695.7	834.8	1,001.8
Cost of goods sold: sales	766.9	920.3	1,104.3	1,325.2	1,590.2	1,906.3
Cost of goods sold: other	32.5	39.0	46.8	56.2	67.4	80.9
Total cost of goods sold	1,202.0	1,442.4	1,730.9	2,077.1	2,492.5	2,991.0
Gross margin	2,382.4	2,858.9	3,430.7	4,116.8	4,940.1	5,928.2
Sales and marketing expenses	230.9	277.1	332.5	399.0	478.8	574.6
General and admin expenses	1,684.5	2,021.4	2,425.7	2,910.8	3,493.0	4,191.6
Bad-debt expense	127.4	152.9	183.5	220.1	264.2	317.0
Operating income	339.6	407.5	489.0	586.8	704.2	845.0
Interest expense	52.5	63.0	75.6	90.7	108.9	130.6
Income taxes	56.3	67.6	81.1	97.3	116.7	140.1
Net income	$230.8	$277.0	$332.4	$398.8	$478.6	$574.3

Since HMC is a closely held company, and dividend policy is under direct control of the current owners, the most common approach to valuing the entire company would be to base the value on the discounted present value of the expected future earnings of HMC. If we apply the dividend discount model to discount the future earnings of HMC as of the end of 2008, the value of Home Medical Care will be equal to the sum of the present value of the earnings from 2009 through 2013, plus the present value of the company at the end of 2013 as determined by the value of all future earnings growing at 10 percent per year indefinitely.

The present value (PV) of the next five years' earnings using a 22 percent discount rate is computed as follows (using earnings from Exhibit 15.4):

$$
\begin{aligned}
\text{PV of 5 years' earnings} &= \$277{,}000/1.22 + \$332{,}400/1.22^2 + \$398{,}800/1.22^3 + \\
&\quad \$478{,}600/1.22^4 + \$574{,}300/1.22^5 \\
&= \$227{,}049 + \$223{,}327 + \$219{,}622 + \$216{,}040 + \\
&\quad \$212{,}491 \\
&= \$1{,}098{,}529
\end{aligned}
$$

At the end of year five (calendar year 2013), the value of the company should be the present value of all future earnings growing at 10 percent per year and discounted back at a 22 percent discount rate. Using the formula from the dividend-capitalization model applied to earnings determines the value at the end of year five (V5):

$$
V5 = (\$574{,}300 \times 1.10)/(0.22 - 0.10) = \$631{,}730/0.12 = \$5{,}264{,}417
$$

Note that the 12 percent capitalization rate ($.22 - .10 = .12$) results in a multiple of 8.3 times earnings in the year 2014 (at a 10 percent growth rate, earnings in year 2014 = earnings in year 2013 times 1.1 = \$631,730). The present value of V5 (\$5,264,417) discounted back to year one is:

$$
\text{PV of V5 in year one} = \$5{,}264{,}417/1.22^5 = \$1{,}947{,}830
$$

The total value of HMC is then the sum of the present value of the next five years' earnings plus the present value of V5, as follows:

$$
\text{Value of HMC} = \$1{,}098{,}529 + \$1{,}947{,}830 = \$3{,}046{,}359
$$

This valuation approach places a fairly high valuation on Home Medical Care. This high value is the result of two factors. First, HMC is assuming the company will grow at the rate of 20 percent for the next five years. At the end of the five-year period, the value of $5,264,417 (V5 in our calculations) would be approximately 9.2 times earnings in 2013 (a capitalization rate of 10.9 percent) and would seem quite reasonable given a history of 20 percent growth. At this early stage, however, unless and until the growth prospects of HMC can be documented, it is highly unlikely that a potential buyer would be willing to pay as much as $3.1 million for HMC. A value of $3.1 million is approximately 13.4 times 2003 earnings of $230,800, well above the common rule of thumb of ten times earnings for small businesses.

This example illustrates the substantial value added that can be achieved by successfully implementing a high-growth strategy. For the owners of HMC, their optimal "exit strategy" would be to do whatever is possible to meet their 20 percent growth targets over the next five years, then position the company for sale at a reasonable multiple of earnings in 2013 or 2014. Obviously, this short example is an oversimplified approach to valuation, and many other factors and approaches would have to be considered in a real case. However, this simple case is a good illustration of the fundamental approach to valuation as the present value of future earnings.

SUMMARY

Revenue Ruling 59–60 provides conceptual guidance for valuing closely held companies. This ruling specifies eight factors to be considered in valuing closely held businesses: nature of the business, economic and industry outlook, financial condition, earnings, dividend capacity, goodwill and intangibles, prior sales, and comparable stock prices. The classic definition of fair market value from this ruling is the price at which a property would change hands between a willing buyer and a willing seller who both have reasonable knowledge of the facts.

The value of a real or financial asset is based ultimately on the discounted present value of expected future cash flows. Selection of an appropriate discount rate is a key issue in this calculation. For well-established businesses with predictable earnings and cash flows, rates of 5 to 10 percent above the current Treasury bill rate may be appropriate. For risky businesses, rates of 20 to 25 percent above the T-bill rate may be reasonable.

Valuation requires an understanding of the company, beginning with an analysis of financial statements and creation of pro forma income statements. The valuation process may then apply the conceptual approach of the stock dividend discount model, where value is computed as the discounted present value of expected future earnings. The case in the chapter, although oversimplified, is a good illustration of standard valuation concepts.

KEY POINTS

IRS REVENUE RULING 59–60   Fair market value is the price at which a property would change hands between a willing buyer and a willing seller when the former is under no compulsion to buy and the latter is under no compulsion to sell, with both parties having reasonable knowledge of the facts.

REVENUE RULING 59–60 VALUATION FACTORS
- Nature and history of the business
- Company and industry economic outlook
- Financial condition of the business including book value of the stock
- Earning capacity
- Dividend payment capacity
- Whether or not the company has goodwill or other intangible assets
- Prior sales of stock in the company and the size of the block to be offered

- Market prices of stocks of corporations engaged in the same or similar businesses that have stocks actively traded in free and open markets

GUIDELINES FOR CLOSELY HELD COMPANY DISCOUNT RATES (APPROXIMATE)

Low risk: Treasury bill rate plus 5 to 10 percent
Medium risk: Treasury bill rate plus 11 to 20 percent
High risk: Treasury bill rate plus 21 to 30 percent

16
Sources and Forms of Long-Term Financing

THE MONEY AND CAPITAL MARKETS

Conventional financial terminology divides the external market for funds into the money market and the capital market. The money market encompasses short-term debt securities—that is, securities that will mature in less than one year. Money market securities include such issues as Treasury bills, commercial paper, bankers' acceptances, and short-term certificates of deposit.

The capital market is the market for longer-term funds—that is, sources of financing with a time horizon of more than one year. As a general guideline, securities with a maturity of more than one but less than ten years may be considered to be intermediate-term securities. Long-term securities generally have a maturity of ten or more years.

The capital market also encompasses the market for equity securities. Preferred and common stock have the longest time horizon, since these securities are normally issued for the life of the corporation. Thus, they may be thought of as sources of financing with an infinite time horizon.

This chapter will deal with the major sources and forms of capital market funds. The use of lease financing will also be examined, although leases are not generally included as a component of the capital market. However, from an economic point of view a long-term noncancelable lease commitment for a fixed asset is very similar to the purchase of the asset with the proceeds of a long-term loan.

INTERMEDIATE- AND LONG-TERM DEBT

There are two primary sources of intermediate- and long-term debt: term loans and bonds. A *term loan* is simply a loan that is paid off over some number of years (term of the loan). Term loans are usually negotiated with a commercial bank, an insurance company, or some other financial institution. Term loans can generally be negotiated fairly quickly and at a low administrative cost. Many term loans are fully amortized, which means that the principal and interest are paid off in installments over the life of the loan. In recent years there has been a substantial increase in the use of floating-rate term loans.

Bonds are intermediate- to long-term debt agreements issued by governments, corporations, and other organizations, generally in units of $1,000 principal value per bond. Each bond represents two "promises" by the issuing organization: the promise to repay the $1,000 principal value at maturity and the promise to pay the stated interest rate (the *coupon rate*) when due. Most bonds pay interest semiannually at a rate equal to one-half of the annual coupon rate. The term *coupon rate* derives from the fact that bonds historically had actual coupons attached that could be detached and redeemed for each interest payment. Today, most bonds are held in electronic form, and coupon payments are credited electronically.

Bonds may be sold directly to the public through investment bankers, or they may be privately placed with a financial institution such as a commercial bank, insurance company, corporate pension fund, or university endowment fund. A complete statement of the legal obligations of the issuing organization to the bondholders is contained in a document called the *bond indenture*. If the bond is publicly marketed, a trustee is named to monitor and ensure compliance with the terms of the indenture. In most cases the trustee is a commercial bank or investment banker. In the case of a privately placed issue, the purchasing institution normally acts as its own trustee.

The bond indenture normally specifies a number of restrictive covenants to which the issuing corporation must adhere. These covenants are designed to protect the interests of the bondholders and generally describe various standards that the issuer must meet or action that the issuer may not take. Such covenants might establish a minimum level of working capital or prohibit common stock dividend payments in excess of a defined percentage of earnings.

If the issuer violates any terms of the indenture, the bond is in default. The trustee will then take whatever steps are necessary to remedy the default. In extreme cases, the trustee may demand immediate repayment of the entire bond principal and any accrued interest. Such an action will force refinancing of the issue or can even force the issuer into bankruptcy.

There is a wide variety of types of bond issues. *Mortgage bonds*, as their name implies, are bonds that are collateralized by a mortgage on some fixed asset such as a building, land, or equipment. A mortgage bond may be a first mortgage bond or a second mortgage bond. A debenture is an unsecured bond that is backed by the full faith and credit of the issuer. No specific assets are pledged as collateral for debentures. In the event of default or bankruptcy, debenture holders become general creditors of the issuer. A subordinated debenture is a debenture that is specifically subordinated to some other debt issue. In the event of default or bankruptcy, the subordinated, or junior, debt has no claim on the issuer's assets until the debt to which it is subordinated—the senior debt—is satisfied.

Convertible bonds are corporate bonds that may be converted into common stock at the option of the bondholder. The number of shares of stock into which the bond may be converted is known as the *conversion rate*. Convertible bonds may sometimes be subordinated, giving rise to the term *subordinated convertible debentures*. *Income bonds*, which vary in popularity from time to time, are bonds on which interest is paid only when the corporation earns a specified level of income. In the past, these bonds have been issued primarily as a part of bankruptcy reorganization plans. In recent years, however, income bonds occasionally have been issued by more financially sound organizations.

Two other bond instruments bear mention. *Floating-rate bonds* are like regular bullet bonds except that the coupon rate is tied to some variable rate benchmark, such as the London Interbank Offered Rate (LIBOR). These bonds are comparable to floating-rate term loans. The second instrument is the *zero coupon bond*. Zero coupon bonds are sold at substantial discounts from par but pay no current interest. Investors earn their rate of return solely from the interest accreting as the bond approaches maturity. The return characteristics of zero coupon bonds were discussed in Chapter 14.

Two additional bond provisions are commonly encountered: call provisions and sinking funds. A *call provision* gives the issuing corporation the right to "call in" the bond for retirement prior to maturity. The terms of the call provision typically state that the bonds may not be called until some number of years after the original issue and that the bonds must be called at a premium above par value. Typical terms for a twenty-year, 10 percent bond issue with a $1,000 par value might state that the bonds are callable after five years at a call price of $1,050. Other callable bonds may have a "make whole" provision whereby the call price is based on what the bond would be worth if it was priced at some (usually narrow) spread to the underlying U.S. Treasury rate.

A *sinking fund* establishes a procedure for the orderly retirement of a bond over the life of the issue. Actually, the term *sinking fund* is somewhat of a misnomer since it implies that some sort of a fund is established to retire the bond issue at maturity. This type of arrangement may have been used long ago, but virtually all contemporary sinking funds require the periodic (usually annual) repurchase of a stated percentage of the outstanding bonds. The repurchasing corporation may either buy the bonds in the open market or call in the bonds for redemption. If called, the bonds to be called are generally determined by lottery based on the serial numbers of the bonds. When high interest rates drive bond prices down, open-market purchases at discounts from par value are much more attractive than invoking call provisions.

Bond Yields

The word *yield* can assume a number of meanings in reference to a bond. Four of the most common yield measures are the coupon yield rate, current yield, yield to maturity, and yield to first call date. Each of these yield measures is significant and should be clearly understood.

The *coupon rate* is simply the rate of interest specified on the bond coupons at the time the bond is issued. The coupon rate is thus the interest rate stated in the bond indenture. Once the bond is issued, the coupon rate never changes. If the general level of interest rates rises after issue, then the market price of the bond will fall. If interest rates fall, then the bond price will rise.

After a bond has been issued and is traded freely on the open market, it is called a *seasoned bond*. Since interest rates fluctuate from day to day, the prices of seasoned bonds also fluctuate. This price fluctuation requires that one measure the current yield on a seasoned bond. The *current yield* is measured by dividing the coupon interest in dollars by the current market price of the bond. For example, suppose that the ABC 10's of '11 (ABC Company bonds, 10 percent coupon rate, maturing in 2011) currently sell for $850 per bond. The coupon rate of 10 percent requires an annual interest payment of $100 per bond. The current yield on the bond is thus 11.76 percent ($100/$850).

The *yield to maturity* (YTM) is the average annual compound rate of return that would be earned if the bond were purchased at its current market value and held to maturity. The yield to maturity includes the return from interest payments and the capital gain (or loss) if the bond is purchased at a discount (or premium). For example, if the ABC 10's of '11 were purchased for $850 in 1995, with sixteen years until maturity, the yield to maturity would include the return from the $100-per-year interest plus the $150 capital gain over the life of the bond ($1,000 less $850). The yield to maturity is the discount rate that equates $100 per year for sixteen years plus $1,000 received at the end of sixteen years to the current price of the bond, $850. This discount rate may be solved by using trial and error and present-value tables (see Chapter 11) or by using a calculator or computer spreadsheet. In this case, the yield to maturity is 12.15 percent.

The *yield to first call date* (YTC) is the yield to maturity on a callable bond, assuming the bond is purchased at the current market price and then called at the first eligible date. If the ABC bonds are callable at the end of 2000 at a premium of $20, for example, the yield to call date would be the YTM earned if the bonds were purchased at $850, held for five years, and then called at $1,020. In this case, the YTC is 14.1 percent. The YTC is much higher than the YTM because the bonds are held for only five years instead of sixteen and are then sold at a premium.

LEASE FINANCING

Many businesses lease assets as an alternative to owning them. Conceptually, leasing is similar to borrowing money to buy the asset. In either case, the business has the use of the asset and incurs an obligation either to pay off a loan or to meet a monthly lease payment. The major difference, of course, is that if the business leases, the asset is owned by the lessee rather than by the business. At the end of the lease term, the residual value of the asset will belong to the lessee. If the asset were owned, the residual value of the asset would belong to the business. In either case, however, the business has the use of the asset and incurs a monthly payment obligation. Thus, leasing is considered a form of debt financing.

FASB 13 (governing lease accounting) clearly defines the difference between a capital lease and an operating lease. A lease agreement that does not meet the criteria for a capital lease must be classified as an operating lease. A lease is considered to be a capital lease if it meets any one of the following four conditions:

1. The title is transferred to the lessee at the end of the lease term.
2. The lease contains a bargain purchase option—that is, an option to buy the asset at a very low price.
3. The term of the lease is greater than or equal to 75 percent of the estimated economic life of the asset.
4. The present value of the minimum lease payment is greater than or equal to 90 percent of the fair value of the leased property.

A capital lease is recorded on the lessee's balance sheet as an asset entitled "capital lease asset" and an associated liability entitled "obligation under capital lease." The amount of the asset and liability is equal to the present value of the minimum future lease payments. Thus, for capital leases, leasing no longer provides a source of off-balance-sheet financing.

Operating leases are more in the nature of true rentals than a means to finance the long-term use of an asset. These leases typically are for substantially less than the expected useful life of the asset and often provide for both financing and maintenance. Operating leases also frequently contain cancellation clauses so that the lessee is not locked into a long-term agreement. No asset and associated liability are created under an operating lease.

Firms may prefer leasing to owning for a number of reasons, but the major motivation relates to the tax benefits involved. The owner of the asset is entitled to the tax benefits from depreciation. In many cases, a business may not be generating enough profit to take full advantage of these tax benefits. The benefits can be effectively "passed upstream" to a lessor by arranging for the lessor (often a commercial bank or leasing subsidiary of a major corporation) to acquire the asset and then lease it to the lessee. The lessor benefits by obtaining tax deductions that would otherwise be unavailable. The lessee also benefits because the lessor will normally price the lease payments at a lower rate of return (imputed interest rate) than would otherwise be charged the lessee on a straight loan arrangement. Since the lessor also obtains tax benefits, the lessor's after-tax return will actually be higher than it would be under the straight debt arrangement. Thus, both parties benefit from the lease (and, as one colorful expression goes, "Uncle Sugar totes the note!").

Leasing may also be attractive to a firm with a low credit rating. A lease can often be obtained more easily than a loan can be arranged because the lessor retains title to the asset. Full recovery of the asset by the financial institution in the event of default is thus much easier than if the asset were owned by the lessee. Lessees also find that the down payment on a purchased asset is much higher than the deposit required on a lease. Thus, a lease may aid in controlling the lessee's cash flow. Finally, use of operating leases may increase the lessee's overall credit availability, since they do not show up on the balance sheet.

Sale and Leaseback

A *sale and leaseback* is a fairly common arrangement whereby a firm sells a fixed asset, often a building, to a lender/lessor and then immediately leases back the property. The advantage to the seller/lessee is that the selling firm receives a large inflow of cash that may be used to finance other aspects of the business. In return for this cash, the selling firm enters into a long-term lease obligation. Conceptually, a sale-and-leaseback transaction is similar to remortgaging a piece of property or establishing a mortgage on a piece of owned property.

Leveraged Lease

Most lease transactions involve two parties, the lessor and the lessee. In a leveraged lease transaction, a third-party lender enters into the agreement. The lessor, say a commercial bank, may borrow some percentage of the cost of the asset, normally 80 percent or less, from the third-party lender. The lessor then purchases the asset and leases it to the lessee. Since there is a loan involved in the transaction, the lease is said to be leveraged.

The primary advantage to the lessor in this transaction stems from the tax benefits. Although the lessor invests only a relatively small percentage of the cost of the assets, the lessor has title to the asset and is thus entitled to the full depreciation benefits.

PREFERRED STOCK

Preferred stock is legally an equity security and thus represents an ownership interest in the corporation. The term *preferred* derives from the fact that preferred stock has two important preferences over common stock: preference as to payment of dividends and preference in stockholders' claims on the assets of the business in the event of bankruptcy.

Preferred stock has been described as a hybrid form of security that combines some of the characteristics of bonds and some of the characteristics of common stock. Preferred-stock dividends are fixed in amount, like bond coupon interest, and must be paid before common dividends can be paid. Like bondholders, preferred stockholders do not participate in the growth of corporate earnings; they collect only the dividends promised in the indenture. However, like common-stock dividends, each preferred dividend payment must be voted on and approved by the board of directors of the corporation. Nearly all preferred-stock issues are cumulative, meaning that missed dividends accumulate as arrearages and must be paid off before any dividends on common stock can be paid. Although preferred stockholders do not normally have voting rights in the corporation, most preferred-stock issues specify that if arrearages accumulate to a specified level, the preferred stockholders have a right to elect a representative to the corporation's board of directors. Thus, the board has more than a moral obligation to vote payment of preferred dividends in a timely manner.

As a practical matter, timely payment of preferred dividends is important to the corporation. Corporations with preferred dividends in arrears find it extremely difficult to raise other forms of capital.

Placing new long-term loans and selling bonds or stock is extremely difficult, if not impossible, for such corporations. Thus, payment of preferred dividends is nearly as important to the corporation as timely payment of bond interest. The critical distinction between the two payment obligations is that missing bond interest payments can result in the corporation being forced into bankruptcy. Preferred stockholders, as part owners of the corporation, have no legal right to force bankruptcy for nonpayment of dividends.

Preferred stock is often convertible into common stock at a specified exchange rate, or conversion ratio, of common for preferred. At the time of issue of the convertible preferred stock, the conversion ratio is typically set so that immediate conversion is highly unattractive. Thus, for example, if a corporation issues $100 par value convertible preferred stock at a time when the company's common stock is selling for $10 per share, the conversion ratio might be set at 6.0 to 1 (one share of preferred stock be converted into six shares of common stock). At this conversion ratio, $100 worth of preferred stock could be converted into $60 worth of common stock. However, if the company prospers and the price of common stock rises, conversion may become attractive. In this case, conversion may become attractive if the price of the common stock rises above $16.67 per share ($100/6 shares). Convertible preferred stock is often callable, thus allowing the corporation to call the stock and/or force conversion into common stock in the future. The call feature gives the company the ability to change its capital structure in the future if such a change seems advantageous.

COMMON STOCK

The common stockholders are the owners of the corporation. Normally, each share of common stock has one vote in electing the members of the corporation's board of directors. The board is the ultimate corporate authority and is the group to whom the president of the corporation reports. The board selects the president and approves the appointment of all corporate officers. In a small, closely held corporation, voting control is generally held by one or several founders of the corporation, one of whom serves as chairperson of the board. If one person is the majority stockholder, he or she may serve as president as well as chairperson. In large, publicly held corporations, no single individual or small group normally holds enough shares of common stock to exercise voting control of the corporation. The board members are responsible to the stockholders, and the stockholders have the authority to elect a new board if the performance of the current board is deemed unsatisfactory.

As a practical matter, boards of directors are reasonably safe from being thrown out by the stockholders. Prior to each annual meeting at which directors are elected, current management solicits the voting proxies of the stockholders. A proxy gives management the right to vote the shares of the stockholders who sign the proxy.

The majority of stockholders in large, publicly held corporations either sign proxies or vote with management. Sometimes a dissident stockholder group or an outside group interested in taking over the company also solicits shareholders' proxies. In this case, a proxy fight ensues, and the party with the most proxies will gain control of the corporation. Another corporation may also attempt to take over a corporation by buying up enough stock in the market to exert majority control of the takeover target. This attempt is generally made via a tender offer. The acquiring corporation publicly announces its willingness to buy shares at a given price above the current market price from all stockholders who tender their shares by a specified expiration date. A takeover attempt by another corporation is a very real danger to a corporation with dissatisfied stockholders.

As a form of financing, common stock provides the corporation's "equity cushion." Money paid to the corporation for common stock does not have to be repaid, and dividends on common stock are paid only when declared by the board of directors. Common-stock dividends do not accumulate as arrearages, and common stockholders have no legal claim to any specified dividend level. Normally, as a corporation prospers and earnings grow, the board votes to increase the dividend along with the increased growth in earnings. As dividends increase, the value of the stock increases, and stockholders also benefit via capital gains. Of course, if earnings do not increase, the dividends will not increase and may decrease or be eliminated. The value of the stock will also not increase and may even decline.

Corporations sometimes create two classes of common stock, one class of which does not have voting rights. Thus, voting control of the corporation is retained by one class, but the other class has the ability to participate in earnings growth. The corporate founders, for example, may own all the stock of a corporation. They may wish to raise additional equity capital but want to retain voting control. They could issue nonvoting class B stock, designating their voting stock as class A stock. The class B stock will have a right to participate in earnings and dividends but will not have a right to vote on corporate matters. However, it is relatively rare for large, publicly held corporations to offer two different classes of stock.

DIVIDEND POLICY

A corporation's dividend policy is one of the most important responsibilities of the board of directors. Most dividends are paid quarterly, and each quarterly payment must be voted on and approved by the board. Dividend payments reflect the division of earnings between payments to stockholders and reinvestment in the firm. Establishing a dividend policy requires a compromise between the stockholders' desire to receive some of the earnings through cash dividends and the corporation's desire to reinvest earnings to finance the future growth of the company. As we saw in Chapter 7, a growing firm must plan carefully to finance its growth. Reinvested earnings are a very important source of financing this growth.

Many factors influence a corporation's dividend policy. One of the most important is the corporation's growth rate. High-growth corporations have correspondingly high demands for funds and normally pay fairly low dividends. In fact, very rapidly growing firms, particularly in the early growth years, often pay no dividends at all because all earnings must be reinvested to finance the firm's high growth rate. For the high-growth firm, a zero-dividend payout ratio (dividends as a percentage of earnings) may be highly appropriate.

The stability of the corporation's earnings is also a key factor in setting dividend policy. A high level of earnings stability reduces the corporation's business risk and allows a higher dividend payout than could be paid if earnings were highly erratic. The rate of return earned on equity capital is also important. If the corporation's ROE is higher than the stockholders' opportunity rate of return (the return stockholders expect to earn on the next-best-available investment opportunity), the stockholders will benefit if the corporation retains and reinvests their earnings.

It is important to remember that earnings are reinvested on behalf of the stockholders. Reinvested earnings finance the future growth of the company. Earnings growth, in turn, increases the value of the corporation's stock, resulting in capital gains for the stockholders. In a very real sense, payment of dividends represents a choice between future capital gains and current cash payments.

The corporation's overall liquidity position and access to money and capital markets is also important. A highly liquid corporation with easy access to the capital markets can pay out a much higher percentage of earnings in dividends than can a less liquid corporation. Any outstanding debt repayment requirements and/or restrictive covenants on long-term debt agreements are additional important considerations. Restrictive covenants commonly prohibit dividend payments out of past retained earnings and place a lower limit as the dollar amount of net working capital that must be maintained.

Finally, there are some legal constraints on dividend payments. In addition to any constraints imposed by debt agreements, corporations are also subject to the capital-impairment rule. This rule states that normal cash dividend payments may not exceed retained earnings and that corporations may not pay dividends when insolvent (that is, when total liabilities exceed total assets). This rule is designed to protect creditors. However, a firm may pay "liquidating dividends" out of capital (assets minus liabilities) if the dividend is identified as such. If there are restrictive covenants or debt agreements in effect, liquidating dividends may not reduce capital below the level specified in the debt-restrictive covenants.

The Residual Theory of Dividend Policy

From a theoretical point of view, management should select the dividend policy that will maximize the value of the outstanding common stock. One well-known and generally accepted approach to the problem is the *residual theory of dividend policy*. The residual theory assumes that investors prefer to have a corporation retain and reinvest earnings on their behalf rather than pay them out in dividends if the corporation's return on equity capital is greater than the rate of return investors could obtain by receiving dividends and investing them in another opportunity of equivalent risk. According to the theory, dividend policy should be determined by a simple three-step process.

The mechanics of the process are conceptually straightforward. First, the corporation determines the optimal size of the capital budget by noting where the investment-opportunity schedule intersects the marginal-cost-of-capital curve. This process was explained in Chapter 13 and illustrated in Exhibit 13.3. Second, the optimal capital structure (see Exhibit 13.5) will determine what percentage of the optimal capital budget must be financed by equity capital. Third, the total amount of earnings available for reinvestment and dividend payout are compared to the total dollars of equity capital needed for the capital budget. If available earnings are less than the required earnings, all earnings should be reinvested, and no dividend should be paid. In fact, in this case, the firm will also have to sell some new stock to raise the amount of equity capital required. If available earnings are exactly equal to required earnings, all earnings should be reinvested, but no additional stock will need to be sold. Finally, if available earnings exceed required earnings, then the excess ("the residual") should be paid out as a dividend. Hence, the name *residual theory of dividend policy*.

Dividend Theory in Practice

As a practical matter, many corporations follow the residual theory approximately. Companies in high-growth industries, such as high-tech companies, typically face many attractive investment opportunities. These companies have very high demands for equity capital to finance their growth and generally pay no dividends or very low dividends. Companies in low-growth industries, on the other hand, typically have fairly high dividend-payout ratios.

Very few companies, either high growth or low growth, follow the residual theory exactly. The reason for this is quite simple. Most companies face substantially different capital budgeting opportunities from year to year. Some years, a great many excellent opportunities may be available. Other years, such as recession years, few if any good opportunities may surface. The residual theory therefore may require payment of a very high dividend in one year, followed by no dividend the next year, and perhaps a "normal" dividend the following year. Such an erratic dividend adds a good deal of uncertainty to the stock market's valuation of the firm's stock price. Since investors dislike uncertainty almost as much as they dislike taxes, an erratic dividend policy reduces the value of the firm's stock compared with what it would be with a stable policy. It should also be noted that most investors interpret a dividend cut to be a symptom of financial weakness on the part of the corporation (in many cases, with good reason). Hence, a firm cutting its dividend to take advantage of some extraordinary investment opportunities may deliver exactly the wrong message to the market.

For these reasons, most firms strive to maintain a reasonably stable dividend payment from year to year. The board of directors will not normally raise the dividend until the board members are confident that the increased dividend can be maintained in the future. Some firms that are severely impacted by the economic cycle will maintain a stable quarterly dividend and declare a year-end extra that can be omitted when the economy turns down. Then the "normal" dividend can be maintained even in the face of adversity. A few major corporations maintain a constant percentage-payment ratio, paying out the same percentage of income to the stockholders each year. In one celebrated case, a firm maintained this policy—"a dollar for the company and a dollar for the stockholders"—right up until the quarter in which the company filed for bankruptcy! The existence of this one case supports the argument for a flexible policy.

Stock Dividends and Stock Splits

In order to satisfy shareholders' desire for dividends but still preserve the corporation's cash, corporations sometimes pay a *stock dividend*. A stock dividend, as the name implies, is the payment of a dividend in the form of additional shares of stock in the corporation. From an accounting perspective, a stock dividend is a simple bookkeeping transaction transferring the value of the stock, at market value, from retained earnings to capital stock. A stock dividend of 25 percent or more (where each existing share is paid 0.25 or more shares as a dividend) is generally considered a split. From an accounting perspective, a split requires a simple memo entry showing the increased number of shares. No change is made in the capital account.

From an economic perspective, there is no substantive difference between a stock split and a stock dividend. In either case, the shareholder gains nothing economically. The total number of shares claiming an equity position is simply increased, and each shareholder increases the number of shares held in proportion to the number of shares held before the split or dividend. In short, the pie is no bigger—there are just more pieces, and each shareholder gets more pieces of the same pie. Empirical studies have shown that unless accompanied by an increase in earnings and dividends per share, the price of the outstanding shares generally will decline by the amount of the split. Thus, in the absence of any change in earnings, the price of a stock that splits two-for-one (a 100 percent dividend) can be expected to drop in half.

Stock Repurchases

Companies sometimes repurchase their own stock with excess cash rather than pay a dividend. The theory behind this is that stock repurchases effectively substitute a capital gain for a cash dividend. Stock that is repurchased is called *treasury stock* and does not share in the future earnings and dividends of the corporation. Since there are fewer shares outstanding after the repurchase, earnings per share will increase if aggregate corporate earnings remain the same, and the value of the stock should increase. Thus, barring fluctuations in the stock market (a rather heroic assumption), stockholders will receive a capital gain rather than a dividend.

SUMMARY

The money markets encompass short-term debt securities, such as commercial paper, Treasury bills, bankers' acceptances, and short-term certificates of deposit. Longer-term securities, such as bonds and stocks, trade in the capital markets. Term loans and bonds are the two primary sources of intermediate- and long-term debt. The use of floating-rate debt and zero coupon bonds has increased substantially in recent years. The bond indenture is the contract that delineates the obligations of the bond issuer to purchasers of the bonds. Bond indentures often contain call provisions and sinking fund requirements. Bond yields are measured in terms of the coupon rate, current yield, yield to maturity, and yield to first call date.

Lease financing is commonly used as an alternative to purchasing an asset with the proceeds of a debt issue. Capital leases must be recorded on the lessee firm's balance sheet as an asset equal to the present value of the minimum future lease payments. An associated liability must be recorded also. Operating leases are treated as simple rental agreements. Most of the advantages to leasing stem from the tax benefits involved.

Preferred and common stock are equity securities. Preferred stock is a hybrid type of security, sharing some of the characteristics of bonds and some of the characteristics of common stock. Nearly all preferred-stock issues are cumulative, and many are both convertible and callable. Timely payment of preferred-stock dividends is very important to a corporation.

Common stock provides the all-important "equity cushion." Common stockholders vote to elect the directors of the corporation, and common stock participates in the future growth of earnings and dividends. Setting dividend policy for the common stock is one of the most important responsibilities of the board of directors. The residual theory of dividends maintains that dividend policy should be a function of the interaction of the optimal capital budget and the optimal capital structure. Most publicly held corporations follow the implications of the residual theory in an approximate manner.

KEY POINTS

MONEY MARKET	One-year or less maturity
CAPITAL MARKET	More than one-year maturity
TERM LOANS	More than one-year maturity Quickly negotiated Low administrative cost Floating rates common
CORPORATE BONDS	Intermediate- to long-term Mortgage bonds Debentures Subordinated bonds Convertible bonds Floating-rate bonds Zero coupon bonds Sinking funds Call provisions

BOND YIELDS Coupon rate
Current yield
Yield to maturity (YTM)
Yield to first call date (YTC)

LEASING Capital lease
Operating lease
Sale and leaseback
Leveraged lease

PREFERRED STOCK Hybrid security
Legal form is equity
Fixed dividend
Convertible preferred
Call provision

COMMON STOCK Full voting rights
Equity cushion
Two classes possible

DIVIDEND POLICY Influenced by growth rate, stability
of earnings, ROE, stockholders' tax
bracket, liquidity, access to capital
markets, restrictive covenants, and
legal constraints
• Residual theory
• Stability in practice
• Stock dividends
• Stock splits
• Stock repurchases

PART VII
Special Topics in Finance

17

Governance and Risk Management

During economic boom times, the process by which decisions in a corporation get made sometimes takes a back seat to proper corporate governance and prudent risk management. However, when the business cycle turns (as it always does), and losses are exposed, risk managers and corporate governance experts regain their credibility and respect. It is therefore useful to explore some of the basics of how corporations are run and how risks can be managed to enhance shareholder value. Remember, it is not how much a company earns that determines its long-term value but how much the company earns *and keeps*.

BASICS OF CORPORATE GOVERNANCE

Corporations are, at their heart, a group of consensual, contractual relations among several constituencies. The articles of incorporation or corporate charter is an agreement between the corporation and the state in which it is incorporated as to how the corporation will be run (there is no federal incorporation statute). The charter includes such things as the authorized shares of the corporation, the corporation's name, and the corporation's purpose. Historically, corporations were established for very narrow purposes, often a single purpose, which were carefully scrutinized by state legislatures before the corporation was established. Today, corporations typically have a catch-all provision indicating that the corporation may engage in "any lawful purpose." In return for the charter, a corporation pays a franchise tax to the state, typically based on the authorized capital

269

of the company. Delaware, the state with the largest number of New York Stock Exchange listed companies, derives a substantial portion of its annual tax revenue from franchise taxes. With its sophisticated judiciary and well-established precedent, streamlined business litigation through the Court of Chancery and flexible General Corporation Law, Delaware is well-positioned to retain its number one spot for many years to come.

Charters may be amended after they are originally filed by the incorporators only by a vote of the shareholders. This vote may be a majority vote or a supermajority vote, depending on the charter itself and the laws of the state of incorporation. For public companies, this vote will typically require the filing of a proxy with the Securities and Exchange Commission (SEC) and the hiring of a proxy solicitor to encourage shareholders to vote their shares.

Corporations also have by-laws that "fill the gaps" left by the charter and provide a more detailed road map for corporate governance. By-laws typically address things such as board elections and composition, appointment of officers, and the timing and conduct of corporate annual meetings. By-laws can be amended by a corporation's board of directors if permitted by the state of incorporation and the charter. Otherwise, by-laws too are amendable by the shareholders.

Corporations are ultimately run by the board of directors of the company. The board is elected by the shareholders at the annual stockholders' meeting. Absent supervoting stock or increasingly rare cumulative voting, each share of stock is entitled to one vote per director, and the directors who receive the most votes win. Because they are directly elected by the shareholders, the directors have a fiduciary duty to the shareholders to strive to maximize the value per share of the corporation.

DIRECTORS' FIDUCIARY DUTIES

Under Delaware law, corporate directors have two distinct duties to the shareholders who elected them: a duty of care and a duty of loyalty. The *duty of care* requires a director to act in good faith and strive to exercise ordinary prudential care in making business decisions for the corporation. Directors are not guarantors of their decisions but are, absent a conflict of interest, protected by the *business judgment rule*, which provides a presumption in favor of a director's decision making even if, after the fact, the decision turned out to be wrong. The business judgment rule requires a director to exercise due diligence in his decision-making process and not rush into decisions without becoming fully informed of the implications of the decision he is making. Process, not result, is what is paramount for enjoying the protection of the business judgment rule.

If a director has a conflict of interest and does not recuse himself, then that director will be held to a higher "total fairness" standard. This standard puts the burden of proof on the conflicted director to show that his decision was, in substance, fair to all parties.

The second duty a director has is the *duty of loyalty*. This duty requires that the director act in the best interests of the corporation and not do things that harm the corporation. For instance, a director is generally prohibited from competing directly with a corporation unless the other directors have expressly permitted the competing enterprise. A director may not usurp business opportunities that the corporation could take advantage of or use confidential corporate information for personal benefit.

Failure to adhere to these twin fiduciary duties can lead to personal liability for the director. This type of liability typically is not covered by directors' and officers' liability insurance.

DAILY GOVERNANCE OF THE CORPORATION

While the board of directors is ultimately responsible as fiduciaries to the stockholders, the board does not generally run the day-to-day operations of the corporation. For that, the board will recruit and hire a chief executive officer (CEO). The CEO is frequently the same person as the chair of the board of directors, although some governance experts believe that having a separation of the chair and the CEO is a healthier structure.

The CEO, in turn, will hire a management team, including a chief financial officer, chief marketing officer, and, depending on the corporation's needs, other "C-level" executives. The CEO is responsible for the day-to-day operation of the company and serves as management's representative to the board. The board will hold the CEO accountable for the corporation's operating performance and, over time, its stock price performance.

Managers of a corporation also have fiduciary duties of care and loyalty to the corporation that prohibit them from competing with their employer, usurping business opportunities, or misappropriating corporate trade secrets and confidential information. While directors may be sued personally, the typical (but not exclusive) remedy for a manager breaching his duty to the corporation is termination of the manager's employment.

Under the Sarbanes-Oxley Act, management of public companies has a duty to structure the corporation with adequate "internal controls" so that the company has integrity in its financial reporting and other processes. The corporation is required to report the status of its internal controls in its public filings with the SEC and to affirmatively state whether the corporation has any deficiencies in its internal controls. This process provides current and prospective shareholders with a view on the riskiness of the corporation's internal management systems.

RISK MANAGEMENT

One of the key functions of both the board of directors (often through its audit committee) and management is to appropriately select and manage the risks that a corporation takes as it seeks to increase the per share value of the corporation's stock. We will discuss three of these key risks and some ways that corporations can work to mitigate them.

Perhaps the largest risk many companies face is *counterparty risk*. This is the risk that an organization or person with which a corporation has a business relationship, such as a vendor-purchaser relationship or lender-borrower relationship, fails to perform its obligations. Banks see this risk manifest itself with borrowers who default on their loan agreements. Home sellers see this risk when prospective buyers "fail to close" on a purchase contract.

Counterparty risk can also have a domino-like effect on multiple companies. Consider the following. Suppose that borrower A defaults on a loan to bank B. Bank B is now distressed and is unable to fulfill its obligations to saver C, who has deposited money into bank B. Saver C then becomes unable to pay creditor D for some furniture that C purchased on open account. Creditor D is then unable to pay vendor E for payables D owes E. And on and on. The lesson from this daisy chain is that a company must often look not just at its counterparty risk but at its counterparties' counterparty risk to get a real feel for what could go wrong.

The simplest way to mitigate counterparty risk is to avoid concentration of lenders, vendors, customers, and so forth (i.e., diversify). For a large company, that can often be achieved. For a small, entrepreneurial firm the task is more difficult, especially when a large order from a single customer or a vendor relationship with an "eight-hundred-pound gorilla" is seen as a net positive for the business.

A second major risk companies, especially financial companies, face is *interest rate risk*. Interest rate risk is the danger that a shift in interest rates will adversely affect either the company's assets or its liabilities. For instance, if a corporation has $100 million of floating-rate debt outstanding, it bears the risk that interest rates will rise and thereby increase the company's interest expense burden. Many individuals faced this risk in 2004–2005, when they took out adjustable rate mortgages just prior to short-term interest rates spiking dramatically.

In general, because bond prices rise when interest rates fall and vice versa, a bond investor will bear the risk of unanticipated interest rate increases that reduce the value of the investor's fixed-rate bonds. The lower the coupon payment and the longer the bond has until maturity, the greater the interest rate risk.

Companies can mitigate interest rate risk by balancing the duration (weighted average cash flows) and mix of fixed and floating interest rate instruments between the company's assets and liabilities. For large financial firms, this is reasonably easy to accomplish given the wide availability of interest rate swap instruments. For smaller firms and nonfinancial firms, it can be more difficult. Those firms need to carefully monitor this risk and seek to take steps to reduce the risk when possible.

A third major risk both financial and nonfinancial firms can face is *liquidity risk*. Liquidity risk is essentially the possibility that the firm will not have sufficient cash on hand or immediately available credit to pay its bills as they come due. This risk can arise when accounts receivable go bad (because of counterparty risk), when lenders get nervous and call a loan before its due date, when an unexpected order necessitates an emergency purchase of inventory, and in many other circumstances. The simplest way to mitigate this risk is to keep higher cash balances. However, cash is expensive because money held in cash balances is not invested in productive assets that would earn a return higher than the return earned on cash balances. If the company does not have sufficient profitability, it may need to raise equity to provide that cash, and equity is expensive. If the company does have sufficient profitability, keeping those profits in cash rather than reinvesting them into a high IRR project can be costly. On the other hand, a failure to have sufficient cash can cause financial distress, even bankruptcy. And as Warren Buffett has shown over the past fifty years, having spare cash available when everyone else is strapped can create great opportunities for the buyer of last resort.

This trade-off of safety versus growth, profit maximizing versus conservative stewardship, is at the heart of the tension that makes the free enterprise system go and also at the heart of why the business cycle has not disappeared. At the end of the day, a CEO will need to make a choice of how aggressive he or she will push the envelope of growth while risking potential liquidity issues. Managing that trade-off will go a long way toward determining whether that CEO will succeed in a particular circumstance.

In addition to counterparty risk, interest rate risk, and liquidity risk, a company faces many other risks, such as product obsolescence risk, exchange rate risk (for companies doing business internationally), and succession risk (the risk that a company cannot adequately replace its current CEO). The key for corporate boards and audit committees is to do as much thinking as practical trying to identify the particular risks a company faces and then to identify ways to mitigate or eliminate those risks. Every business must bear some risk. The key is knowing which risks you are bearing and how you can manage them so they don't imperil the organization.

SUMMARY

Good corporate governance and risk management are important features of successful corporations. Corporations are creatures of state law. Key corporate documents include the charter (articles of incorporation) and by-laws. Directors have a duty of care and a duty of loyalty to the shareholders who elected them. Failure to fulfill such duties can cause personal liability. Management and the board of directors need to be cognizant of the risks the corporation is bearing, including counterparty risk, interest rate risk, and liquidity risk. Other risks, particular to an individual corporation, also should be identified and mitigated.

KEY POINTS

CORPORATE DOCUMENTS	Charter By-laws

GOVERNANCE	Ultimate responsibility:
	    Board of directors
	Day-to-day management:
	    CEO and senior management

FIDUCIARY DUTIES	Duty of care Business judgment rule Total fairness standard Duty of loyalty Business opportunity doctrine
RISK MANAGEMENT	Counterparty risk Interest rate risk Liquidity risk

18

International Finance

Total global trade (as measured by exports) has increased from $58 billion in 1948 to $16.1 trillion in 2008, an increase of 27,805 percent or roughly 10 percent per year compounded. That trade, and the corresponding increase in world living standards, has been underpinned by a sophisticated international financial community consisting of multinational banks, global stock markets, and multinational corporations. That community has developed and used an increasingly complex array of tools to facilitate trade finance while minimizing the risks of doing business across national boundaries. We could easily write an entire book devoted to the complexities of international finance, but the goal here is to provide the reader with the fundamentals of several of the most important concepts in international finance.

CURRENCIES

As anyone who has traveled outside the United States can attest, there are many currencies circulating in the world today. With the small exception of a few countries, such as Panama, which have "dollarized" their economies by using U.S. dollars as the country's currency and those European countries that have replaced their national currency with the euro, every nation on earth has a different currency. It is one of the perquisites of sovereignty. As Weimar, Germany, Bolivia, Argentina, and, most recently, Zimbabwe, have seen, however, that perquisite, if abused, can lead to hyperinflation and financial ruin.

A Short History of Fixed Exchange Rates

Prior to the 1929 stock market crash, many countries, including both the United States and Great Britain, were on the so-called gold standard, under which a nation's currency was directly convertible into gold at a fixed exchange rate. If a country ran a balance of payments deficit, gold flowed out of the country. If the country ran a balance of payments surplus, gold flowed into the country. This mechanism was subject to periodic breakdown if a country ran low on gold, as the United States did during the 1893 panic (J. P. Morgan had to assist President Cleveland, as the United States did not have a central bank at that time). Nevertheless, the fixed exchange rate regime was seen as a form of discipline for countries to maintain a balance of interest rates and trade so that gold was available for commerce.

The Great Depression of the 1930s served to challenge the primacy of the gold standard. Countries went off the gold standard as domestic economic needs took precedence over orderly international trade relations. Protectionism, in the form of the Smoot-Hawley tariff of 1930, also dramatically curtailed trading between countries, exacerbated the Depression, and helped lead to war.

As World War II drew to a close, the Allies saw the need to reestablish a global financial framework to facilitate trade and commerce among the nations. In 1944, leading Allied economists and financial teams met at the Mount Washington Hotel, located in Bretton Woods in New Hampshire's White Mountains, to work out a plan for the postwar order. The result of the conference was the famous Bretton Woods agreement, which established a new fixed currency regime with the dollar as the anchor and the dollar, in turn, tied to gold at a fixed price of $35 per ounce. Bretton Woods also led to the creation of the International Monetary Fund (IMF) and the World Bank as well as the General Agreement on Tariffs and Trade (GATT), the forerunner of today's World Trade Organization (WTO).

The Bretton Woods arrangement worked well for more than fifteen years, but with the advent of meaningful inflation in the United States in the 1960s in part because of rapidly growing government spending under President Kennedy and then President Johnson's Great Society program, the system started to show strain as that decade wound

down. As a result of escalating commodities prices caused by inflation, the United States was forced by Gresham's Law ("bad money
drives out good," i.e., bad money in circulation causes people to hoard
their good money) to remove silver from its dimes and quarters beginning in 1965, reduce and then eliminate the silver content of its fifty-
cent pieces, and no longer print silver certificate paper money but
instead issue only fiat paper money. By August 1971, President Nixon
was forced to "close the gold window" after an 1893-like run on U.S.
gold and effectively end the Bretton Woods exchange rate regime.

Floating Exchange Rates

Since 1971, exchange rates have largely floated. That means that each
day the exchange rate between two currencies can move in price.
One day, it may take $1.50 to buy one euro. The next day it may take
$1.48 or $1.52. Currencies have, therefore, become like all other commodities, with their value determined by supply and demand in the
marketplace.

The downside of floating exchange rates is that firms that do business internationally now must account for another form of financial
risk: currency translation risk. With fixed exchange rates, a firm could
generally do multiyear planning for operating in a foreign country
without worrying about the value of the foreign currency changing in
a way that made business less profitable, absent an exchange rate
"devaluation." Now that risk is very real.

The exchange rate of a particular currency with the U.S. dollar
can be stated in one of two ways: either how many dollars it takes to
buy one unit of the foreign currency or how many units of the foreign
currency it takes to buy one dollar. Historical practice often comes
into play here as to which way the exchange rate is typically quoted.
The exchange rate for Japanese yen is typically quoted as how many
yen per U.S. dollar. The euro and British pound, conversely, are generally quoted as how many U.S. dollars per euro or per pound, even
if the rate is less than 1-to-1.

An exchange rate between two foreign currencies, from an American's perspective, is generally called a *cross rate* because it can be
calculated by multiplying their rates relative to the U.S. dollar. For instance, if the yen is 100 yen per U.S. dollar and the dollar is $1.50 per
euro, then the cross rate would be 150 yen per euro.

For the business manager, the key issue with floating rates is how to manage the currency translation risk. We address some techniques for doing so in the next section.

FUTURES, OPTIONS, AND SWAPS

Beginning in 1973, in reaction to the introduction of floating exchange rates in 1971, a variety of securities and other contractual mechanisms were invented to help businesses hedge their currency translation risk while simultaneously providing speculators such as George Soros and others a mechanism to bet on the future movements of exchange rates. We discuss a few of the most common here.

Private parties can hedge currency risk through the use of *forward contracts*. These contracts are privately negotiated agreements under which one party (often a commercial bank) agrees to purchase another currency from the counterparty at some fixed rate at some defined point forward in time, hence the term *forward contract*. All the terms of the agreement are negotiated between the parties, including the quantity of currency, the rate, the time for forward delivery, and the mechanism (physical delivery or cash settlement). Each contract is a one-off deal, and there is rarely secondary trading or securitization of the contract. The bank may hedge its risk by seeking to have an offsetting contract with another party, but often it just bears the risk for its client.

Futures contracts, in contrast, are traded on an exchange, such as the Chicago Mercantile Exchange. The terms of the contracts are standardized with respect to such key terms as the quantity of currency, the rate, the time for delivery, and the mechanism for settlement (generally cash settlement). In this way, the Merc facilitates liquidity in any particular contract, albeit at the expense of the individual tailoring that a forward contract can provide.

Option contracts are a third way to hedge currency risk. With an option, which is the right but not the obligation to enter into a particular contract, one party pays a price (called a premium) to have the right to buy (for a call option) or sell (for a put option) a certain amount of currency at a defined price (called the *strike price*) at a particular point in time in the future (called the *expiration*). Option contracts are priced based on elaborate financial models, many of them derived from the famous Black-Scholes option pricing model developed by Fisher Black and Myron Scholes in the early 1970s.

A final way to hedge risks, including currency risk and others, is through *swap agreements*. Swaps are privately negotiated arrangements between parties under which one party agrees to trade (or swap) a risk it bears with a counterparty in exchange for an instrument that does not have that risk. For instance, one type of swap is called an *interest rate swap*. Here, one party (e.g., a borrower) bearing interest rate risk through, for example, a floating interest rate will agree to swap the floating rate for a fixed rate from the counterparty. There may be an explicit fee associated with the swap, or the terms of the swap may be established in a way that the fee is embedded in the terms of the swap. The borrower benefits by locking in a fixed rate; the counterparty benefits from the fee income it generates for the swap and, depending on the counterparty's own interest rate risk, may also benefit by better matching its mix of fixed and floating assets and liabilities.

Swaps can also be used for hedging currency risk whereby one party agrees to swap a stream of cash flows in one currency for that same set of cash flows in a different currency.

Swaps have come under some scrutiny of late because of the apparent role of one type of swap, called *credit default swaps* (CDSs), in the financial panic of 2008. Credit default swaps allow one party to swap its credit default risk to a counterparty. The default risk party pays the counterparty an upfront fee and a series of annual fees until the expiration of the swap in exchange for the counterparty's guarantee of payment of the face value of the swap contract in the event that the underlying company defaults on the payment of its debt securities. In effect, the counterparty is writing a type of insurance contract that guarantees the payment of the amount of credit at risk in the event that the underlying party cannot make its payments on time. While a full explanation of how credit default swaps work and the risks, both contractual and systematic, associated with them is beyond the scope of this book, suffice it to say that while CDSs do help some parties hedge credit risk, they also present challenges that regulators and market participants have only started to understand.

MONEY MARKETS

The international money market, which refers to international debt securities with maturities of twelve months or less, has become dramatically more liquid in the past fifty years. This market, which is largely based in London, involves debt securities denominated in several different currencies, with the U.S. dollar being the most prevalent in what is called the *Eurodollar market*.

A Eurodollar is technically any dollar located outside the United States. More practically, Eurodollars are borrowed in the London money market at what is called the London Interbank Offered Rate or LIBOR. The ninety-day LIBOR is one of the most popular rates for serving as a benchmark short-term rate. It can be thought of as a proxy for what it costs one bank, such as J. P. Morgan, to borrow from another, such as Barclays, for a short period of time.

The Eurodollar market got its real push in 1963 under President Kennedy with the introduction of an interest equalization tax. This tax made repatriating dollars more expensive than keeping them abroad and caused international banks to look for a way to borrow and lend in dollars outside the United States.

Today, the Eurodollar market is a large, liquid market. Banks lend to each other at the LIBOR. Banks then use LIBOR as a proxy for their cost of funds and charge their best customers some spread over LIBOR. Except for the unusual spike in LIBOR during the post–Lehman Brothers collapse in the fall of 2008, LIBOR has generally been a very steady, liquid market.

Interest Rate Parity

The interest rates charged in the international money market are tied to the exchange rates of the underlying countries through a concept called *interest rate parity*. In essence, interest rate parity is a no-arbitrage condition that must, on average, hold over time. Under interest rate parity, the difference in the forward exchange rate for two countries' currencies must equal the difference between interest rates in those countries. Here's an example to illustrate the concept:

In practice, a speculator can bet against interest rate parity happening in actuality. This is what happened with what was called the

FIGURE 18.1   INTEREST RATE PARITY

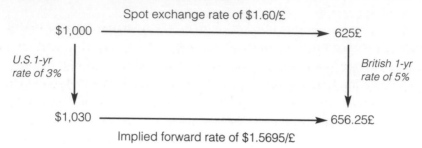

Spot exchange rate of $1.60/£

$1,000 ⟶ 625£

U.S. 1-yr rate of 3%

British 1-yr rate of 5%

$1,030 ⟶ 656.25£

Implied forward rate of $1.5695/£

Note: If a speculator believes that the actual spot rate one year from now will be different from $1.5695/£, then there is an opportunity for profit.

"carry trade" under which hedge funds borrowed money in Japan at low interest rates on the assumption that the yen would not appreciate sufficiently to offset the interest rate differential. However, the stability in the yen/dollar exchange rate that had persisted from mid-2002 until July 2007 broke down when the yen appreciated from 121 per U.S. dollar in July 2007 to 90 per U.S. dollar in January 2009. Hedge funds that had borrowed in yen were stuck with massive losses. Interest rate parity reasserted itself.

CAPITAL MARKETS

In the immediate aftermath of World War II, the American capital markets stood unchallenged as the world leaders. While Berlin, London, and Tokyo had all been badly damaged by bombing during the war, New York stood unharmed. With American GDP constituting more than a third of world domestic product and the U.S. dollar acting as the anchor to the Bretton Woods system, American finance was the most important and largest part of world finance.

Over the past sixty years, New York has gradually decreased in importance as a global financial center. Tokyo, Frankfurt, Hong Kong, and especially London have grown to challenge New York as the preeminent global financial capital. With the growth of China's economy and the rising price of crude oil, Hong Kong and Dubai have the potential to become increasingly important during the twenty-first century. American companies can use these markets to raise money, either via a dollar-denominated Eurobond offering or in an alternative currency such as euros or yen if the company wishes to diversify its currency exposure.

The rise of other major market centers has created a system in which trading occurs virtually around the clock, starting with the opening of the New Zealand and Australia markets on Monday morning and ending Friday afternoon when the New York markets close for the weekend. For the business manager, these changes introduce both risks and opportunities. A company can now choose to list its shares on one of many different financial markets around the world. Financial firms need individuals in many geographic locations in order to provide top-drawer service to demanding global clients, and global risk managers need to be alert for more hours per week to changes in market conditions, interest rates, and exchange rates and how those changes affect business conditions.

SUMMARY

World trade has boomed over the past sixty years, increasing the quantity of transactions involving foreign currency. With the end of the Bretton Woods regime in 1971, currencies floated, introducing a new risk for business managers. New ways to hedge risk, including futures, options, and swaps, were introduced to complement the traditional forward contract. Global money and bond markets have broadened and deepened over time. London has grown to rival New York. Hong Kong and Dubai have significant potential for the future.

KEY POINTS

CURRENCIES	Bretton Woods fixed rate regime
	Post-1971 floating rate regime
FUTURES, OPTIONS, AND SWAPS	Forward contracts, futures, and options
	Interest rate swaps
	Exchange rate swaps
	Hedging exchange rate moves
MONEY MARKETS	Eurodollars and LIBOR
	Interest rate parity
CAPITAL MARKETS	Benefits of international diversification

19

Mergers and Acquisitions

Corporations, especially publicly traded corporations, strive to increase their earnings per share (EPS) over time. One method of increasing EPS is to increase the sales of the firm's existing divisions while maintaining level operating margins. Alternatively, the firm could seek to increase operating margins with constant sales. Both of these approaches are considered "organic" in that they involve improving the yield on the existing business being "farmed." A different approach to growth, and the topic of this chapter, is for the firm to seek to merge with or acquire another corporation, with the resulting corporation's size and earnings enhanced by the combination.

A BRIEF HISTORY OF MERGERS AND ACQUISITIONS

Mergers and acquisitions (M & A) transactions have been a part of the business landscape since at least the late nineteenth century and the era of J. P. Morgan, John D. Rockefeller, and Andrew Carnegie. Rockefeller built Standard Oil largely through *horizontal acquisitions*, that is, acquiring his competitors in the nascent oil industry and then systematically reducing costs of the acquired company by integrating its operations into Standard Oil. Carnegie benefited from *vertical acquisitions*, that is, acquiring companies in his supply chain, including, most famously, Henry Frick's coke business. Morgan is renowned for many things, including organizing enormous trusts, or business-holding companies, such as the creation of U.S. Steel through a leveraged buyout (using debt and preferred stock) of Carnegie Steel in 1901.

During the twentieth century, mergers and acquisitions went through a series of ups and downs tied largely to the performance of the stock market. During the 1920s and 1960s, and again in the 1980s, with Wall Street booming, M & A activity hit historic highs. The 1920s saw straight combinations of firms within industries. The 1960s saw the apogee of the conglomerate approach to acquisitions with companies such as LTV and ITT. The 1980s saw the use of large amounts of debt, especially high-yield "junk" debt, as the means to finance acquisitions of companies with cheaply priced assets, often through so-called leveraged buyout firms such as Kohlberg, Kravis & Roberts or Forstmann, Little.

As we end the first decade of the twenty-first century, M & A is going through another transition. With Wall Street in retreat as a result of lower asset values and increased government regulation, strategic horizontal mergers are becoming the flavor du jour. Strong banks are absorbing weak ones either before or after the FDIC forces the issue by seizing the weak institution. Chemical, pharmaceutical, and commodities firms are linking up in an attempt to increase their global reach and reduce their cost per unit of production. Leveraged buyout firms (now rebranded as private equity firms) have cut back their activity after losses suffered on 2007 and 2008 vintage investments and because of the reduction in debt availability as the global economy deleverages. Deals that are being completed have lower levels of debt and therefore either a lower price or more equity.

So how do corporate executives evaluate potential acquisitions? Should investors cheer or be wary of acquisition-minded executives? This chapter will explore several key topics in M & A to provide the reader with a basic guide to understanding what this high-powered world is all about.

HOW COMPANIES CAN WORK TOGETHER

To begin with, mergers and acquisitions are not the sole, or even the primary, way that companies do business together. Most corporate business in the world today is done through simple commercial agreement, often in the form of a written contract. If the transaction involves the sale of goods, then the provisions of Article 2 of the Uniform Commercial Code (UCC) provide a ready-made set of contractual rules for companies to follow. Vendor-customer relationships are often governed by purchase orders (POs), a short form of contract that typically has numerous standard provisions and a few blank spaces to enable the parties to fill in such things as price, quantity, and shipment date of the goods involved.

If the two parties involved have a need to work together to jointly pursue a business opportunity, a different arrangement may be put in place. If the parties are likely to work together on a single project over a finite period of time, they will often enter into what is called a *strategic alliance* or *teaming agreement*. Under such an arrangement, the parties work together in a collaborative way but typically do not exchange equity or otherwise create any permanent entity to mark the relationship. A strategic alliance or teaming agreement will typically be memorialized in a written memorandum of understanding (MOU) or similar document that sets forth how the parties plan to work together.

If, instead, the parties intend to work together for a lengthy or indeterminate period of time, a more permanent sort of relationship is the *joint venture*. Here the parties will typically form a new, third entity. They will divide the ownership and control of the new entity between themselves and determine who will contribute what resources to the new entity so that the joint venture can succeed. The primary advantage of a formal joint venture is that the two entities can remain focused on their core businesses while letting the joint venture pursue the new opportunity. The downside is that governance issues and economic fairness issues (making sure that the parties who put most into the joint venture get the most out of them) often create friction over time and cause many joint ventures to disband.

The most permanent form of relationship between two companies is when one company acquires the other so that the acquired company becomes a subsidiary of the purchasing company. An acquisition eliminates governance and economic fairness issues because 100 percent of the upside of the acquired company is now controlled by the buyer and, likewise, the buyer calls the shots on how to run the acquired company going forward.

An acquisition can take several forms, the most common of which are the *merger, stock acquisition*, and *asset acquisition*. A merger occurs when two companies legally become one. All of the assets and liabilities of the company being merged out of existence become assets and liabilities of the surviving company. A stock acquisition causes the acquired company to become a subsidiary of the acquiring company. An asset acquisition causes the assets but not the liabilities (unless explicitly assumed) to become assets of the acquiring firm.

HOW AND WHY TO DO AN ACQUISITION

As the reader may guess, there are good and bad reasons to do an acquisition or series of acquisitions. At the time of a transaction, corporate management of the buyer will generally sell the deal to the company's board and other constituencies by describing how the transaction will generate synergies and thus cause the combined company's worth to be greater than the sum of the individual parts pre-acquisition. This is a simple extension of the NPV rule for capital budgeting we described in Chapter 12. If the acquisition will create positive present value when weighing the outflow (the acquisition price) versus the future inflow (cash flow of the acquired company plus any synergies), then the transaction makes financial sense. The difficulty is often in determining what exactly are the outflows (especially if stock is being used to make the acquisition), what are the inflows from the acquired company, and what are the synergies— both revenue synergies and cost synergies.

Some common synergies may include the following:

The combined company will save on costs:
- One company has lower existing costs because of efficiency, scale, or another reason.
- Surviving management will manage the combined company's costs more effectively.
- The combined company has greater economies of scale—for example, greater purchasing power with vendors, thus getting a lower price per unit.
- The combined company will have cheaper financing costs because of one company's better credit rating or balance sheet.
- In a vertical merger, transaction costs of negotiating contracts are eliminated.
- Employee costs are reduced via layoffs.
- Taxes are reduced if the acquirer has NOLs (Net Operating Losses) and is not limited by Section 382 of the Internal Revenue Code.

Revenue is enhanced:

- The combined company can use both firms' distributors and other channels.
- The combined product offering makes the company more attractive due to "bundling" opportunities.
- Provided it does not violate the antitrust laws, the combined company is able to raise prices because of its greater market power.

Evaluating these potential synergies and navigating the thicket of legal, accounting, financial, and other land mines frequently causes companies involved in a potential M & A transaction to hire a group of advisors to assist the company in evaluating and consummating a transaction. This team often includes an investment bank, a law firm with expertise in mergers and acquisitions, an accounting firm, and, in some cases, a valuation firm.

The investment bank (even if it is part of a larger financial institution), such as Goldman Sachs or Morgan Stanley, serves as the primary financial advisor to the company in a transaction. In practice, this means putting together a financial model to analyze the cash flows of the combined company on a pro forma basis, evaluating comparable transactions in order to render advice on price, offering advice on tax and accounting structure for a transaction, and, in some cases, helping raise capital needed to get a transaction completed.

The law firm, such as Skadden, Arps, or Cravath, is typically responsible for the drafting and negotiation of the transaction documents, including any documents associated with related financings. This job includes reviewing appropriate tax, employment, environmental, corporate governance, securities, real property, and other applicable international, federal, state, and local laws to ensure that the transaction does not run afoul of any of the myriad legal requirements that corporations are subjected to in the twenty-first century. Working with the company's financial advisor, the company's law firm will also spend significant time with the company's board of directors advising them on fulfilling their fiduciary duties of care and loyalty to the company's shareholders. This involves ensuring that the *process* by which an M & A transaction occurs (especially for the selling firm) is done in a careful, deliberative, transparent way.

The accounting firm, such as PricewaterhouseCoopers or Ernst & Young, will advise the company on the proper tax and accounting treatment of a transaction and may also assist in valuing certain specific assets. A company will frequently request a "comfort" letter from the accounting firm on certain accounting issues and also will need a consent letter from the accounting firm if a publicly registered securities offering made in connection with the transaction relies on prior SEC filings that included the accounting firm's audit opinion.

THE POLITICS AND ECONOMICS OF ACQUISITIONS

For any potential M & A transaction to reach completion (what is called "closing"), it is necessary to satisfy both the human element of the transaction (the politics) and the financial element of the transaction (the economics).

The key political elements of a transaction are (1) which entity will survive or be the parent company, (2) what the new company's board of directors will look like, and (3) who will run the company day-to-day from a management point of view. When a large company acquires a much smaller company, the politics of a transaction are largely dictated by the larger company. The smaller company will typically become a subsidiary of the larger company and may have token representation on the board of directors of the parent. Management of the parent will remain in the hands of the existing management, while management of the smaller company will either remain at the subsidiary or exit. Of course, there are always exceptions to this generic description. Historically, one of the most famous exceptions was when General Motors acquired Hyatt Roller Bearing in 1916. Hyatt was run by a young executive named Alfred Sloan, who went on to become CEO of General Motors in 1923 and build GM into one of the largest companies in the world.

When the M & A transaction is a "merger of equals," the politics become trickier. Board positions are often allocated in a fifty-fifty manner or close to it, there may be an "office of the chairman" or "office of the CEO" formed to share management authority, and the choice of surviving entity may be driven by tax or other considerations rather than by size. As you might expect, murky lines of authority or shared power can frequently lead to difficulty and conflict, as they did in the aftermath of the infamous AOL-Time Warner merger of equals.

The economics of a transaction are also a delicate issue for negotiation. The buyer will frequently offer a price based on whether the transaction will be *accretive*—that is, will increase the earnings per share of the acquiring company. The seller will typically seek some *premium* over its existing stock price (if the company is public) or a price in line with publicly traded comparables or recent publicly disclosed M & A transaction multiples based on price to earnings, price to EBITDA (earnings before interest, taxes, depreciation, and amortization), or price to sales if the company is privately held. Academic studies suggest that in nondistressed sale situations sellers typically do better over the short run than buyers in negotiated transactions, suggesting that buyers typically "pay up" in order to get a transaction done. Despite this short-term evidence, most large publicly held corporations (including success stories such as Cisco, GE, and Microsoft) use M & A as a way to grow their businesses.

LBOs, HOSTILE TAKEOVERS, AND REVERSE M & A

In addition to the plain vanilla form of corporate merger, there are several other types of deals broadly called M & A. They are addressed below.

Leveraged Buyouts (LBOs) are purchases of the stock of a company in which a significant percentage of the purchase price is paid for with the proceeds of a bank loan or other debt offering. As described above, the formation of U.S. Steel was one of the earliest LBOs: Andrew Carnegie, the owner of Carnegie Steel and the linchpin of the future U.S. Steel, took promissory notes (i.e., debt) as a significant portion of the approximately $400 million purchase price that J. P. Morgan paid for his company. LBOs only became prominent in the late 1970s and 1980s with the rise of the LBO shop. Pioneers such as Henry Kravis and George Roberts at KKR, Ted Forstmann at Forstmann, Little, and former Treasury Secretary William E. Simon and Ray Chambers at Wesray became famous for using large amounts of borrowed money to acquire larger and larger companies. The 1980s culminated with the famous battle for RJR Nabisco (ultimately won by KKR), chronicled by Bryan Burrough and John Helyar in their book *Barbarians at the Gate: The Fall of RJR Nabisco*.

The debt used in LBOs often took the form of high-yield (junk) bonds, raised by Michael Milken at Drexel, Burnham, Lambert. Milken had studied the subprime debt market for many years and had concluded that a diversified portfolio of "fallen angels" (formerly investment grade–rated bonds now below investment grade) could outperform a portfolio of investment grade bonds even after accounting for default risk. Milken expanded this thesis to postulate that newly issued junk bonds could behave similarly. Milken was successful in the 1980s in convincing institutional buyers, such as life insurance companies and savings and loans, to allocate a portion of their portfolios for these bonds and thereby created a new market for low-rated debt. Unfortunately, Milken also skirted the securities laws in connection with certain record-keeping and disclosure obligations and ended up serving time in federal prison before being rehabilitated as a philanthropist and global strategic thinker on education and health care.

Milken's debt financing, in addition to funding LBOs, also was used as a tool to finance *hostile takeovers*. A hostile takeover is any acquisition in which the target's board of directors does not consent to the transaction. The primary mechanism for such a deal is through what is called a *tender offer*, whereby the potential buyer or "raider" makes a cash offer directly to the shareholders of the target company, thereby bypassing the target's board of directors. In the early 1980s, such offers were commonplace.

However, three major events altered the landscape to dramatically reduce the incidence of hostile takeovers. First, companies created so-called poison pills, under which companies issued convertible preferred stock to existing shareholders with provisions that made a potential tender offer prohibitively expensive. Second, the state of Delaware (where a majority of publicly traded companies are incorporated) passed a new provision of the Delaware General Corporate Law called Section 203, which made a "hostile" buyer acquire at least 85 percent of a target company in order to consummate a hostile takeover. Finally, Congress passed a revision to the tax code that limited the tax deductibility of certain high-yield debt (the so-called HYDO rules), thus reducing the attractiveness of junk bonds as a means of financing acquisitions.

Reverse M & A

While many corporations seek to grow through acquisition, some companies seek to add value by divesting parts of their businesses. This *reverse M & A* can take several forms.

The most common form of divestiture is a simple sale of a division or subsidiary. This approach uses the same structures as an acquiring firm: asset sale, stock sale (if the business being sold is in a separate subsidiary), or merger (again, if the business being sold is in a separate subsidiary).

A second form of reverse M & A is the *spin-off*. With a spin-off, a corporation will issue a dividend of shares of the subsidiary to be spun off to the corporation's shareholders. Typically, the corporation will dividend at least 80.1 percent of the shares in order to have the spin-off qualify as a tax-free spin-off under Section 355 of the Internal Revenue Code. The shareholders of the parent corporation will participate in the spin-off on a pro rata basis based on their ownership percentage in the parent corporation.

Prior to the spin-off, the parent corporation may take steps to extract cash from the subsidiary in one of several ways. The parent corporation can do a 19.9 percent IPO, whereby the subsidiary is taken public and all or a large portion of the proceeds are then allocated to the parent corporation. Alternatively, the parent corporation can transfer certain debts to the subsidiary so that the parent corporation ends up with a less leveraged balance sheet after the spin-off. Along with the debt transfer, the parent may have the subsidiary use a portion of the subsidiary's cash to pay a dividend to the parent corporation.

Two forms of corporate transactions similar to the spin-off are the *split-off* and the *split-up*. With a split-off, a shareholder in the parent corporation can elect to take shares in the subsidiary being split off but ends up with fewer shares of the parent corporation. With a split-up, a shareholder elects to take shares in one part of the split company or the other. Because most shareholders like having parts of both the parent company and the entity to be divested, split-ups are less common than spin-offs and split-offs.

SUMMARY

Acquisitions can help a company grow and increase its earnings per share and overall value. M & A has been around for more than a century and has waxed and waned with the fortunes of Wall Street. Because of the complexity of M & A transactions, corporate boards frequently hire advisors, including law firms, investment banks, and accounting firms, to assist. Transactions can create value if there are synergies that make the value of the combined firm greater than the sum of the individual companies. Poorly structuring the politics or economics of a deal can lead to value destruction. If a subsidiary no longer is core to a company's mission, it may be divested by a spin-off or other reverse M & A transaction.

KEY POINTS

HISTORY OF M & A	Relationship of M&A to stock prices Horizontal and vertical acquisitions
HOW COMPANIES WORK TOGETHER	Contracts, strategic alliances, joint ventures
HOW AND WHY TO DO AN ACQUISITION	Cost synergies, revenue synergies, investment banks, law firms, accounting firms
THE POLITICS AND ECONOMICS OF ACQUISITIONS	Mergers of equals, accretive acquisitions, premiums
LBOs, HOSTILE TAKEOVERS, AND REVERSE M & A	Private equity firms, tender offer, junk bonds, spin-offs, split-offs, split-ups

INDEX